## About the Author

Vivien lives in London with her daughter and partner. She is a dedicated mother, family caseworker and a first-time author.

# The True Mother

**Vivien Rose**

# The True Mother

Olympia Publishers
*London*

www.olympiapublishers.com
OLYMPIA PAPERBACK EDITION

Copyright © Vivien Rose 2023

The right of Vivien Rose to be identified as author of this work has been asserted in accordance with sections 77 and 78 of the Copyright, Designs and Patents Act 1988.

**All Rights Reserved**

No reproduction, copy or transmission of this publication may be made without written permission.
No paragraph of this publication may be reproduced, copied or transmitted save with the written permission of the publisher, or in accordance with the provisions of the Copyright Act 1956 (as amended).

Any person who commits any unauthorised act in relation to this publication may be liable to criminal prosecution and civil claims for damage.

A CIP catalogue record for this title is available from the British Library.

ISBN: 978-1-80074-405-9

This is a work of creative non-fiction. The events are portrayed to the best of the author's memory. While all of the events in this book are true, some names and identifying details have been changed to protect the privacy of the people involved.

First Published in 2023

Olympia Publishers
Tallis House
2 Tallis Street
London
EC4Y 0AB

Printed in Great Britain

# Dedication

For my daughter.

# Acknowledgements

First and foremost, I would like to thank my daughter, my soulmate for being the light in my life, for bringing such joy to me as a mother and who makes me proud every single day. I love you infinitely, darling. Writing a book about the story of this tumultuous time in our lives is a surreal process. I wish to thank my incredibly patient and loving partner, who always believes in me, and makes me feel that anything in life is possible. Who supported me day and night when I was glued to the laptop writing. Thank you for sharing your beautiful heart with me, I love you. I could not have come out of this ordeal without my family, who were part of my emotional turmoil. Your support reached deep into my heart and guided me towards that light at the end of the tunnel. A special thank you to my sis, who has never left my side and is the best sister anybody could wish for. To my mum who despite being thousands of miles away was my absolute rock. You are the strongest woman I know. Thank you for sharing your story with me about your similar experience of losing your children and the pain that lingered in your heart until the day we were freely allowed back into your arms, sadly, corruption and justice did not blend well in the late 80s, your children were removed from you despite your biological connection. Your heart can finally rest easy, knowing that justice was served to a true mother, and that history will never repeat itself. A family's support is for life. I love you all so dearly. To my friends – you know who you are – who have always stood by me during the worst time in my life; your company and support helped me to live through the hardest period in my life. An additional thank you to my dear friends, whose testimonies imprinted on the judge's decision. I will forever be grateful to you all. To the man who made my daughter's existence possible, I will forever be grateful for the gift you have provided. You will always remain such a special man in our lives. I would like to thank Olympia Publishers, for believing in my story and for your support nurturing my work from manuscript to book. And finally, I owe a debt of gratitude to my lawyer who fought with me every step of the way. Without you, I may not have got my daughter back. I will be eternally grateful, and I will never forget what you did for me. 'Love has colourful meanings, hold on to it, embrace it, and celebrate it.'

# Prologue

Let's have a baby! Easier said than done. Having a child is a life-changing event, but when two women embark on that journey, everything that surrounds the plan is life-changing, even before the baby is conceived. Where to begin? This is a perplexing moment, when everything appears to be a jumbled-up thousand-piece puzzle. A never-ending online search and boundless lengths of internet forums, trying to convey the journey of conception, in this modern world of diverse possibilities. Feeling overconfident, believing you've broken the code and figured out the best approach to make the baby plan a reality. But then, with a sharp pause, you realise that going to a private clinic is certainly a costly adventure, and that failing to conceive is beyond stressful, forcing you to pull the plug on the established plan. So, what's next? What else can two women do? More online searches, more reading, and more uncertainties. Although, one day, the search stops at home insemination! Relaxed environment, no clinical pressure, affordable! But, where to get a special seed? Unless there is an unknown birth or a scientific miracle, two women don't have one. It's a difficult decision: do you go with a formal and unknown donor bank, or do you go with someone you know who is willing to help? Things can still go dreadfully wrong when you believe you've got it all figured out, successfully have a child, and become a parent. If you establish your family solely on trust, ignoring the necessary papers, and you are not the one who carries the child, but the relationship breaks down horribly, the law will determine the legal aspect of your relationship with the child based on biology. Whether it's a vengeful ex-partner, non-biological ties, or both, you're just unprepared for what's to follow. I was certainly unprepared.

# Chapter 1

## The Email

'Heartbroken, in the light of lies.'

The unbeatable smell of freshly baked pizza – oh my favourite pepperoni and mozzarella cheese topping on a crispy thin base – and the taste of a crisp citrusy glass of Rosé in a local North London restaurant in the company of my very good friend, is something I have sorely missed. I am sensing a different sort of negative sensation lingering within me which I could not understand as I am finally free from the unhealthy effects of my relationship, yet in the background of my happy mingling, I feel swirls of discomfort in my stomach. The company of my friend is successfully distracting my mind, and those sensations, by a simple gesture of laughter – a reminder of the person I used to be before it all happened. Inside I am lost beyond the broken pieces of my entire being which I will, in time, piece back together - but for now relaxation and a smile was my facade. After the final sip of wine, I say goodbye to my friend, but for some reason I cannot shake off this lingering strange feeling. The pale crescent moon shines like a silvery claw in the night sky, but its power is not enough to make me feel relaxed. I follow an urge to look at my phone and as I browse through some newly received emails, there it is, the strange feeling directs me to an email from my ex-partner Shona. Why am I anxious? Something is not right. I hope Tia is all right. With trembling hands, I dare myself to face the words that are enclosed within. What is this? I scroll fast though the text with my eyes. No, no this cannot be. An ocean wave of nausea crashes through me at high speed, throwing me out of balance. Tears well up. Breathing shallow. I begin to read the words from my worst possible nightmare: My ex-partner has notified me that I am no longer allowed to see our daughter. What? How dare she! We had a verbal custody agreement. Heat erupts from below, my face flushing from my elevated heart rate as I read the contents of this complicated text. I'm also a mother to our child, so why does Shona think her biological status gives her the right to make this decision to suddenly wipe me out of Tia's life? Oh no! She really has every right, by law, she's Tia's one and only legal parent. I'm a devoted full-time mother, but legally my name is not even present on the birth certificate. Although, that was not supposed to be the case. Well, we tried to conceive through a clinic at first when we started planning for a baby, where, if we were successful, we both would have gone on the birth certificate automatically.

Unfortunately, the clinic's IUI sessions were unsuccessful, so we thought of another, in fact, a more natural way to try for a baby. It wasn't very straightforward, it took a lengthy search through an online sperm bank to examine different unknown donors, but we exhausted our search as no one resembled me, not even close. As a result, we came up with a fantastic idea, and that was to try and consider someone we know and who would be up for helping us. Without hesitation, we asked my dearest friend Gregory.

'Hi, Gregory! How are you? We are sitting here thinking, whether you would be interested in being our donor to help us to have a baby? It may come as a shock, we understand, and take your time but please let us know when you are ready. No worries if the answer is absolutely *no way*.'

I remember sitting on the bench in the local park, feeling quite anxious whilst awaiting Gregory's response. My gut feeling whispered to me, that his response would be quite quick, although however much I know and adore him, I couldn't tell if his answer would be a *yes* or *no*, more likely a *maybe and let's meet and talk about this*. He was potentially the perfect choice, as his vibrant character, values and outlook on life resembles mine, and that was an important aspect of my non-biological input into the conception. Additionally, and immensely important, was the fact that I trusted this man, more than I would trust anyone else. Twenty minutes later my phone peeped and there it was, his response.

'Hi, Vivien! I am good, good. Absolutely shocked from your message and I had tears in my eyes when I read it. Wow, I mean thank you for thinking of me as the right person for this decision. I am in, yes, I want to help you and your partner to become parents. When do we start? Let's meet for a beer this week to discuss things further, okay?'

We felt elevated, out of this world, beyond the whole universe! We have a donor, and we will continue to conquer the conception plans and hopefully, soon a baby bean will successfully begin to grow into a beautiful baby who will be loved unconditionally.

'Gregory, that is amazing, you have just made two women very happy! Yes, of course, we will meet and answer all your questions. Yay!'

We all agreed for Gregory to be a known donor but without any legal entitlements or financial responsibilities. It was an exciting start to our journey, but we had to create a donor agreement first, which all parties and the solicitor witnessed and signed. Home insemination was certainly a more relaxed option, although, we had no certainty of knowing that we were doing it *right* ha-ha. Was I ever clumsy? Oh, yes, but I think it all rounded up well as we did manage to get that precious plus sign on the stick. The pregnancy was the first moment that I became a parent, an exceptionally beautiful feeling of picturing that tiny seed growing into a fully developed baby, who I could barely wait to hold and snuggle with. The nine months of pregnancy were a rollercoaster of joy, excitement, pain, discomfort but in my case, I was part of every moment and felt connected to that little seed inside Shona's uterus. When she was just a few minutes old, I was there to hold her, wrap her in my warm hugs, and shower her with smiles to reassure her that the world awaiting her is a crazy place, but she will always be loved and safe. However, the beautiful experience of becoming a mother was overshadowed by everything else. I feel so stupid writing this today, but I was fooled, mislead and manipulated from that moment. Was this Shona's plan all along? Did she see this day coming from the start and secured herself as the only legal connection to Tia? Before we had Tia, she did clearly say that she would prefer to raise a child from school-age, skipping the new-born stage of sleepless nights and first-time parenting challenges. I never understood this. Becoming a parent comes with unconditional terms and there is no break clause until a child is an adult. Shona knew how committed I would be as a parent, and she could have not been more right. I was the one tending to Tia's needs most of the time; waking to her cries at night, monitoring her fevers when she fell ill, experimenting with solids and bottled milk until Tia's interest was satisfied, holding her little hands as she learnt to take her first steps alone and forming early boundaries that were important. Shona tried, at times did well and had opportunities for having the same input daily, even more so as I worked, but there was a lack of patience and innate interest within, that failed her. Over four years have passed since Tia was born and she will be joining reception class in just few months. Shona's timing is convenient for her, exactly what she always wished for. This can't be. If Shona's selfish safety plan was a trap, then I fell right into it. Was she going to ditch me in an event of separation all along? Just a month since our separation and she has already put her safety plan into action. Not a phone call, no discussion, but an email. One email, telling me that my daughter will not be returning into my care. That's it. It's as if she pressed the delete button and expects me to disappear without a trace. Let me pause there for a second. When we discussed conception, signed the donor agreement, there was nothing mentioned about the issues that occurred when it was time to register Tia after she was born. Shona automatically entered the birth certificate, with a plan to add me as a parent shortly after her housing matter had been resolved. I must admit that her personal circumstances were believable back then. Today, I realise how absurd her story was and I naively followed her lead. I did not suspect that I would be disregarded one day, even if the relationship broke up. Months and then years had passed in the relationship and Shona as the biological mother set all the rules. Not only that I did not get added to the birth certificate, but later, when doubts kicked in and I started to think about leaving Shona, I found that she had indeed remained legally a single parent. How do I know? Shona told me herself, after the breakup when I remained in the family home, she flashed the tenancy agreement in my face and her name was the only one present, including the council tax where it clearly stated a single parent residency. I signed the tenancy agreement, but when was I removed? I asked Shona the very same question and what I did get in return was an arrogant smirk. Whilst I paid rent into Shona's account, funded our weekly food shop and holidays, a simple phone call to delete my presence from the 'home' made me even more legally invisible in Tia's life. After Tia's birth I pushed harder as I desired the birth certificate and my parental responsibility, but as life had continued, things started to change for the worse because of Shona's abusive outbursts, so any of my rightful requirements became more of a challenge. Doubts and paranoia affected her nature, and our relationship and Shona refused my rights as she predicted my departure once Tia was to become legally my child too. It was a domino effect, starting with me pushing harder for the paperwork and Shona overreacting out of insecurity due to her growing aggravated behaviour during the relationship. Therefore, the relationship remained but I started to feel very different, scared and fearing this person who she was becoming. I contacted the registry office, without the biological mother's approval, but they didn't accept anything else as proof of me being a parent. I was a full-time mother, 24/7 with my daughter, but none of the officials seemed to care about that or have exceptional terms in place for same sex parents. It made me so frustrated. I was advised to contact the courts and seek legal representation to challenge the biological parent, but as far as what they could see, there was only one parent evident and that was the biological mother. When I began to mention the court application, Shona used to go ballistic and threatened me to 'not ever dare to do that' as she would change the locks and I would never see Tia again and she would never agree for me to have parental rights. In addition, her threats were followed by calling the police and reporting me for trying to break in and abduct her daughter by falsely claiming that I am also her parent. After a thorough search, I found that if I applied to the court, it would be months until my case could be heard, and I could not face the disconnection from Tia. So, I sucked up to all her nonsense and continued with the family life, only for the sake of my child, to keep her safe, looked after and happy whilst I continued to push the paperwork on Shona. Bless Tia, she was oblivious to it all as I hid the troubles very well, until the breakup period, when Shona couldn't stop her angry outbursts even in front of our daughter.

Walking away from the relationship was a move that had to happen as my heart finally said: enough is enough. There was no longer a way to continue to live in harmony and provide the best life for our daughter as a couple. I was mentally and physically exhausted from trying to keep the failing dream of a family alive. There was something my father would often say about his relationship with my mother: *One person pulling the cart alone will eventually one day fall.* I realised how hard it truly was when only one person was trying to fix everything, only wishing for the other to just lift the handles and pull the cart along. So there I was, sitting next to my daughter holding her little soft warm hands, staring into her innocent little face – having to explain to her that I will be moving out of the family home was just the hardest act I had to ever carry out – worse, I never thought it would have to be to my little precious darling – I felt tension, wanting to just bite my nails, I felt so sick in my stomach, holding my tears back – you can imagine that this was very incomprehensible at that time to a four-year-old – I wished to be able to just make up a joke and giggle together but sadly it was time to break the truth.

'I will be moving out, sweetheart, but I will not be leaving you, I will always be here for you just some days when you will be with Mummy Shona, I won't be here at the same time but Mummy Vivien will never stop loving you and the exact same days spent with me, we will always make the best out of them.'

Her chestnut brown eyes filled with tears, her tiny hands gripping at my blouse.

'No, Mummy, don't go, I want you to be here when I wake up.'

She pleaded with her sobbing voice, waiting for my response, to convince me – oh God, if that was so easy – to stay for her, but we were both at a great risk if I remained.

'Mummies love you so much and we will always love you but we don't do very well living together, darling, and we no longer make each other happy. We did try very hard to make it better, but it didn't work. I am so sorry for you to hear this and I wish I never had to cause you this disappointment. You will have the same time with Mummy Shona and I, and still come with me to the nursery. We will be here for you every step of the way.'

My chest felt heavy, I could barely stop myself from crying as I had been here myself and felt this pain, at the age of five watching my own parents separating and promising to myself to never let that happen if I once had a family. I worked so hard to keep my promise that I forgot to realise how unhealthy my relationship ended up being. It is always more painful when children are involved in a relationship breaking down and seeing their little sad faces is something I still shed tears about to this day. It was not about me selfishly breaking free but the thought about the well-being of my daughter and the possibility for her to have a better and safer life, was at the forefront of my mind. Even if that sadly has to be in two separate homes.

I sit down on a nearby convenient and vacant bench, lean back gently as I stare at the gloomy distant sky. I take a long deep breath to inhale some calmness into my soul and wipe my teary smudged phone display on my jeans so I can continue reading the rest of the text in the email. *I will not let you see Tia again so DO NOT expect her tomorrow as she will not be coming.* My calming breath is rapidly turning into one giant heavy drop as I read Shona's words. Every word is going through me sharp as a sword – it is a cruelly wrenching feeling – tears run down my face, how can she say these things to me? How can Shona make such sudden decisions without considering the emotions of our little Tia – she will be searching for me, falling into despair for being abruptly removed from a mother whom she loves and adores. Tia is going to be ripped away from her relatives, her peers and everything she's known since she was born. Her world is packed with people who love her to bits – social networks that will detach from Tia simultaneously with me. Blissful memories of being part of my child's everyday life with happiness shining from her heart are suddenly overshadowed by Shona's threat that has finally come to fruition: *she is being taken away from me.* As a mother who truly connects with her child despite non-biological strings, I could not possibly go an hour without knowing that she will return to my arms for those hugs she needed every day of her life. Knowing that nights will come when she calls for me and I won't be there, and days will pass she will ask about my absence, but no answers will be given to her. Who will I become to my daughter if she won't be able to see me anymore?

I follow the urge to call the person I would always turn to for comfort and guidance, my own mother. She is the right person at this very moment as I feel everything around me is falling apart. I still have my music on – "You've Got the Love" by Florence + The Machine – playing through my headphones. Music feeds my soul, it is a daily companion. As I dial my mum's number, her voice replaces the playing music in my ears but as my mum picks up the call, her voice makes me crumble so I just need to take a minute to let my cry subside. I clear my throat, clench the tissue in my hand and I began to talk, in a quavering voice.

'Mum, I received a terrible email from Shona, and she has decided that I am no longer going to be part of Tia's life, meaning that I will not see her ever again. Is she out of her mind, Mum? She cannot do this!'

I can barely grasp my breath to let more words out, rubbing the legs of my jeans to calm the tension rising within me as my watery eyes slowly dry up by anger, unfairness, and betrayal. Shona has also mentioned in her email, that she has no intention ever for me to be legally present in Tia's life, including her sincere acknowledgement of Tia's loving connection to me, but if I do not stay in a relationship with her, I will lose Tia. Is this another threat just to get me back, using our daughter as a bribe? What mother uses their child for manipulative games? No way, absolutely no way that I will ever return to her, nothing in the world would make me do that. What am I going to do, my baby girl, waiting to see me tomorrow and that will not happen. I love her with my life, and we have never spent a day apart. This cannot be real! Shona may calm her currents and change her mind, as morally this is not acceptable. I am a mother, parent to Tia, and I have every right to see her!

'What? That monster! I could rip out every single piece of her hair, one by one, because that is the only way she would feel the pain she is about to cause you both. Little sweetheart Tia, our little shining star! She will be asking about you, what will she say to her? How does she imagine this will work? '

My mum is furious, I can sense the feelings churning within the phone lines across the two thousand miles separating us from being able to hug. I could clearly imagine my mum's piercing brown eyes, shoulder-length mahogany hairstyle that frames her round face, sitting down with her legs crossed and her hands on her chest, gently rubbing – she would do that for self-soothing in any discomfort even though my mother is a strong woman, who has a heavy past herself. My mind starts to race, projecting images of events that haven't even happened, my palms becoming sweatier with anxiety at the thought of their reality. Shona has a plan, shit what if she has had a backup plan the entire time? The events make sense now as Tia's dramatic handover scenes when leaving my home every time since the agreed childcare arrangements.

'Mum, I'm so scared. I am not on the Birth Certificate and I don't have the donor agreement. Shit, Mum, I am legally a nobody to Tia. Shona is the birth mother, and however nasty it is, she can do whatever she wants.

My voice begins to tremble as the reality has hit me.

'If she is being serious and will not let me see Tia, how will her little heart cope?'

Sudden thoughts fleet across my mind, the effect it can have on Tia is posing a primary worry. From my role at work and knowledge obtained from studies, I know that a child being suddenly separated from their loving carer will enter a stage of protest followed by despair, ending with denial – the longer the separation lasts, the more development and behavioural disruptions it will cause. I just think about the duration of this needless suffering given to little Tia. Basic needs of a child can be taken care of, but it is more important to respond to the child's emotional needs accurately and sensitively and offer love and affection. Children, from birth form an attachment with this special person, whether it is through biological connection, or non-biological such as with adoption or in my case the 'other mother'. In our situation, our daughter formed this attachment with me, since her birth. I am not the one who gave birth to Tia but being a mother goes way beyond genetics as children connect with the person who is there in every tough moment with that child, figuring out ways until the baby reacts happily and when you respond with a smile and your eyes meet. I have naturally formed this connection with my daughter. I had tried my utmost to help my ex, but her attitude was not in the right place. Do not get me wrong, she liked the idea of being a mother but she struggled with patience and persistence, just being there, and bearing the title of a mother expecting things to just naturally happen without any effort, was not enough. Shona often stressed that the bond should happen naturally, not with hard work and she eventually just left things to me whilst she took a step back – with an attitude that she already has the given motherhood title, leaving me to do the work and in a way earn mine. However, I didn't have to work hard, our bonding was smooth and synchronised – we use this term when we encounter moments of almost reading each other's minds or saying out loud what the other is thinking or reaching for something simultaneously. As a mother and child, we are best friends. You might think that I am the fun one, and Shona is the disciplinarian. Imagining two women becoming parents, sharing roles in a balanced manner, agreement and harmony. Wrong. Besides the fun side of our relationship, I have always been the one forming the boundaries and dealing with various milestones. You also might wonder, was Shona not around much? Yes, she certainly was but she left each time a challenge arose, for instance bottle feeding, eating solids, fussy mealtimes, tantrums etc. and she loved the time to herself – which I thought had been essential after birth especially and throughout a relationship, but it became more frequent, more of a routine. In a way, we all have humps and bumps but not having been able to build a good relationship with Tia, is her own fault.

What is she thinking, by forcing me and my daughter apart? That she can fill that void with emptiness and lies and pretend I never existed? Tears refill my already sore eyes, my body begins to tremble, my fingers cannot remain steady, and I give in to the temptation of feeling naively so stupid to ever trust Shona. I am terrified to think about how painful it will be for Tia. She will have no choice but to adapt and forget about me with some serious brain washing from Shona in my absence. I can feel my chest closing in – I have to stay positive and stop overthinking.

Suddenly, silence enters our phone conversation. My mum has been here for me this whole time, listening intently, but I find my mum's speechless manner worrying.

'What are you thinking?'

She patiently exhales.

'I feel your pain darling, I felt this exact pain when your father did this to me.'

My mum shudders at the thought of it.

'Oh my god! What is this universe doing? Repeating history?'

I look up to the sky, as if searching for some answers. The sky is a blank slate, yet to be filled with meaningful words. I clear my throat of the hard lump that has formed and try to get any sense of this dreadful moment in my life, I gently squeeze my rough amethyst pendant hanging on a thin rope around my neck – a habit I have formed to calm my nerves.

'I believe that things happen for a reason, on this occasion what is the reason, Mum? Why am I supposed to live through the same experience?'

My mother is the strongest woman I have ever known, and sadly did experience the pain of losing her children. She left my father, the unhappy marriage with a hope for a brighter future ahead for her three children. Little did she know that shortly after her successful exit, she would stand empty-handed without her children, without their infectious nature fulfilling the importance of her motherhood, her existence. What happens to a mother when the roots attached to every part of her are being torn away? Subdued. Aggrieved. Much like a tree that stands firm during the cold seasons, waiting for the warmth of spring to blossom to serve its function – but just like the trees that just take a break from the harsh winter weather, they never lose their emphasis on sustaining the growth of their roots, making their purpose stronger and not allowing the winter to defeat them. How smart is Mother Nature but so is a mother by nature – if her children are taken from her, she'll draw courage from within, and she'll strike back with far greater intensity than anybody might possibly imagine – Mama Bear, as my daughter would say. Unique traits that characterise a mother, whether biological or non-biological, are about what you mean to a child and the connection that unites you both.

You may wonder how my *biological* mother lost her right to her three children. The thought still makes me feel so unsettled as my memories are vague, I was only five years of age when it happened. Unlawful acts and corruption kept me away from my mother for four years. Back in the late 1980s – in an Eastern European country overshadowed by a Communist government – money in your pocket made the rocks move and my father was qualified for this *privilege*. The day when my mum packed her bags and left with us was a moment I will never forget, along with the moment when my father pulled up at my grandfather's house where we stayed for some time and dragged us away from our mother. I remember her crying and screaming for help, but no one came to her aid – it was a rural area, where on late and cold evenings people were tucked away in their homes – we were ripped out of her arms and I will never forgive my father for his cruel act. My mum's first move, as she didn't have a car to come after us, was to call the police – that was the moment when she realised she was alone, the police advised her that our father was also a legal parent and to achieve getting any contact with the children would be through resolving it with our father or filing a case to the court – being a biological mother was of no advantage. My distraught mum contacted our father and his response was: *You will only get to see your children if you come back to me.* My mum didn't take that threat easy and she applied to the court, besides she tried to see us every day but she was turned away, reported to police for trespassing and warned by her lawyers to stop harassing the children because she would be portrayed in front of the judge as *incompetent* to look after her children, coming across as *mentally unstable*. This is a fact, my mum had to step back otherwise she risked losing us and as for my father, he had the police contact and the best lawyers in the country. Yes, my mother was literally powerless against my father and the only thing left for her, was to fight. Unfortunately, she didn't have much money to continue with the courts and state funding was not available. Social services deemed my father to be more of a stable parent due to his finances and the support of his parents. He also became friends with the social services professional – well, perhaps *more* than a friend – we didn't have much of an input although we were interviewed but my father told us what to say. We were scared of his strict parenting – he never hurt us, but we were intimidated by his authority. My mother ended up losing all three of us and had only limited visiting access to us after school or the weekends, of course agreed with my father – many unsuccessful visits, where we sat in the window and told not to respond to her ringing the doorbell. Often, we drove past her in the car, we were told to turn our heads but I always managed to send a little wave. As I got older, I also got braver – just about five years after the separation – all three of us started to regularly sneak over to the restaurant where our mum worked, not far from our school. It was risky as everyone knew our father, but we didn't care, we missed our mum and we could no longer obey our father. We gradually sealed the wounds of the past and slowly mended our mother's bleeding heart.

'You will make this right because there is justice to those unique individuals who deserve it, just remain positive. I will light a candle of hope for you and my sweet granddaughter, I will be here every step of the way. '

My mum has never really been religious but life has brought her into bad times where she found praying and candles hopeful. Candles, right I do have my bases covered – ha-ha, laughing to myself – I sound like such a fool, but I guarantee you, they're really enlightening at this very moment, even though they're only at a spiritual level.

Mum clears her throat so that she can address my question in the best way she can.

'I know, dear, I'm sorry, but the only way to see this is that you have a far better chance than I had back in the' 80s with your father, and to address your question why, I can only say that you have to do this to make it right and become legally visible, which Shona has denied you all these years. You can make things right, once and for all. What else is she saying in the email?'

Oh, the e-mail, reminiscent of the past, has briefly made me forget its awful substance, still sitting on the bench, talking to my mum, not mindful of the number of people who may have gone by me tonight. I mulled over the words used to describe me in the email, violent, aggressive, and inappropriate. Absolute garbage, well-planned and organised lies to portray me in a way that represents her own self, to defend herself, to keep my daughter away from me, to make me look mean and unstable to look after Tia. This email is the start of her game because I did not return to her and she can't manipulate me anymore therefore what's left is to cause me pain by denying me of my greatest treasure in this world – my lovely little Tia. Shona knows this is hurting me badly. Punish me for what, for taking the courage to walk away from her abusive manner and endless promises? I must not let her make me feel guilty as she is at fault for driving this relationship to this point, to the *dead end*, there was no hope for this relationship not after what she has put Tia and me through, we cannot live like that. I have reached my limit before, and before that and I discovered the many layers of agony until I realised, I am taken for granted, unappreciated, violated, mentally suffocated and physically exhausted. Walking away was not an easy decision, I have not walked away from my daughter but away from a toxic relationship. I made it clear to Tia that our relationship, our love will not ever come to an end. She needed to be reassured that the love we share, is a love that can't be broken and that I will always be there for her no matter what.

 What does Shona mean by informing me not to show up at the flat, email, call or text because she will report me for harassment and will no longer let Tia witness my behaviour outburst? Is she seriously this twisted in her mind, to blackmail me to seem like I am the mean one with issues? Oh my God, she is building a wall made up of lies, to keep me potentially away from Tia, for good. Is she asking me to just leave them alone? Oh, no way, I will leave her alone despite her disgusting lies but I will never leave Tia alone, never. Tears run down my face, crying just explains how my heart feels, I have been holding on for too long. My mum is listening to me intently, letting my crying flow free, in a place where I am free to do anything, in the arms of my mother, even if that has to be over the phone, still precious to me.

'Mum, I'm seriously worried about Tia. What is she going to be told? Is Shona going to reshape her little brain to forget me? I am going to be completely alienated.'

I am chewing tight on my lower lip as I inhale a deep controlled breath to temporarily ease this nervous tension coming from my inner thoughts.

'Darling, no one, not even Shona will change the mind of little Tia about you, your special relationship can conquer anything and everything, she loves you so much, you have nothing to worry about and you can make up for the lost time if it comes to the worst – if there is any luck, in the coming days she will change her mind. You've got to respond to her email, remind her who you are in this union and what are the damages that Tia can potentially suffer because of her selfish actions.'

My mother always has something positive to say, she is instinctively therapeutic, often friends would come to her place for a coffee and discuss their life problems, sometimes even my mother has her own problems, but when someone needs her, she would put those aside – her words would cover me with a blanket of comfort, but my horrible feelings are hardly patched up this time. The final part of the email addresses the mediation I sensibly organised in the early phase of our organised post-separation childcare arrangement, for a simple reason – I did not trust the verbal agreement. I explained to my ex that having a family mediation with an independent professional who could help us to work out our issues including parenting arrangements and financial responsibilities, and could serve as a guide for us both to follow in Tia's best interest. Shona clearly stated that she won't be attending the proposed mediation because she will no longer allow me to see Tia therefore any mediation is pointless. I suddenly realise, yet another possible trigger to my ex's abrupt act – this is all for no longer obeying her ways, for not returning to her, this is all about her – angry and frustrated because the reality of the break up has just truly hit and not only that but also her guilt is kicking in for ruining the relationship and losing me. Sickening is the fact that she can't handle her emotions nor accept her loss, instead she is opting for revenge and that is by causing me pain where it can hurt me the worst – my mothering heart. Shona knows me well enough, how determined and positively motivated I am, that I'm going to fight, but it's going to be a fight for the truth without legal ties – I'm a mother, I love my daughter, and I am ready to truly prove my connection to her with all honesty and hope that professionals will assess Tia and their findings will confirm my claim. Tia is four years of age, do not underestimate her, she is intellectually advanced for her age, and she will happily draw or talk about me, things she knows about me, things we used to do together, my family – who she feels close to, especially my sister, my mum and her favourite little cousin Charlie. Friends, who she has spent day-to-day life with, in my nursery, since she was just a few months old. I cannot move an inch from the bench I have sat on for the past half an hour or so, with my earphones in, still intently conversing with my mother. I am practising the 'Hot chocolate breaths' – hold your tummy as you would hold a warm cuppa, inhale the aroma of the cocoa deep in and then exhale into your cuppa to cool your drink – the strangest things come to our surface from our subconscious as I read about this technique in an article on an aeroplane years ago and I have not used it for a while.

'I must remain sensible despite the upsetting and untruthful words in the email. Mum, thank you so much for being here for me tonight, I really needed it. Good night, I love you.' My brain is shuttered, my soul battered but I have one more thing to deal with – respond to *the email*.

As I press the end button, my music resumes, I enter my email app and begin to type up the response to my ex's email, and it has to be done now:

*Hi Shona, I am truly shocked to receive your email but we both know that I am very important in Tia's life and you cannot demand to keep her. I am her mother too and she needs me in her life, it is not your decision to make. I understand that you may feel upset but this is a harsh act and your biological traits give you no right to separate me from my daughter. I very much hope that you come to your senses so we can come to an agreement and no one will need to be hurt. I would like to see my daughter tomorrow as per our arrangement or as soon as possible.*

I read through my email response and press send. It has left me feeling rather frustrated, as I feel like going against my urges to actually drive over there and demand her answers. Although, what would acting out these emotions do to my chance of gaining access to my daughter, probably less than the chances I could possibly have now. I shall wait for a better tomorrow, Oh, the time is late, almost eleven p.m., it is time to go home so I slide my finger across to my Uber app to book a ride. Flicking through my music library, nothing seems to fit my tune, finally I land on Mogli and her song Wanderer – perfect. My cab is here, the wait has been hardly two minutes which is great as I just want to curl up in my bed, go to sleep and hope to wake up knowing this all is just a bad dream or that this is the beginning of my strenuous journey to get my legal visibility once and for all.

'Had a lovely evening, Ma'am?'

The dapper Uber driver kindly begins a polite chat whilst smiling in his rear-view mirror to capture my face in return.

'Not how I imagined my evening would ever be.'

# Chapter 2

## The Disappearance

'Like a sword, the sharp ache of panic pierces my soul.'

Standing anxiously peering out of the patio window, my eyes were drawn to the ominous grey clouds overwhelming the sky – a storm was brewing, both outside and in my gut. As each second passed by, the ticking of my living room clock became more profound as the hands drew uncomfortably past one o'clock. The pitter-patter of the raindrops scattered across the window mesmerised me for a few moments but my worrying thoughts kept fighting their way back to the forefront of my mind. The subdued air got heavier as the realisation dawned on me. As I place my hand on my chest, I can feel my rapid heartbeat pulsating under my fingertips. Pursing my lips and taking a few breaths to try and release the heavy weight piling upon me. It is now way past the agreed time. I have been waiting for half an hour on this particularly gloomy Wednesday afternoon, how much longer should I wait? I can no longer hold my nervousness, so I pull out my phone. No text messages. No missed call. No email. No sound of the doorbell. I step outside, seeking shelter from the downpour of rain under the twisted rough branches of the Oak tree that proudly stands on the nearby green space. The Oak tree that offered endless hours of play showered me with warming memories of laughter and excitement spent with my little darling. Rain droplets slipping in between my fingers as I lift my hand to make that dreaded call. Just keep hope, there will be an answer. Come on, please.

Voicemail greeting is the only answer. No, no! How dare she? Who would do such a thing? I feel desperation, torture, heartbreak. So, I leave a voicemail *Hi, Shona, please, call me back as we need to talk! You have no right to keep my daughter away from me. Tia will not understand my sudden absence. Don't cause her pain, she is little and will miss me. Please rethink your actions, only for Tia's sake.* As I pressed the end button on my screen tears began to well up in my eyes and run down my face. I feel like a saucepan about to boil over. How can she use our daughter to hurt me, what for leaving her? A cruel and selfish act that I am not going to allow to happen. The wild swaying of the tree branches mirrors my feelings. I bury my face into my hands, allowing my crying to flow free.

I must do something! I wipe my face of tears, swallowing the lump in my throat, and taking a deep breath whilst starting the car's engine. Windscreen wipers have begun to swish in a rhythm to match the rain hammering against the screen. Blasting the music, I have to get my girl. It is time to face my ex-partner. Traffic is piling up ahead of me. I can hardly handle the wait. My fingers tapping to the beat of the music playing on the radio. Katy Perry's song "Roar" seems perfectly right in this moment. The lyrics paint an image in my mind of a wild lioness protecting her cub from poachers. My wild thoughts are suddenly splashed away by a car that drove fast through a large puddle. Memories of my darling Tia enter my mind as she loves driving through large puddles and would giggle from the amusement. Sadness fills my heart. I could not bear to not hear my daughter's laughter again. We had spent every day together since the day she was born. No, this can't be happening! Finally, as the road gradually empties, the traffic spreads out at the crossroad. London with no traffic is like a Sunday without a British roast dinner. It just doesn't seem right. A long exhale leaves my body as now I am arriving at my destination. A twenty-minute drive has seemed like forever. Pulling over, I quickly park the car. The rain stops and only puddles remain, decorating the pavement. I begin to walk, hopping over them, but my colourful flip-flops keep filling with muddy water that makes my feet slip out. Flip-flops, what was I thinking? With my focus elsewhere I keep treading over every possible crack in the uneven lay out of the concrete path leading to the block of flats entrance. Hardly bothered by any of them, I approach the door. I can feel a sudden heat rushing through my body. Do I feel fear? Yes, I fear the consequences that my uninvited visit to Shona might bring. I recall her previously repeated dissonant threats.

'If you ever leave me, I will change the locks. If you try to get back in, then I will call the police to report abuse. What have you got as proof really? Nothing! I am the biological mother residing in this flat formally and don't think I won't cause a scene; I will say you are harassing us and trying to break into the flat!'

I start to feel uneasy! Would Shona do that? Would she really cause this scene in front of our daughter? What am I thinking? Of course she would! Tia witnessed many of Shona's angry flare-ups and Shona did not seem to ever be concerned about her observing every detail. Her agenda is probably to hurt me, to punish me for taking the courage to walk away from her. As a biological parent, she truly holds the key in her hand and can use it to her advantage. I am standing here hesitantly, staring at the doorbell which reads number 21. Forever wondering, whether I will stand a chance with the police? It has occurred to me, of course I could potentially look like a looney to the police. Although Tia could tell them who I really am, would she be allowed to even come near me or talk to me if Shona would portray me for being an abuser? A million scenarios flooding my mind like a tsunami. My daughter had no home in my womb, but she will always have a home in my heart. I recall the words I whispered into her ear when she was born: *I will always make sure you have the best life and grow up happy and healthy.* Tia's large eyes stared back at me like she understood. Since that moment, I had a promise to fulfil. I would be there every night, snuggled up and reading the words out of her favourite books, reassuring that my little darling went to bed happy and knowing that she is loved and safe. To be there day by day to show her the wonderful opportunities each day has to offer. Side by side with smiles on her face or tears in her eyes. My job would be to be there, to make things better. To not just make things go away and comfort her little heart but to explain the meaning of the world and use every given opportunity to teach her a life lesson. Oh, how much fun we always have, laughter would fill our days. This fragile little human means everything to me.

Okay, this is not the time to reminisce. My decision is buried deep amongst the right and wrong thing to do. Here I am still standing in the moment of constant mind disharmony. I need to let Tia know that I did not leave her side and that I will do anything to be with her. Am I foolish to trust in some kind of justice? My shaking wet hand reaches out to press the number 21 button. The loud sound of the intercom is making my stomach swirl and my heart plays a rhythm that does not match my lungs. Oh! The beeping stops. Silence fills the air. No answer. No one is home. I can't just leave without seeing her or at least knowing she is all right! Protective mother instincts kick in. The Lioness lay just beneath the surface. I am out of my mind not knowing where she is. What shall I do? Frustration and my lack of control is dwelling deeper within me with every minute of the unknown. The colours of yellow and orange paint the sky as the Sun is setting behind the surrounding buildings. Time is pushing me over the edge. I brace myself and after sitting outside the block of flats for at least couple of hours, decide to leave as I realise, I would not see my daughter that evening. Where is Tia at this late hour when it is almost her bedtime? Feeling defeated as I walk to my car, the adrenaline still coursing through me, I sit behind the wheel to gain composure and allow Radio1 to distract me for a bit before igniting the engine. I have to take another round around the block before leaving the area completely. There is no mutual friend I could call, and I have no numbers of any of the family members apart from Shona's mother who has not been involved much but something triggered me to message her. At the end we did get on well and had nice meals and chats during her visits. A ray of hope strikes within me, so I pull over and fiddle with my phone to search for her number to dial. Yet again no answer. I opt to send her a simply written message to just kindly let me know if she has heard from Shona. Obviously, I am not expecting a response at such a late hour. Hope is my only saviour tonight, tomorrow or maybe every day from now on. Why am I being punished like this? Clearly, Shona did not like my decision to separate on that horrifying night and most certainly she resented handovers after the separation. It does not surprise me that Shona's lack of involvement in childcare or family duties may have resulted in our daughter's preference to stay with me. Upsetting as it may be for Shona, Tia has naturally found home with me, she felt safe and loved. She kicked up a massive fuss over leaving me at each handover that was in place for some weeks then. Cried, closer to screamed each time, repeating, *I don't want to go with Mummy Shona, I want to stay with Mummy Vivien.* It broke my heart into pieces every single time, but I did what a loving mother would do, I reassured her about the arrangement, showed my understanding to what she was saying and gave her all my love. It worked verbally but as I said *goodbye* she grabbed around my neck and wouldn't let go. It was painful to watch her hurting. I cared about her wellbeing; it was the only important aspect that mattered the most. Tia showed us both what her heart truly desired with the strong emotional bond we shared. However, she had two parents and I just had to make sure to continue doing my best to settle her while she adjusted to her new life routine. It was not going to be easy for anyone, especially not for a four-year-old. The relationship broke down and there was no return to how things were before, there was only a way forward, as a separated couple. I feared for Tia's safety more than my own. Things she witnessed were sad to even think about. Children need to grow up seeing their parents' role modelling a loving relationship, living in harmony, communicating and laughing together so they can feel safe to be able to explore the world around them . I did not leave my daughter, I left the relationship that I no longer could keep alive. I remained in the family home after the break up while things calmed down and an arrangement to take care of our daughter Tia was in place.

Over the course of continuously stressful handovers, the final issue that I assume pissed off Shona the most was the one in the park. That was the last handover before the dreadful email I received on that Tuesday night. The dramatic scene Tia caused on the street. Anger aroused from Shona that afternoon when our daughter was due to go back into her care as arranged. I vividly remember that day, it was sunny and warm, and Tia enjoyed a fun play in the park with a friend. We skipped out from the playground, holding hands with joy dancing in her eyes. Shona walked behind us, slightly disconnected and withdrawn. However, I at least tried. This day was arranged for Tia to spend a couple of hours with friends in the park and see her two mums together. It was meant to portray the separation more positively to her and with the hope to ease her handover experience. Sadly, it did not go to plan. The second I turned toward Tia's little face as I uttered *goodbye*, the light in her eyes had vanished, and her happy face broke into a cry. Her little body clung to me; her arms wrapped tightly around my leg unwilling to let go.

'No, I don't want to go, I want to stay with you, only you,' Tia bawled.

Shona's jaw tightened at those words; her temper began to rise. Something that immediately worried me, because I've seen it more than enough.

'Don't be silly Tia! I am your mother and you come home with me. If you don't stop these ridiculous scenes, I will make sure you don't see Mummy Vivien anymore.' Her words were laced with bitterness and exasperation.

'Vivien, you have to help me and make her come with me! Look, everyone is watching!' Shona shouted as she tried to grab Tia away from me. Tia was getting more stressed; her cries became more intense along with the grip she had on my jacket. She did not want to let me go.

'I don't care that everyone is watching. Tia is really stressed out and we need to calm her down. That is the most important thing. Threatening her is utterly unacceptable and it will only make things worse!'

'Darling, do you remember that we said you will be going back to Mummy Shona after the park?' As I gently kneeled to Tia's eye-level and spoke to her softly.

'Yes, but I don't want to go. I want to go home with you!'

'I understand but look, in a few days you will come back to me again. It wouldn't be fair to Mummy Shona if I got all the turns. Would it? I am always there with you in your heart, no one can take that away from us and a few days apart is just time, and we will make up for those days. You will have a good time.'

When I thought that my words had sunk in, I slowly released her arms. In that instant she began to cry even harder.

'Tia, come on let's go. This is absurd now.'

Shona was noticeably becoming very impatient.

'No, I don't want to, you just go.'

Tia shouted back at her. Shona got closer and managed to grab Tia to put her into her car. Unfortunately, it was without success as she wriggled and kicked out of her arms to run back to me. Still crying and devoted to her plan. Shona got very angry then. I must say, I began to feel even more worried. I was prepared to call 999. Shona could have been unpredictable given her anger issues – hence the breakup. I felt a little at ease as passers-by filled the street to enter their parked cars. Shona looked around, aware of the drama Tia was causing and Shona being in the negative light. She shrugged her shoulders and let out a frustrated verdict on the situation.

'Okay, go! Go with Mummy Vivien as you are way too upset but I will see you tomorrow, okay? No crying or clenching onto her tomorrow though.'

'Okay Mummy, bye bye.'

I had never seen Tia so relieved in her little life. She still cried as she let out those words. Shona marched away towards her car and hurriedly sped off.

Still no sign of Tia. No contact from Shona. I just feel so hopeless, and I am running out of options. I obsessively check my phone display but no call or message from anyone who could have the tiniest information about where my daughter is. I am getting worried. I dial the person who is always there for me.

'Hi Viv, is everything okay?'

A sense of relief hits me as I hear my sister's voice on the other side.

'No, Tia didn't come back to me.'

'What did you expect? That she will happily bring her into your arms again after those hysterical handovers? I told you that she didn't like how Tia kept preferring to be with you and not her. She knows the only way to end this, is to remove your daughter from you as that is the only way she can make Tia 'try' to love her as much as she loves you!'

My sister's words may come across harsh, but so truthful and that's why she has always been the best sister, the protective kind who wouldn't sugar-coat a situation or talk too much crap. She tells you the real deal, whether it is lovely or the hard truth. I have to drive to see her now. With tears all over my face, I knock on her door. My sister gets overprotective over seeing me hurt so she hugs me tight and pulls me inside her flat. Late or not we would always have a coffee, regardless of the time, it is our thing.

'Sit and talk!' she demands in a shaky voice, almost crying.

Stirring the freshly made black coffee with a shiny spoon that reflects my cried-out eyes, sitting in my sister's kitchen facing the view of the orange sun set covering the sky as a warm blanket. The evening is surprisingly warm for a May month and the high road traffic noise fills the kitchen. I am sitting here, feeling so hopeless, so lost. Wishing for this moment to be a bad dream. I can't just simply speak, words seem to be stuck in my hurting chest and as I try to speak, only a faint crying sound creaks out of my throat. I remove myself, leave for the bathroom and rinse my face with cold water. I need to get my strength back; I have to set my mind to think clearly and carefully without an irrational move that could jeopardise my chances to get my daughter back.

'So what are you going to do Viv? You need to find a solicitor and act fast. I cannot believe that she did this to you and to Tia. She knows breaking the connection between you two is the only way to cause you suffering. It is not something a true mother is capable of doing. I bet Tia is asking every minute where you are.'

I must say, I did not just settle with a verbal childcare agreement with my ex but I have not had enough time to start legal proceedings. I had been too preoccupied by settling our daughter and getting her used to a new routine, that I did not manage to act quick enough. I didn't think my naivety would lead to this. Such an idiot.

'Why for not just one second could I have realised that

Shona could turn reality into my biggest nightmare. I am so worried and scared.'

'Don't worry we will get through this, and I promise you, you will see your daughter soon but you have to get the best solicitor, fast.'

I nervously fiddle with my spinning ring, feeling uneasy with the thought of applying to the courts and going down that route. Anger is rising within me like spreading wildfire. No, this is not what I promised my darling child when she was born. Courts and social services were not meant to be part of her journey. I begin to panic as I imagine Shona telling Tia horrible lies to alienate me, to blame me for leaving and maybe even to forget about me. Nausea washes over me.

'Viv, wait until tomorrow as Shona could change her mind and get in contact with you. You could imagine the tantrums Tia could throw at her for not seeing you.'

My sister knows her niece Tia very well and the edgy nature of Shona too. There is nothing more I can do today, it is getting too late. I wish for the next day to arrive so I can shine some light on my sorrow. My sister is seething, I haven't seen her this upset before.

'I can't believe this Viv, I will drive over there and bring her back to the mother she belongs with. Who can do such an evil thing? I have disliked people in my life, wanted to cause pain to many but I would never hurt my own child. If I would ever break away from my husband, I would not be able to face my son's everyday expectations to see his father. I would never make him hurt for our faults. Stay strong, sleep on it and tomorrow will bring some good news, trust me.'

As I drive back home, in silence, without music, lost in my thoughts focusing on the street lit road. Police sirens make me jump up in my seat, so loud one car after another followed by an ambulance and fire engine. Oh dear, something bad must have happened. It has just made me worry even more. If anything is going down in London, how am I potentially able to protect the only precious being in my life? Shivers run down my spine as I try to reassure myself. She is okay, safe and she will be all right waiting for me and no matter what everyone will say, nothing can come between our true connection. We will get through this, the right way. The eyes of the law will recognise our inseparable love.

I couldn't sleep much last night, as my thoughts kept me awake, so I got out of my bed to begin my search before work commitments. Sipping my freshly brewed coffee, I browse through the top listed Family Law Firms in London. I scroll down and something like a magnet pulls me towards the *firm*. That is it. I call the number listed on their website.

'Good morning, can I help you?'

A warm friendly voice answers the phone.

'Good morning, yes please. I wish to speak to a family solicitor at your law firm.'

'Sure, that would be possible. What is it regarding, if I may ask?'

'I separated from my female partner a few weeks ago but she is denying access to my daughter. I have no legal ties so I need to speak to someone about my options.'

'Sure, Gloria, our family lawyer is at court today but we can book a phone appointment for tomorrow.'

'Okay, yes please.'

'What time would be the best for you?'

'The earliest please?'

'Ten o'clock?'

'Yes, great thank you.'
'Speak to you on Friday at ten o'clock.'
'Yes, goodbye.'
'Goodbye.'

I feel warmth filling my chest slowly. Friday! I will find out what I can do, how to get back my daughter and gain my legal rights. Suddenly, for a moment I am not feeling so *invisible*.

Working from home is not easy today, I am distracted and lost. All I feel like doing is cancelling all of my clients for the day and curling up in the comfort of my duvet. But I have to be strong, I have always told that to myself. So I put on a brave face adorned with the best smile I could muster to deliver the best day I could for the cheerful little ones in my nursery. My colleague Rachel walks in, her eyes scanning the room I assume for Tia as she always has done.

'Hi, where is Tia today, is she not feeling well?' she asks with concern. I turn towards the kettle trying to shun away the tears that quickly form in my eyes.

'Are you okay? What is the matter?'

I am unusually quiet, too focused on not letting my mask crack.

'She is not coming, and I don't know when I will see her again,' I begin with a trembling voice.

Rachel studies my face; I can see the confusion growing in her mind.

'What? How did this happen?'

Rachel has known my daughter since four months of age and seeing her daily as part of the early years provision team made her form an adorable bond with her. My daughter adores her as she is smiley, cheerful and always playful with all of the children. They used to enjoy poking her feet through the holes on her odd socks. I chuckle a little as I remember this unique trait. It is a blessing to have such a wonderful member of the team that I can rely on, especially today. I am really finding talking about the situation difficult because I have not yet had a chance to fully understand what is happening and where my daughter is. How could I possibly answer all these questions when the reality still hasn't sunk in with me?

I find myself peering through the front window almost filled with hope that Shona will come to her senses. As the day has moved from one hour to the next without any changes, I decide to send a text message to Shona, simply pleading for her to make contact with me to discuss *the email* she sent the night before Tia was due back in my care as arranged. I remind her to prioritise Tia's wellbeing over the anger she is feeling towards me. I am not prepared to accept her demanding approach of abruptly removing her from my life. I become more restless with every word I type, the anxiety triggering again within me. I quickly hit send and await a response, even though I know it will not arrive. With my working day over, I feel relieved that I have had time to myself to reflect on the situation and attempt to think clearly about my next actions. I pace around the house, the air lingering with emptiness. I make my way to Tia's room, I need to feel her energy. I crawl into her Peppa Pig bed and pull the mountain of soft toys over me. It feels like a ginormous hug from my daughter as her scent surrounds me. Although the sound of the doorbell startles me out of my dreamy moment. I bound down the stairs towards the door like an excited puppy, thinking that my daughter could be on the other side. My excitement drops as I open the door, it is not who I deeply wished for to appear. It is my sister,

who looks surprised by my expression of disappointment.
'Not who you expected? I am sorry Viv.'
My sadness is taken by her powerful, bear-like hug. After a long moment she lets go and flaunts a bottle of Merlot in my face. No words needed, I am in absolute need of a glass to finally unwind.

My sis suggests ordering in my favourite cuisine; Indian, but I cannot find the inspiration to enjoy any of those vibrant flavours. I couldn't find the will to eat anything. I pour us a glass of wine and I pick some cashews to snack on as we settle on the sofa deepening into a chat about the 'what if's'. The sound of my phone's ringtone straightens my posture as I lean towards the table to answer the call. Is this the call that I have eagerly anticipated the whole day?

'Hello?'

'Hi, this is Gloria, the family lawyer from the firm,' a raspy but strong voice responds.

Although this is not Shona as I had hoped for, it is a pleasant surprise. My heart begins to beat so fast as things feel like they could start to move forward. As our appointment is not until the next day, hearing from her is the first positive thing that has happened since that horrific *email*, announcing to me not to expect my daughter anymore.

'Yes, hi! Thank you so much for calling me back so soon.'

'I wonder if you have time to speak to me now as I will be in court tomorrow. An unexpected turn of events, I am sorry. I have heard about your inquiry and it seems important to not leave this matter until next week?'

I look towards the clock which displays 18:25, it has made me realise that my case could stand a chance as it seems like an out of hours call.

'Oh, that is so thoughtful. Thank you. Yes, of course, I have all the time.'

My sister smiles and mouths the words 'You see, there is hope! She will know what to do'.

I feel emotional as I begin to recall the events from the past few weeks to the lawyer, my shaky voice is evident, and I am in pain. After a brief monologue I stop and pass the turn to the lawyer who takes a deep breath and answers.

'I must be honest, this will be hard without any legal ties to your daughter but we will do everything to get her back. I am sorry to hear, I know that both you and your daughter are suffering right now.'

I know it, she is the one.

'This is what I shall suggest first!'

I sink into my comfy sofa cushion, place the blanket on my lap and listen attentively to her advice.

# Chapter 3

## Realisation

'The cloud of doubt has cast a shadow.'

I am literally glued to the sofa, staring at the blank wall, waiting to hear about this plan. I need a plan, desperately, I need something that can distract me from wanting to go over to Shona's place, again and again until I get to see Tia. I am afraid that I would invite myself into another of her traps. I must be ahead of her, at all times and take action before she becomes aware.

'Firstly, have you got Tia's birth certificate and if so, is your name on it?'

Gloria began with what I have feared the most. I can feel an immediate unease in my stomach as my answer is clearly not going to go well.

'No, I don't have the birth certificate and unfortunately my name is not on it either.'

Giving a clear answer, I am immensely aware of transmitting confusion at this very moment as I would pose the same question myself: parent and not on the birth certificate?

Sadly, on the other hand, I am the only one with the answers.

'Oh, I see. Would you mind briefly explaining why your

name was not added to the birth certificate when Tia was born? I am sorry if this is not easy to talk about, but I need to understand your situation to be able to draw up legal feedback.'

Gloria exhaled hesitantly. She has probably encountered many interesting stories in her profession, but mine in particular must be mind puzzling already. I pull the blanket towards my chest and clench on to my amethyst crystal, it is time to face my naivety and it is time to start talking. I bite my lower lip to ignite my facial muscles to speak.

'It is difficult to talk about anything right now, related to my daughter, as she hasn't come back to me, and my contact has been cut completely loose. But I need to start opening up about the past, so I can get her back in my life and gain my legal recognition as a mother. It is a long story, Gloria, but I will try to sum it up for now. My ex-partner's living situation was supposedly at risk if she had claimed me at the time of our daughter's birth, and she would have lost her eligibility. She reassured me, though, that the resolution was in progress and asked me to wait until her circumstances improved and she sorted things. I was promised to not worry and that as a parent I can be added to the birth certificate at any time. Well, so I was told! I pressured her as often as it was necessary, but back then I was not worried, Gloria, as I trusted her! Since then, weeks, months, passed and I was denied being added to the birth certificate, and so was my application for parental responsibility as both required my ex-partner's agreement. What began to happen was my awakening to the fact that I was accused of claiming my legal rights to Tia so I could flee at any time and leave her behind. I am sorry, there is no short way to explain this, shall I still continue from this point or is it enough for now, Gloria?'

'Oh, no, please continue.'

'Okay, thank you. So, basically, my ex-partner may have been jealous of the love for my daughter and may have found that somehow threatening to our relationship. Therefore, she may have secured my stay by not having the legal rights for Tia, so I don't ever leave her. It may sound absurd but when the arguments began to rise, because of this sensitive subject, everything started to shift. Here I am today, and my ex-partner's latest email confirmed that she had no intention to get me legally registered, unless I resume the relationship. I had suffered years of emotional manipulation and abuse, and the moment when I came to realisation, our relationship was on the verge of a breakdown. Many attempts to fix things failed, there was no other way than out.'

I release my hand from the clench to wipe the tears away from my eyes. To avoid sabotaging my ability to speak, I managed to hold them back from flowing down my cheeks, but I was unable to stop my voice from shaking. Lately, it seems like an emotional reaction, when I mention my daughter's name.

'Oh, I see, I am so sorry to hear what you have gone through, and there are definitely many more details I will need to know if you decide to proceed. I must say without civil partnership and no formal parental recognition in any means, your case will be a little more difficult but not impossible. Nonetheless, I will do my utmost to help you to get your daughter back, it just may take some time until we can get things sorted, so please be aware of that. After receiving an application and observing the case urgency, the family court establishes a hearing date.'

Gloria emphasised the facts, which to be honest, has left me quite bewildered. Although, true, what a pickle I have got myself into, but I will get out of it, whatever it takes. I need someone like Gloria, who is professional, articulate, honest, direct, vibrant and knowledgeable in diverse custody cases as I am absolutely certain that the situation I am in will be a rare one for the judges to untangle.

'Okay, may I ask, how long does it usually take for an application to be accepted by the courts? I am a mother who has been denied access to her daughter, the longer the detachment phase lasts, the more Tia will suffer but her safety is also questionable because of the physical abuse that was occurring especially prior to the breakup and...'

'Wait, Vivien, you haven't mentioned domestic abuse. I am truly sorry to hear what you went through, that's awful – can you tell me more about the abuse and has your ex-partner ever abused Tia?'

Images of those harsh treatments enter my mind, immediately filling my chest with heaviness and my heart palpitates.

'No, Tia was never physically abused but she witnessed the abusive actions against me. The one abused was only me, luckily nothing ever happened to Tia, not physically anyway! I would have never let that happen, but Shona occasionally threw in some emotional burden on Tia which was in a way mended by some kind explanation from me to avoid having an effect on her innocent soul and wellbeing. Many remarks have left Tia in tears, and at times in absolute distress. For instance, when she was blamed for the pain her birth delivery caused or may have blamed Tia for not respecting the fact that she is not listening to her own biological mother. It was such a shock to see my little girl so vulnerable. Something hit me, deep inside, my protective instinct arose with time more but I persisted in the relationship for my daughter. However, it had become unbearable, Shona's temper grew from rare to frequent. I began to feel scared because she was blinded by anger when she struck. I did draw an end to the relationship a few times but I was promised change, sadly each trial was short lived. Instead, she pushed me over the edge of my fear, my patience, and my emotional limit. I had no other option, no more chances to give, no more sacrifices to make, nothing was left. I had to make it end.'

I hardly took a breath during my discourse. Swallowing doesn't seem to move the lump in my throat, taking a sip of water out of my bottle barely makes a difference. This is literally the hardest topic I have ever had to discuss, it is way too emotional but essential as the person who will potentially represent me in front of the judge, must know my story. No story, no court case. My story is all I have to get my little darling back.

'I see, I am sorry, I understand that this must be hard for you to talk about and thank you for sharing all of this with me tonight, and yes, we can talk about things in more detail when or if you reach the court stage. Your suffering, which your daughter may still be exposed to, will certainly make a big difference in your application to the court. We might be able to move faster than I had projected at the start of our conversation but again, please keep in mind that courts set dates that could be weeks or months away but I will do my best to speed this process up for you.' Gloria sounds warm, affectionate, and even if not what I wanted to hear, still reassuring. I need someone right now who I can trust and who believes my honesty is strong enough to fight for my rights as a mother, to earn justice.

'One important thing you must do in the meanwhile, and that's to book a mediation and see whether your ex-partner will attend and willingly cooperate. Not a worry if she doesn't, we will only need mediation as your attempt to try and compromise with your ex-partner, before applying to the court, as per court requirements. This will save us time because judges do, at first instant, ask whether mediation has been already sought. Therefore, on the first date of the hearing, we will be a step ahead this way. I will email you a solicitor I know, he covers family mediation and operates in your local area.'

'Thank you, that would be great and I will contact his office straight away on Monday. Gloria, you calling me tonight means so much to me, you cannot even imagine. I have hope, however scared I feel of the outcome or the court hearing time frame. Besides my family and friends, you are someone who can not only help me legally, but also mentally.'

Shortly after our separation, I had proposed mediation, suggesting a debate to form a structured and witnessed parenting plan to satisfy both our interests regarding the child care arrangements to support Tia in the best way possible. The meeting was never set because Shona may have rejected the idea of mediation as mentioned in my response to *the email* the other night, and she could have also realised that the relationship was clearly over – because of the mediation suggestion – and so was my access to Tia. However, I will set a mediation appointment despite her previous rejection, and if she doesn't turn up then her actions may just threaten her case and hopefully, strengthen mine. This ambivalence haunts me, feelings of excitement for making steps towards seeing Tia again and hopefully claiming my lawful rights as a mother. Being a female partner doesn't mean I'm 'the other mother' or 'the other one', I'm a mother, and I have always been from the moment Tia was conceived.

'I think I have sufficient information from you today, Vivien. Please, do let me know once mediation has been arranged and keep me posted. If Shona doesn't show up or will not agree, we will begin processing your application. Does this sound okay, Vivien?'

To be honest, I feel no hesitation, my gut and mind are in sync and I am going to follow this sensation, the same that I had felt during my search process when this law firm stood out from the crowd. A clear arrow pointing towards my destination!

'Yes, that's perfect, thank you. I would like you to represent me in the court and prepare my case.'

I feel a dash of excitement, a hint of positive vibe, a gentle relief of tension. I have, for the first time, opened up about my relationship to a stranger, who has signed up to change my life, to attempt to make me visible as a parent.

'As for now, however stressful this is, try to respect your ex-partner's wishes because if you keep continuous electronic contact, she can report you for harassment and that could jeopardise your case. Stand strong, be the person who you have always been in Tia's life and we will get to the bottom of this. Please provide our law firm details to the mediator when you arrange an appointment and if the meeting is unsuccessful, we will exchange a signed document and begin your court application. The mediator will send an invite to Shona on your behalf, so it is very formal. We will be in touch, if your ex-partner will show up and you come to an agreement, you will not need our legal representation. Best of luck, Vivien, and speak to you after the mediation stage.'

'That's great, thank you so much for finding time to speak to me at such late hours and I will call you to let you know how the mediation has been. Bye for now.'

'Bye and try to rest, Vivien, everything will be all right one way or another.'

The phone line fell silent. I reach for my headphones and exhale. Wow, what a mountain of information, I feel so overwhelmed, in a way excited yet anxious and that's because I may possibly face Shona if she turns up at the mediation. How will I react? How will I hide my anger that I feel towards her? She not only has betrayed me but may have betrayed our daughter too. She cut me off like I am an absolute nobody whereas to Tia I am everything. Our daughter shouldn't be part of any of this, it is not the way it is supposed to be. Besides, what may she be told? Shona may try to alienate me, as that's the only way she could paint a negative image of me in Tia's mind.

Could Shona change the perspective of a four-year-old, reset her sense of belonging and delete the mother to whom she is so lovingly connected? With many possibilities, the answers to my questions transpired. I am left feeling absolutely petrified.

I turn to my sis, who has been sitting on the sofa the whole time, her eyes wide open and her face full of curiosity. She begins to pour wine into both of our glasses. 'So, what did the lawyer say, come on I can't wait to hear.'

I let out a deep exhale as I place my phone face down on the arm of the sofa.

'Basically, I have to arrange a mediation and if Shona doesn't show up then Gloria the lawyer will begin the application to the court. Sis, it was so hard telling her about everything that has happened, what you did gather anyway.'

'Mediation is a great idea, but she won't show up and you know it but let's see. Of course, it was hard, you are hurting and be prepared that the court might be your only option so things may get even harder. Viv, you are the toughest woman I have ever known. We all make mistakes, yours was that you trusted a woman and she betrayed you at the end, but you did come to your senses and made the right decision to walk away. It's going to be a tough journey, I know, but you're not going to let her take the most precious thing away from you in your life. What matters is that you have great legal support now and I'm going to be here every step of the way, whenever you need me.'

She reaches out to hug me and that's what I need right now. My sister's bear hugs take me back to my childhood, when I used to crawl into her bed during a stormy night or after a bad dream. She always let me in and hugged me tight. The hugs still feel the same today, comforting and like home.

I suddenly exclaim about the donor agreement! That reaction makes us both jump on the sofa. My sis looks rather freaked out, but I couldn't help the exciting thought that has just occurred to me.

'Gregory has been searching for his signed copy because you know I don't have mine, Shona may have it hidden somewhere or may have got rid of it. Trust me, I searched everywhere, but it was gone straight after the day we signed it. I called the solicitor's office around the time when I began to feel suspicious and worried but they didn't keep copies of any witnessed documents that were not prepared at their firm. We prepared our document from an online source and had it only witnessed at the solicitor's and I was informed that they do not keep copies, unless the solicitor had also prepared the document for us, so ultimately untraceable. I need to contact Gregory, he hasn't got a clue about what's happening nor feel the urgency to look for the donor agreement.'

This is so ridiculous, I left the relationship with one condition, to have a clear childcare arrangement so that we can continue to provide the best support to co-parent Tia. We both sat down and discussed the number of days that Tia should spend equally with each of us, and we reassured Tia that she would spend equal time with both of us, even if it had to be in two different houses. However untrustworthy Shona was, I wouldn't have thought of her using Tia for her own selfish revenge, to hurt me for taking the courage to leave her. I mean, what does she think I am going to do, live in fear and constant threats? No, that's not what I ever imagined my life to be like or my family to be like. I prioritised Tia's safety and I will always prioritise my daughter over everything else in my life, she is my world. I have never left her! I left the person who was making our lives miserable, but to be honest, the emotional and mental torture weighed over the physical outbreaks. Walking around Shona, was often like skating on thin ice, anxiously expecting a crack to appear beneath the feet. The key contributions to the cause were having an opinion, making a personal decision without her consent or attempting to organise a social event. An absolute yes to the fact that family life is a team life, and that has always been respected, but being suppressed as a person makes it almost impossible for the team to work efficiently. I have always taught my daughter to freely express herself, to tell the truth, regardless of the consequences, to stand up for herself and to be part of a community where she can explore her interests, have a say and practise her agency. Albeit, I was not modelling my values to Tia, as I could no longer be who I am in that relationship and once the abuse built on top of everything else, my limit I had already exhausted, had been surpassed.

I begin to type a message: *Hi Gregory, when you get a chance please call me, it's important.*

Uneasy emotions pass through me, such as worrying about disappointing him or failing in the ability to protect Tia. Frankly, I don't even know where to start when he calls me.

Gregory and I have been friends for at least seventeen years, he is like family to me. I was nineteen years old and all alone when I arrived in London, making friends was not easy in such a large city especially when my English wasn't so polished. One person, my dearest friend still today, Sofia, was the only one who spoke my language, walked my paths, and missed the same very thing as me – family. Together we went through a lot more than just adjusting to the cultural diversity of this city, the new flavours that were foreign to my palate and don't get me started on the weather as I think I slept in my hat and scarf even in the summer. We had to make ends meet and find work simply by looking at the off-licence windows every day and hoping for the best. Somehow, we did always succeed at finding paid work. One thing we did love doing was getting on a random double-decker bus and endeavouring to see every corner of London. One journey in particular led us to an international bar and restaurant which served food and drinks from our country – wow was that an extraordinary discovery? Oh, hell yeah! It had become our favourite place to visit for as long as it remained open – it shut three years after – and we started to meet people from various backgrounds. After a few weeks we made friends with Gregory and his girlfriend, they were both super cool and showed genuine interest in our small country and never judged our poor English, in fact we laughed together when mistakes were made but we didn't mind being corrected – that's what made the learning through our socialising such fun. Gregory, in particular, helped us a lot, with paperwork and later on I wouldn't have been able to start my business without his support. I had more than friends, I had a family. Today we have our own families, but Gregory and Sofia are both still in my life and they always will be.

My reminiscing is interrupted suddenly by a call. I look at my display and it's Gregory, I didn't expect him to call me back this quickly. On the other hand, I am truly blessed with such caring people surrounding me.

'Hiya, how are you doing, is everything all right?'

His deep slightly hoarse voice greets me so cheerfully every time, no matter the circumstances.

'Hi, I am so glad you have managed to call me so soon. I'm okay, but for the past few days I've been stressed because Shona has stopped my access to Tia, and I have to apply to the court to get custody.'

'What? That is unacceptable, she can't do that! You are Tia's mother, and she needs you!'

Gregory's voice has changed, it has become heavier and more concerned.

'I know, I am so furious, you cannot imagine! It is not fair, but because all the past years Shona managed to keep me legally detached from Tia, it's biting me back now as I have no other choice but to apply for mediation and if that fails, apply to the court but before I begin this excruciating process, can I ask, have you ever found that donor agreement?'

'Shit! Shit, no I haven't, I looked everywhere, and I just wonder whether I did get a copy to take home? I do have the draft we wrote up, but it is unsigned.'

'I am more than certain that you did get a copy, and now I wish even more than ever that we didn't ask for three copies immediately at the meeting with the solicitor as then I would have my copy, hidden and safe, ready to serve its purpose. Without that agreement, I stand a very small chance of proving my existence in Tia's life to the judge and convincing him of my truth.'

Suddenly, the world seems to collapse around me.

'I am so sorry, I will keep looking, maybe I will go to my parents' house too and look into some old files, maybe the document got lost somewhere during the move.'

I feel like an idiot for not keeping that document safer, I guess I have always trusted a wrongful person and our agreement. Call me naïve, hey?

'Don't worry, everyone involved in Tia's life knows that she has two mummies, and in particular how close you two are and the special bond you share that even strangers can see and trust the judge will see that too.'

'Ah thank you for your lovely words, it is so true but I still need to prepare a case with all my evidence as only the judge can put that legal stamp on my rights as a mother, once and for all. I hardly trusted the childcare arrangements going smoothly, particularly because Tia had always gone against Shona during handovers and refused to return to her care. I was prepared to involve the court, but I never imagined such an act of cruelty that would separate a child from her mother.'

'So, what are you going to do? Can you not go and knock on her door and ask to see Tia? I mean what can she do, you have every right to see her.'

'I did attempt to visit Shona, but that was unsuccessful, as no one answered the door. However, my lawyer has advised me to respect Shona's wishes, as it will present a more positive outlook on my case. Also, the continuous visits and attempts could potentially be used against me as harassment. Plus, if Shona ever called the police on me, she may fabricate a scene of my attempt to abduct Tia by breaking into her property, portraying me as a crazy ex-partner. Something she has threatened me with in the past! I cannot risk the slightest thing going against me, as my case is uniquely sensitive already! I could not only lose my tiny chance in getting Tia back but lose her forever, I cannot risk that, and it is not worth the gamble.'

'Oh, God that is awful! Yeah, right! To be honest, because of the legal position as a single mother, she would get the protection during a report and you would be seen as a threat, however untrue that scenario would be. I will do my best to find this agreement but if there is anything I can do to help in the meantime, like testify or anything just let me know. Let's meet for a chat anyway, I will be in your area next week so we can catch up, okay? Keep strong and keep me posted if there are any changes.'

'That would be fab, please try and look everywhere as that agreement is my golden key. I look forward to seeing you next week. Bye.'

'I will do my best, bye-bye, see you then.'

I need to arrange a mediation meeting with the recommended solicitor as soon as they are available and emphasise the urgency of my case. I can't just sit around waiting for the donor agreement. Has Shona possibly calmed down and could take mediation into consideration? The weekend ahead, with a work-free mind, will help me to search and collect material for my case. I have to search and find any possible articles or discussion forums on custody battles between same sex couples. There must be some kind of guide to help my case, people with whom I could speak, something, anything.

'Sis darling, sorry I hardly managed to chat with you but you being here feels really comforting – thank you. I guess you grasped everything from the calls I had tonight, right?'

Sis is collecting her stuff to leave, as it's getting late for us both. Funnily, that's often not the case for an immediate exit when we get ready with shoes and jackets on, as we get into chatting, making it difficult to leave.

'Yeah, the lawyer sounds ace, she seems like she knows what she is doing, and I like her approach towards your case. Shame about the donor agreement though, none of you have it even though it is such an important document. Okay, don't worry something else will help your case, I am here for you in everything! I am so angry with Shona for doing this to you both. Maybe I can try and talk to her over the weekend and see if she responds. I am Tia's godmother and I do have a right to seek her safety. Okay Viv, I need to go because your lovely nephew will be up bright and early tomorrow. Bye, love you.'

My nephew, Charlie, this sweet three-year-old boy, always full of energy and always up to sweet mischief. I adore him to bits, and I have my way around him, even if he gets hyperactive, instead, it becomes fun play. Charlie and Tia have an incredible connection, they spend a lot of time together, more like siblings than just cousins. When I visit, Charlie running to me for a cuddle at the sound of the bell fills my heart with warmth, love, and hope that Tia will soon run for that hug too. Of course, nothing and no one can replace Tia, but I take everything that can heal my wounds temporarily, until Tia is able to heal them completely. My sis and her family decided to relocate to the UK, just a few months before my break up with Shona, and start their lives here in London, but our family reunion – after so many years having a long distance relationship and seeing each other only when we had a chance to travel abroad and vice versa – was short lived and heavily affected by the negative pressure from Shona. In terms of moral support and helping them to settle, Shona seemed supportive and understanding about me spending slightly more time with my family. However, that did not last much longer than the first week or so, and fights over me having my attention elsewhere began. When my sis visited, Shona would complain about us being loud in our native language – it felt offensive towards my identity and my family background – although, in Shona's presence we spoke in English out of respect, however hard it was for my sis who spoke very little at that time. In addition to everything, I tried to tune things down to keep the harmony at heart, especially for the kids who could finally spend so much time together, and for my sis, who needed less stress, not the opposite, to worry about my already deeply troubled relationship. Sadly, it gradually developed to a degree that my sis avoided coming to our place to mitigate the arguments and she frankly felt bad that her arrival was causing further issues in my life. It was not my sister; it was just any person who was close to me, and Shona saw it as a threat just as she has always done with anyone close to me.

However, that time I was already back to myself, very much aware of unhealthy sings- should this be signs, and I didn't let Shona treat me like no one else should matter to me, but her. Shona's jealousy towards me spending time with my family was bizarre to me. I no longer let her threats scare me and I stood up for myself more and more with every argument. That's not what Shona may have liked at all, and she surely showed me how much she didn't.

The sound of the boiling kettle disrupts my musing, pouring hot steamy water into the cup fills the air with an aromatic scent of cherry cinnamon tea. So much happiness in one cup, with one deep breath, I inhale this pleasure to lighten my worries. I balance whilst holding my hot cup of tea as I settle on the sofa and pull my soft mustard yellow blanket over my crossed legs and switch on the television in search for a show that can distract my mind away, even if just for a little bit – Gogglebox seems to be the perfect choice, I need that easy laughter to fill this empty evening and distract my crowded thoughts.

The sun is shining already, children's voices surround the outside space, on the streets. My eyes feel swollen and sore, I remember crying myself to sleep, but I have surely had a long-needed lie-in. Although all I want to do, is curl back under my duvet and turn away from the world which I cannot possibly face right now. Images of Tia running into my bedroom, tumbling into my bed with her sweet energetic giggles and wrapping me in her small arms for those morning cuddles, fill my tender aching heart with warmth. We are part of each other, regardless of the non-biological traits, and I will not crumble, and I will not stop until I have her back with me. I pull my arm out from under the duvet, which seems like a hard move, observing the messages from my sister, asking me to call her urgently. I jump up and pull myself into a sitting position to make that call, slightly oblivious of the news that awaits me.

'Morning, sorry I have just woken up. Is everything all right, what happened?' Despite being awake for such a short time, my voice is excited and high pitched.

'Morning Viv, that's okay. I have an update for you but you won't like it.'

My sister's tone quickly lowers my excited expectations.

'Earlier this morning, I called Shona, but she didn't answer so I texted her instead. I asked her about Tia and whether I could see her. I also added, I don't want to get in the middle of the two of you, and that I'm only interested in Tia's well-being. Anyway, she replied that Tia is doing just fine and settling well in her new life, so it wouldn't be a good idea to see anyone from your family. Wait, that's not all, on top of that she added to stop harassing her because she finds it very stressful.'

'What? Harassment? You haven't even ever contacted her, like at all? Sis and what new life?' I feel sick and dizzy at the same time, kicking the duvet off me as heat flashes through my body – I am feeling enraged!

'What is she doing, is she trying to completely change Tia's life and make me disappear from the picture?'

'I know, I am afraid that's exactly what it seems she may be attempting to do. I don't think Tia is as all right as Shona said she is, but we don't know. Tia is probably adapting to not seeing you and just getting on with her life, but she must be missing you and crying after you but may have been asked to stop. You know how Shona could be, she may have found a way to stop Tia from her emotional outbursts, somehow.'

I am just shocked and angered by her actions! How can she remove her from everyone who loves her, Tia must be protesting and feeling utter despair.

I can't imagine Tia getting used to new life, without me in it. I can barely feel anger, it is sadness I feel. Tears mount into my sore eyes. My heart has just shattered into tiny little pieces.

'Thank you for trying though, Sis. I am so gutted that she couldn't even let you and Charlie see Tia. She is not only cutting me off, but she is cutting off everyone who can remind Tia of me. I am not in much mood to talk, speak to you later Sis but thank you again, I appreciate it.'

I curl back under the duvet, thinking what will happen with time, who will I become to Tia? What if Shona is going to choose to go down the alienation route – a process through which a child becomes estranged from a parent as the result of psychological manipulation of the other parent which may result in child's hostility, disrespect or hatred toward the alienated parent? This unknown and wondering is frankly racking my brain, but the difficult reality is hearing that Tia is getting used to a new life routine, and how Shona is making that happen is gut-wrenching.

# Chapter 4

## Exploring

'Invisibly take a stride towards equality.'

Chewing the tip of my pen, I stare at the blank page opened in my notebook. I am feeling lost as my life is taking a direction I didn't think it would. My mind feels numb, and my hands feel utterly aimless. I am my own grey cloud and I don't feel like myself, at all. My former toxic relationship drained my spiritual wellbeing, my happy balance, my smile, but one thing I gained is courage. Whilst I search for my scattered pieces and return them to the place they belong, I will gradually unlock new forms of energy that may be necessary to fight for my rights. I am incomplete without Tia, I stand alone, nonetheless, my heart is filled with mothering armed warriors and the deep love of my daughter. I will not accept defeat, nor loss, and will treat this situation as a pursuit of new beginnings. The definition of loss is when you have no hope left but I do, and that is my child, who helps me to see the world in different ways and who makes me feel grateful everyday by simply calling me *Mummy*. Becoming a mother changes one's perspective on life, as when a life journey moulds to fit your child in, they become you and they need you at every tiny step they take. No matter how old children become, how much less hugs they may ask for or how much less time they need to spend with the parent, when peers suddenly become a big part of children's lives. Not to be mistaken, children will never stop needing their parents, and as they grow older, they will learn to know the feeling of comfort that they have their back, no matter what. I am coming for my daughter, as I need to reassure her, to not ever feel alone in this big world. She could be feeling a sense of failure, abandonment as she needs me right now, but I am not there as I promised to always be. Tears begin to fall across the empty page in my notebook. How am I supposed to answer all the requirements from my lawyer if I don't have any evidence to add to my statement draft? All I must give, is my honesty, and how much that will satisfy the judge is extremely difficult to predict. I cannot help this strong confidence that pulses from within, a faint belief in justice. I have never had any experience with a court matter in my whole entire life. Could the judge simply acknowledge the biological parent's rights and automatically disregard me as the other non-biological parent? Has there even been a similar case of a legal custody battle between same-sex parents? How do heterosexual couples relate to same sex couples, really? Well, without regards to the background, cohabitation and marital status apply to all the parents out there. Maybe the choice to co parent, single parent, get married or join in civil partnership, defines the beauty of the diverse family unions of the modern world. There is no longer a term of a *normal family*, as each union forms their unique individual version of a family. However, heterosexual couples join the parenting world, by having both of their biology involved, there none of them carry a *non-biological* status, during or beyond the relationship. Unless the conception requires a female egg or male sperm donor to gift the couple with a child, but the process is not possible without a legal NHS or private clinic procedure. So, they are entered on the documents as parents, but in my case, no biology and no documents. Of course, they may not be excluded from disputes over fighting for their children during a custody battle, but their fight most likely excludes obtaining the proof of their parenthood. Whereas, with the same-sex couples, the cases may hugely vary. There is the question of biology, and often none or just one parent might be biologically involved in the conception process, and lacking complete legal documents, separation can become as nasty as mine is proving to be. There are also the single parents, who may be the biological parents or used a known or unknown donor or pursued their baby dreams via an adoption route. The possibilities are entangled! However, if the legal factors don't apply and you are that parent to the child with no biological connections and no formal documents to prove that parenting relationship to the child, and go through a dramatic aftermath of a stressful break, then you may be rocking in the same boat as I do, at this very horrific moment in my life. So, to meet the statement content request, that could satisfy the judge, requires attention to the smallest speck of a detail. At the very bottom line, the emotional connection between the child and the parent is possibly more proof when determining the custodial case for a child, and that is my primary mission to allocate evidence for. Why would a parent who wants the best for their child and loves them so much be legally denied access to them? Rationally, it makes sense, theoretically, as bound in the eye of the law, probably things are not so lightly concluded. Nonetheless, a judge has a safeguarding and legal obligation to protect a child, and from that aspect I have nothing to worry about as I pose no harm to Tia. The court hearing, if I do get one, will be an interesting one for any judge because they will need to deliver a well analysed decision based on an unconventional family foundation.

I begin to draw around the splattered teardrops on the blank page, my hand is navigated by my imagination and one tear drop slowly transforms into an image of a ballerina dancing freely on my page surrounded by butterflies transformed from other random looking teardrop splatters. Suddenly, I feel a sense of ease, some kind of warmth has entered my body, whispering sound waves of inspiration into my ear. I have always connected with my creative abilities; indeed they do guide me and show me the way. Drawing is not about the skills, but about the satisfaction it provides to my senses. The same effect I receive when I write poems, as the words collide in my mind and the lines present on the paper. Every poem, ever written, is the immediate reflection of my thoughts. I find any form of art calming, encouraging, knowledge building and motivating and its expressive and creative nature helps to balance my thoughts. Momentarily, I need this specific stimulus process, more than ever before. Instead of discarding the sheet of paper as garbage or a mistake, I interpret the tear drops into something that can make more sense and whilst I enjoy the pleasurable art, my mind is performing its own form of art. It also makes me think, I am a human being, and mistakes are part of a life, and my mistake was the lack of emotional intelligence to recognise the toxic traits of Shona. However, I will never pack my past away in a box and just label it as a mistake, but instead use that mistake as a lesson into my future self, and not ever allow it to repeat. A transformed *me* who shall not be misled by a narcissist, nor shall ever adapt to suit their needs, satisfy their ego or provide them with energy to fulfil the purpose of their existence. Narcissists are attracted to kind-hearted and vibrant people, with confidence and high self-esteem and they have the intelligence to get them trapped in their web by some kind of unnatural force. But, eventually that kind hearted person will become weak, with no energy left to possibly regenerate. Recognise these signs? Then you know the relationship, however addicted you may feel to be, is unhealthy or to say, toxic of a kind. The only part of this past mistake that will be forever cherished, is my beautiful baby girl Tia. Her existence must never be referred to as a mistake!

I reach for my iPad, take the pen out of my hand, because an idea has risen to the surface, thanks to my inspirational teardrop ballerina. I know what I must do, and that is to search for everything, simply anything that can connect me to Tia. So, shopping deliveries, any sort of bank transfers, bills of any kind, address related emails or text messages. Grouping such atypical evidence could do no harm, in fact, it may serve its purpose right. The statement requires proof of three years in Tia's life, so I must find any absurd relevant material that could resemble the required information from the court statement. Doing my best will certainly be better than simply saying I have nothing to prove. Let's face it, I can't expect the court to accept my application otherwise. I need to act fast, as any time Tia spends away from me, the more she adapts to her new life routine, where I am not present. As I have always passionately studied children's development and used my knowledge in practise, my understanding about stress factors that may affect children, especially at young age, I am well aware of and the possible effects my detachment could have on Tia. Some minor everyday stresses that can naturally occur in children's lives, could in fact strengthen their resilience and coping mechanism, when faced with stresses later in life. Although, parental role modelling of their own coping mechanisms during stressful periods, is a significant contributing factor to achieve this positive outcome in children's lives. To learn that challenges cross one's path, but to face and try to solve them, takes practise, just like everything children acquire to develop as they grow and mature. As a person, I always felt like I wanted to avoid any stress, and wrap my baby in a protective bubble where they can be safe. That changed with the years of my expertise in the field of early childhood studies, when I learned that it may not be the right way to parent a child. As parents cannot avoid unprecedented life events, which could be more severe than ever experienced before, children just need that reassurance and the feeling of security, that however bad the situation may be, that parent is there to provide comfort and make everything better. Tia witnessed abuse in her family home, but I kept her safe and away from the negative vibe as much as I possibly could. What she managed to store in her mind and convert into her little world of understanding, was out of my control. However, the separation, the night when Tia's safety was also compromised, must have rocked her nest of comfort and left her terrified from not knowing the reasons of my absence. Additionally, past separation, Tia was involuntarily moving between two homes, always remembering to pack the important bits, which can be a tricky task even for an adult. Tia struggled since the shared care, as she simply refused it, in fact already at such a young age, raised it with me, every time when she was due to head back to her other mum. What she missed there, was me, the one who developed that nest of comfort for her, and that nest is where I am. That may have been the reason why she refused to leave me, because she had to depart from where she felt at home and that was a heart breaking experience for us both. I felt ever so hopeless seeing her tears, demanding only one thing, to stay with me, and besides my comforting and boasting support, there was nothing else I could do. But Tia is strong and smart for her age so she may have settled and adapted well into her new routine, involving separated mummies and two separate homes. However, the unpredictable happened, and she was snatched away from everything she had ever known, me and the world of people that love her immensely. She must be confused, especially if I may be negatively portrayed in her mind, and that is if Shona is indeed attempting to wipe me out of Tia's life. What I know is that I am hurting, and I cannot shake off the sensation that Tia is hurting too. I feel the pain in my chest, as there is a big hole of emptiness and the hollowness of this sinkhole echoes nothingness to me. How will I survive this harrowing time? How will I stop the hole from sinking deeper? Something hard has just hit my window urging a sudden chill up my spine, and out of my thought hole. Oh, what was that? Another hit bounces off the window, sounding like a small rock, it clatters again, what is happening? I swiftly get up from my desk and open my violet curtains to look for immediate clues, feeling slightly puzzled as there is no physical evidence as to where the hits were coming from. Is someone playing a prank on me? It must be! I walk downstairs, and open my front door and there I finally see a familiar face looking very excited to finally see how much she scared the utter creeps out of me.

'Emilia, you got to be kidding me.'

'Hello there.'

Emilia appears from behind the front gates, in an absolute guffaw, her arms flailing all over her petite frame and performing the most powerful laughter I have ever experienced at 7:30 a.m. on a Saturday morning.

'You are crazy, get in the house!'

I am laughing at the same time, when my heart is still pounding. What is she doing here so early, absolutely bonkers.

'I thought you needed a cheer up! I saw your light, and I knew you were awake. So, my surprise worked huh? How are you, girl? Do you fancy our local for a slice and coffee?'

My bestie has come to my rescue to save me from the sinkhole, the timing couldn't have been any better but the laughter slowly fades away. I accept the hug that squeezes hard, from such a dainty person looking immaculately casual, as always in her favourite hoodie, tracksuit bottoms and pair of Converse All-Stars. We had planned to establish a routine, where we would meet in the local bakery and spend hours chatting, undisturbed, surrounded by the most amazing smell of cakes and freshly brewed coffee. Couple of times that we visited already, we were standing in front of the cafe doors, enthusiastically waiting for the sign to turn to 'We're Open'. Customers would stare at our empty cups of coffee surrounding us at the table and at the amount of cake selection on our plates, but we didn't take any notice. We would be deeply involved in our conversation, either about work, life, our children, viewed TV series, recently read books or about food. To my delight, the sound of a delicious coffee is perfectly suited for my needs right now. So I pull my jumper over my head, slip on my trainers and pick up my keys, before I shut the door behind. Early mornings are so peaceful, almost magical, as the traffic is rare and the sound of the birds is what my ears can fully embrace. After a short walk, we arrive at the cafe, and choose our favourite spot, right at the window that is engulfed by the heat of the baking ovens and the steam from the busy coffee machine. This time it was not a usual Saturday chitchat, but I admit to Emilia that her surprise visit is gratefully welcomed. The small number of friends that I have, all play an important role in my life, some have been in my life for long years, and some I have formed friendships with in the past years. But each and every person is special to me in their individual true amazing way. Loyal friends, who share the same morals and values, but live very different lives from me. We make each other laugh and what makes all the years of friendship count is honesty, support, understanding, selflessness and non-judgemental opinions. Additional factors to our meetups, without a doubt are good food, tasty wine and freshly brewed coffee. Emilia is one of my closest friends, and she has come over to be here for me, to listen to me, and do what we would do when one of us is in need.

    I am slowly sipping my favourite hot white Americano, but I do not seem to have the appetite for my favourite cake. It's inviting richness overwhelms my senses, it provides a moment of tranquillity amidst the hustle and bustle of life. I could inhale this beautiful smell daily. Hmm, I should get a coffee scented candle or incense stick, a mental thought taken. After an hour or so, trying to update Emilia over my recent traumatic ordeal, which has made me feel lighter, but sadder. The more I talk about Tia, the harder it gets to accept that she is not in my life. As I turn towards the window of the cafe, to take in the outside buzz of people and the sound of traffic slowly filling up the air, that was just not long ago peaceful with birds chirping and flitting about, I spot someone familiar. Carol with her daughter Jackie, who attends the same Saturday morning Gymnastics club as Tia does. We used to talk, whilst waiting for the girl's session to end. Suddenly, their appearance on the street triggers a thought in my mind. I place my cup down on the table and run my fingers through my hair as I turn towards the clock that shows 10 am. My attention to Emilia, apologetically stops and I attempt to pull her away from the table. I feel a rush of exciting tingles all over my body, the adrenaline rush following a perfect idea.

'We must go, come on Emilia. We can still make it! Hurry!'

'What? Make it where? Vivien?'

Confusion crosses Emilia's face as she joins me on the run to the car. Out of breath, we both take a seat in the car, and I start the engine to embark on a journey of a possibly positively enriching moment. Oh my goodness, she has got to be there, please be there, please just let me see your little shining face!

'I am sorry, Emilia, the Gymnastics club is about to start at 10:30 a.m. and we can totally make it. I will stop around the corner, just to get a glimpse of Tia, to heal my heart, even if just for a short time.'

I exclaim in a rather unusual high-pitched voice. Excitement is rising and I wish the car could fly above the traffic ahead. Argh, I will not make it this way, the roads are way too busy! I quickly signal and take a sudden turn to the left, and attempt to overtake the traffic taking the side road. Oh no way, now a rubbish truck is blocking the road ahead. This cannot be happening. I am going to run out of time and miss the opportunity to see Tia. I look in my rear-view mirror, but a tail of cars has already built up, because of the truck, so my backup plan to turn around, flies right out the window. Time is certainly moving faster than the truck ahead. So annoying! Finally, as the truck reaches the end of the road, we are finally able to turn right on to the road that leads to the community centre where the Gymnastics lesson is, looking at the clock in the car, about to start in few minutes.

'No way, we are late, thanks to the truck. All I wanted was to see my baby girl!'

'I understand, but look, I will stay with you to keep you company, let's wait for the lesson to end and watch out for Tia leaving.'

That's a brilliant idea Emilia, I jump up like a spring in response. Half an hour wait is nothing, and anyway no time limit applies, when it concerns my little darling. After a pleasant chat, half an hour has flown by and the wait is over, and I pull myself up in my seat at an angle to see the exit door of the community centre. The car is in a safe distance, hopefully not to be spotted by Shona, as she would take a turn in the opposite direction from where I have parked. People slowly spread out from the outside space of the community centre. Where is Tia? Could she possible be behind the other children, for some reason? The doors of the community centre open again, my heart stops a beat, my chest is tight, and I hold my breath in as my body freezes. A child is slowly appearing through the doors. Yes, yes, yes? My body shudders, the excitement drops, and I exhale a heavy breath, as the child within my sight is not Tia. My heart begins to beat in an unusual rhythm, and my chest is left feeling tighter than before. Emilia puts her arm on my shoulder to offer solace, but there is nothing she could say or do to make me feel any better.

'I am sorry, Vivien! I know how much you wanted to see

her. Maybe come around again next Saturday and every Saturday, if you can, and try to see her.'

'Absolutely, I will try and drive over next Saturday again, but beat the traffic with time to spare. I wish I could drive over and spot her going into her nursery, but there is nowhere near the school nursery or around the building, where I could park without being seen.'

I am about to take a turn at the traffic light to drop Emilia home, when I notice Carol again, walking down the street with her daughter Jackie. I park a little ahead, leaving Emilia in the car, and get out quickly so I can meet her coming towards me.

'Oh, hi Vivien, how are you? How is Tia, is she not well as Jackie missed her in the lesson today.'

Carol seems startled over seeing me alone, her eyes quickly searching for Tia over my shoulders. It's too early for me to tell people, too early to know any answers, simply too early to get the rest of the world involved. What do I do at this moment actually? I need to say something, anything, but staying silent in the middle of the street. Awkward!

'Tia is with her other mum, sorry Jackie that you missed her in the lesson earlier, but hopefully you will see her next time. Carol, I will give you a call at some point later today, but I need to go now.'

Cowardly, I decide to flee the scene. If I started telling the truth about Tia, Jackie would be listening too and that I could not just easily ignore. Carol accepts my rushing body language and quickly says bye, as I move away in the opposite direction back to my parked car. I offer Emilia a lift home and thank her for the lovely time and her patience. We agree to meet soon for our next cafe meet up, with a reservation, depending on how I will feel socially. The moment Emilia lets go of our hug and leaves the car, I let out the waterfall of tears, and cry as heavily as my body feels the need to. My baby, where is she?

I slam the door behind, fling my keys on the hallway shelf and throw myself into the large soft cushions placed randomly on the sofa. Argh, I can't believe it, Tia is being deprived of her favourite lesson too, she loves gymnastics, and she has the whole term left to attend, her whole routine is seemingly thrown out of whack. But it may be just a one off and as Emilia said, I can try again next Saturday. I switch on the speakers, scroll through my playlist and select Lindsey Stirling, a modern violinist that I have only recently discovered. Her music blows my mind as it's so vibrant and upbeat. I turn the sound on a higher volume, a sound of music fills the space in my small house. I take a deep breath in and a deep breath out, clearing the heavy weight left inside me after my crying episode. What needs to exit my body, must come out! After a few songs, I begin to feel a little restless. Shall I or shall I not? I shall! I pick up my phone, the call hits the pause button on my music playlist as it dials Carol's number. She picks up after the second ring, which surprises me. I explain things to Carol, in simple terms, no heavy details and the only reason why I have made that decision to involve Carol is that I may need her help. It may sound selfish but there is not much for me to hold on to. Carol can lead me to Tia, she can let me know if she sees her or meets up with Shona, as we met in the park on a couple of occasions altogether before.

'Vivien, this is terrible, poor little Tia and yourself too. I am so sorry to hear! I will keep our conversation confidential, and that is not because I am taking sides, but to keep in contact with Shona, and act as if I know nothing about her cruel move. Tia and you are so wonderful together, and she visibly loves you dearly. I will keep you posted on any updates!' Carol reassures me, but should I trust her? Trust will not come so easily to me, since my betrayal. Well, I have nothing to lose, besides, I will not share anything that could get Shona's attention, even if Carol would turn around in the future. I am intrigued whether Shona will ever contact her for a play in the park or show up for any more Gymnastics lessons. After a brief goodbye to Carol, I hang up, the music hits play again and the song "Shatter me" by Lindsey Stirling comes on. Perfect timing as I am utterly shattered, both physically and mentally.

I heavily walk up the stairs, sit back in my desk chair by the window and gaze outside with the notepad drawings in front of me, without any written notes whatsoever. Looking at the drawings I made earlier where the tear drops dried up around the ballerina and the butterflies, I begin to wonder whether anyone out there has experienced a similar situation to mine. I open the internet search engine and start typing in words *rights of a biological mother UK and* as I read through the very first summary on a legal law firm site, it confirms the worst, and that is a biological mother can in fact do anything she wants, however cruel or unfair that is to the child involved, unless the other parent is on the birth certificate or has parental responsibility to the child. Other than the court, no one else can physically make the biological mother change her acts. Also, the site confirms that from their experience, mothers often act out of revenge or spite. Biological mothers seem to have a strong belief in keeping the children to themselves after their separation, thinking they belong to one else but them. No, I can't rely on heterosexual couples, whether married or not, there is always a father, regardless of the history. This is far from my position, as I am not a father nor am I biologically connected to my child, I am a nobody in the eyes of the law. Their circumstances differ from mine, as the biological father gaining custody could be challenging, but not so complicated as mine. What they need to present to a judge is their plans and intentions in their child's best interest. I keep reading that the father has the same rights as the mother in the eyes of the law, unless the court finds them to be a threat towards the child's welfare, they in almost all cases get visitation or shared custody of their child. If I am offered an opportunity to prove my parental relationship and that's if, I will convince the judge of my mothering nature and the importance of my presence in Tia's life is in her best interest. That poses a question, how does this process work? Will social services visit Tia and compare her testimonies with mine? Given her young age, her voice may still be considered, via a play session type of an interview I suppose.

Anyhow, the internet search results are focused on heterosexual couples, which is useful, but I need very different answers here. So, I reword my search into *same sex couples* and luckily many results load up on the screen. I am pleasantly surprised, but as I read along, I also realise that civil partnership and marriages seems to be dominant in some cases, and some forums state insemination through a clinic that legally provides an immediate parental recognition on papers, including the birth certificate. Great, nothing on the forums about home insemination with a known donor. Home insemination is not an uncommon way to conceive, but probably what is common, is getting the legalities right from the start. Reading after reading, I can't find anything that relates to my case, no forums, no articles, no books, no court cases related to at least one parent who had no legal ties to their children, and managed to win over the courts. These results leave me feeling trapped. I will not stop looking for clues, someone must have gone through this, and someone must have parented a child since their birth, but legally didn't manage to sort things out for some believable reasons. What if it is actually true, what if this position I am in is extremely rare and what if the lawyers will find it too rare to even deal with it. An invisible mother, completely bare! I need to file a statement that will present the rareness of my situation, but one that will also present the rare relationship between a child and non-biological mother. My heartening hopes go for the court to accept my case and give me a chance to prove myself. I just need to be heard! I deserve that one opportunity!

# Chapter 5

## Desperation

'Law and order, where to start, what I desire is nowhere in sight.'

Working under this emotional pressure is daunting. Constantly thinking, assuming and discussing possibilities in my own head is stopping me from focusing on my work, which needs one hundred percent attention. If I stop my productivity, everything else may just fail. I need to pull myself together, even if everything that has been happening is pure disappointment. I decided to take the risk, and drove to the nursery location, on Tuesday this week, but I didn't spot Tia going in either, and that has made me really suspicious as to what Shona is up to. Has she left on holiday with Tia? In the end, nursery attendance is not mandatory so she can go whenever and wherever she wants, with only a simple notification email provided. As I was leaving on Tuesday, I spotted the nursery teacher going into the building, so I took the chance and dropped her an email. She has always been so kind. Her input into settling Tia into the nursery was effortful. She found settling in a little challenging, as the detachment from her comfort bubble of my nursery setting, where I would be around, including her friends and the staff that she adored very much, was difficult for her at the start. With time, after working in partnership with the nursery staff, who offered much patience and understanding towards Tia's shy nature, she managed to settle. I remember her coming out with a huge smile, running with full on power for a hug to me was a good sign.

My email said, 'Dear, Ms Gardener. I hope you are well. I just wanted to find out whether you have been notified about our separation. Also, whether you know about Tia's whereabouts as I was refused contact with her, against my will. I would appreciate any information you could offer.'

A response followed up fairly quickly, sooner than I had anticipated at the time.

'Hi Vivien, it is lovely to hear from you! Sadly, I am no longer allowed to provide any information regarding Tia to you, as Shona asked the school nursery to remove you from the parent contact list and you are also refused any collection rights to Tia. All I can share is that Shona has presented the school with safeguarding concerns, and we have a protocol to follow to protect Tia's welfare. I am really sorry, as you are such a lovely mother to Tia, but this is out of my control. Best of luck with everything, and I hope you get to sort things out and see Tia again soon. She must be missing you.'

I was truly shocked and deeply saddened to read her response email. I am barred from the school, simply put. I had nothing else left for now, but of course to respect the decision the school made based on the report Shona filed in. When I called the school, after the email, out of a general curiosity, I was advised to seek a court order to change the statement that is filed at the school as now it's the biological mother who is listed as the only one with legal rights for Tia. My heart was torn into a million pieces, as my case got worse, and the school statement filed by Shona could jeopardise my application. I panicked over the thoughts about what Shona has possibly planned for her next steps, as I feel in my gut, that the school nursery barring is only the beginning. Visibly, Shona is using her rights and that is making her powerful, leaving me terrifyingly powerless.

Today is the day of the mediation I arranged, and an invite has been sent to Shona to attend. Today will determine whether we can come up with an agreement without going to court. Today is partly a decision day. I need to better myself at work, so I am going to choose a tactic that may just work for me, at least for now. I will try to switch off my Tia brain while at work by occupying my mind with all the pleasures of dealing with the little children in my care. I have lately been hiding more in my office, but that has not worked well as my mind was constantly on fire over the past news. Children offer the entrance into the world of an imagination, where I can get lost in time, and hope for that innocent entertainment. Tia has always known me as a loving, happy, bubbly, playful, adventurous and energetic person and that's who I will aim to remain, ready for her return. I will make every effort to keep my untiring perseverance and relentless energy in place, for Tia's and my own sake. This is what is going to keep me inspired. Will it work? That depends on the length of time spent apart from Tia. How long will it take to fix the gap and what damage will our detachment cause?

The clock strikes 6 o'clock, as I sit in the waiting area of the solicitor's office, ready for the mediation appointment. Although, the solicitor's assistant has informed me that they haven't heard from Shona and are predicting her non-attendance. The time is passing by, and I am still just sitting in the waiting area, refreshing my email page, just in case Shona reaches out to me directly. Nope, nothing, no email, no call to the solicitor's office either. It's past 7 o'clock, the time limit has been met. No contact means no mediation. I am advised that a signed document of the attempted mediation will be copied over to Gloria, who is awaiting the outcome of today's appointment. Sadly, today, I am left with no other choice than to apply to the court for shared custody and that long fight for parental responsibility, to keep our union with Tia forever safe. With my head tilted down, I walk away from the solicitor's office. Again, another disappointment. How much more is set to block my journey towards my visibility? My phone suddenly rings, silence enters my mind, what if its Shona calling that she has changed her mind and is prepared to agree for me to continue seeing Tia and to arrange an equal shared care. As I pull my phone out of my bag, I realise it is Gloria. What was I thinking, it is time to come to terms with Shona's intentions that are seemingly nowhere near allowing me back into Tia's life.

'Hello Vivien! I have received the papers as the mediation was unsuccessful. I am sorry to hear that you couldn't sort things out with you ex-partner. How are you feeling? Are you still going for the court application, and if so, feel free to come to my office this week Friday as I am not in the court then? It would be great to meet you face-to face, to discuss the court application and go through every detail in more depth this time?'

'I am disheartened, but Shona mentioned her disinterest in her email, so I hardly expected her to change her mind and realise that what she is attempting to put Tia through, may harm her wellbeing in the long run. Yes, please, we must start the application and file it to the court as soon as possible. I will free myself to see you on Friday, and I look forward to meeting you.'

The conversation was short and to the point, but what else was there to say? There were no high expectations, and turning to the court for help, is the only option left in my case. The impact of a court process could be emotionally damaging to Tia and applying to the court, means the time spent away from Tia is looking more like weeks, than days. It has only been over a week now, but I honestly struggle, as I miss her sweet voice, her adorable smile, and the feeling of her gentle arms wrapped around my neck. These thoughts make me tremble, teary and weak! I can feel the looks of passers-by, as my tears are visibly running down my face, but I am lost in the moment and the world around me just does not matter. I am a hurt woman, who has been abruptly disconnected from her loving child. I finally get to the car, wiping my tears away, I follow a 'stupid' instinct probably out of desperation, which is to call the police. I no longer care what papers I am on or not, I just want my baby back, quicker than the court can potentially provide. I place my thumb to unlock my phone and look up the closest Police station that I can personally visit, as I need to speak to someone and report my daughter's abduction. Tia is being separated from me against her own will and this is certainly not all right, nor can be legal either. I was in a long-term relationship with Shona, regardless of no legal papers. Would the Police believe me, and try to contact Shona to at least check on Tia's safety for me? As of now, I am very worried as Tia didn't turn up for her Gymnastics lesson or her school nursery daily sessions. I am a distraught mother looking for help, for information, for anything that can get me just a tad closer to my little darling. I find the directions to the Police station and start my engine to begin the journey. I am driven by desperation, and I am going to try everything that is possible with a pinch of hope.

'Madam, are you here to report an abduction by another woman who is the legal parent of that child?'

'Yes, we separated a few weeks ago and we had a shared care in place to take care of our daughter, but out of the blue she cut contact with my daughter, refusing my presence in her life. I get no responses from her, and our daughter hasn't been showing up for her usual commitments such as her weekend club and the school nursery. Please, is there a way you could contact her and find out whether she is safe? I am so very worried.'

'Okay, were you and your ex-partner married or in civil partnership? Do you have a birth certificate or any documentation of your parental rights to this child?'

'No, we never married, nor did we enter a civil partnership, nor do I have any documentation. To cut the story of the why nots short, I may have been manipulated to never have my parenting relationship to our daughter documented. I am a full-time mother, who has spent every day of her life with her child, day and night. All I need is to know whether she is all right.'

The police are staring at me, as if I was some kind of a mad woman. I feel like screaming, this is so frustrating. I am beginning to feel hideous!

'Madam, I am very sorry, but there is not much we can do from here. Your child, as you are claiming is your child, is safely residing with her biological parent and that is not referred to as an abduction, I am afraid. The best for you would be to hire a lawyer, and get the court involved. All right? I am sorry!'

There it is, the biological mother, protected in the eyes of a law, and as for me, I am more invisible than I had felt at the start of the abrupt separation. I hope my situation is not a lost cause, and my journey will hit a dead end. Just as I am about to leave the station, one of the police officers appears from the back of the office window suggesting to contact an organisation called *Stonewall*. Right by the station, there is a subway, so I decide to get myself a takeaway meal, as hunger has struck, and I need food to be able to untangle today's stresses. I sit down with my meal at an available table, place my earphones in and play my music. What is playing is not of my interest, but I need a key element to cut me away from the outside world. It's too much to take and music is the therapy for my soul. Taking slow bites into my six-inch barbecue chicken toasted sub, I take a quick look at the Stonewall website and find some information on their *dissolution and divorce* section. As I am reading into it, I notice a highlighted point that people not falling into the categories mentioned i.e., legal parent, husband/wife, guardian, should seek permission from the court, along with applying for parental responsibility down the line. This is a great site, but besides some contact advice to seek legal presentation, there is not much more for me to absorb. Every little helps, so I put an end to my search for now and try to accept that the application to the court, is presenting to be my sole option. I take my last sips of Coke, tunes in my ears are making my mind dance over the thought that I am making something legally happen, however nervous that makes me feel. For so many years I was lied to, misled and deprived of my legal rights as a mother. Now, this moment in my life, is shaping up to be the end to threats and the beginning of a fresh start. If only Shona could be civil, placing her own agenda aside and focusing on Tia primarily, this nightmare would vanish with a blink of an eye! Why put a four-year-old child through a legal battle? It is unnecessary! Tia may not comprehend much either way, although witnessing her parents separating in a manner that presents co-working and positive attitude, would have laid out a blanket of comfort for Tia to snuggle with. Anger, revenge, punishment may cloud the mind, disabling a person from thinking clearly and reasonably, resulting in irrational acts. Sadly, things don't always go as planned in life and pain is part of our growth, our survival. Eventually when things settle, and the pain disappears, we may realise that standing up against such great challenges has made us only stronger, not weaker. Right now, I am feeling my spiritual defeat as all I can feel is the pain leaching on me. I need to find the inner power to transform this pain into a new source of energy, but my brain has never mentally trained me for this moment. What it needs is some kind of resilience, a protective wall I can lean on, and focus on taking that mental pause and reenergise. Foremostly, I must not look back and count the days spent without Tia. I fear that the days will turn into weeks, and the worst if the weeks turn into months. I feel the panic overtaking my mind, my breathing is becoming shallow, so I place my hands over my face, close my eyes and begin building my protective wall. I inhale deeply, sucking in the fresh oxygen like a vacuum, and exhale all my worries, leaving my inner *me* feeling a little less panicky, and a little more brave. After this exercise, I have a clear access to my soul, and I sense Tia's imprint, deep inside. I can feel her so close. I can almost touch her, smell her scent. I can feel her hand touching mine. She is here, with me, and I whisper into her ear *I love you my little darling and I am coming for you.* I can see her little smile shining bright, those piercing chestnut brown eyes open curiously wide and as she gently brushes her ash blond locks from her face, with her small hand and she whispers back to me *I know, Mummy, I am waiting for you, don't be long.* I can feel our arms wrap around each other, and the sensation of that magical warmth fills us both equally. That is it, I have got it, my protective wall, the ability to focus all the wrongful and negatives on my loving connection to Tia. I will fuel my days with our memories and take every day as a new day, as to fool the reality of time.

I place my empties into the nearby rubbish bin and begin my way back to the car. Ah, I just want to go home! My phone suddenly rings, it is my sis, so I answer it straight away.

'Hi Sis, you won't believe the day I had…'

I am sitting in the office waiting for Gloria to invite me into her office and I frankly have butterflies in my stomach from the excitement. In the meantime, I have had some email responses from some of the organisations I searched for the other night after the Police station visit, such as Family Lives, Children and Family Court Advisory and Support Service (Cafcass), Citizen Advice Bureau, but they all seem to merge into one jar of advice and that's for me to seek legal representation with a recommended contact list attached. I do not see the importance of contacting more lawyers, explaining everything all over again as there is no time to waste. Besides, I have a good feeling about my chosen law firm, as they have a reputable background of successful cases, with highly experienced lawyers. In my case, Gloria, who will draw up my application to the court, and represent me. I mean, if I get that opportunity to be heard by a judge. It ought to be! I do know for a fact that this will cost me a great deal, as I don't qualify for free legal support as advised by the Citizen Advice Bureau, but there is no price set when it comes to Tia, and I do need the best lawyers in town to help me get her back! This seems to be a rare case, as I cannot find stories of any similar cases in the courtroom before so I need a strong, confident support whom I can trust to win my case.

'Hello Vivien, nice to meet you finally. How are we doing today?'

Gloria's look does really match her voice. Strong pointy features, light green eyes and shoulder length straight cut light brown hair. Her energy is calm, patient, but also strong and powerful. I get a sensation that anyone crossing her could trigger her strictness coming to the surface. Excellent, this is exactly who I need!

'Lovely to meet you too. I am okay, suffering, but trying my best.'

'I understand, of course, this is very difficult to even just hear about. I have two children, and however much they annoy me sometimes, I could not bear ever losing them. Have a seat please, thank you for coming. Now let's get things going, the quicker the better. At this stage I need to know a few more details to draft your final statement. I will do the drafting after our meeting and email it over to you so you can have a read and add anything else you wish to include.'

Gloria opened her case file printed onto A4 sized sheets that appears to be a draft of my statements with sticker notes ready to take details for further amendments.

'Let's start with some latest updates, besides the mediation, as I am aware of that and I already attached the report to your open statement.'

I begin, my voice is shaky, and I feel suddenly anxious

and tearful at the same time. Talking about this situation is making me crack and conversing is one of my strongest natures. This is different, this is not something that comes to me naturally.

I have updated Gloria about my attempts to see Tia, my email to the school nursery teacher, my sister's text to try and get a response from Shona and the parent who could possibly provide information on Tia. So much has happened, just over a week or so. It seems like I am carrying out some kind of an investigation.

'Vivien, from now on, however hard that will be, you have to stop driving around to try and spot Tia. Unfortunately, because of the given circumstances, and as I mentioned before, this is a very sensitive case, and if you are ever spotted in your ex-partner's area, she will file that as harassment and that will go greatly against you. I absolutely feel and fully trust your story and I can see how much you love your daughter and your life together, but we have to continue to portray you the way you have always been – the positive parent. This approach will work, as your story is the key to the door that will lead you to the winning side. What I can advise you to do, is to send postcards weekly to Tia. Children friendly, age appropriate, with no emotional messages so probably positive updates of what you have been up to. It is also a good idea to choose cards with images that Tia will find familiar and connective with you. This will show the court that you have never stopped being in touch with Tia, regardless if those postcards will get to Tia as please be prepared that your ex-partner may keep them away from her. Therefore, it is important to take pictures of the postcards on your phone, before you send them off, for the records as evidence to present to the judge. I would suggest one to two postcards per week. Okay?'

This is all so overwhelming, so much that I wouldn't have thought of as wrongdoing. I trust Gloria, her attitude is spot on, I admire the enthusiasm and as I am the positive parent in this ordeal, I absolutely agree with this approach all the way until the end, no matter what obstacles will cross my path. Feeling a rush of excitement as there is a huge chance that a judge will accept the application and set an early – unexpected – hearing date. I can't stop picturing this scene in my mind, all over again, where Tia sees me in the court hallway and runs into my arms, shouting *Mummy* and as I hold her tight in my arms, I tell her how much I love her, how I did not abandon her. That I fought for her with every minute of the day, thought of her every second of every minute. I may be getting carried away but this boost of hope has made me feel like I am on a roller coaster, slowly aiming for the high point, and the anticipation that is slowly building within, preparing me for the drop. Once on the top, there is no way back, but the speed ride ahead, that feeling of being weightless and letting go of all my fear. Seeing all the problems and issues from afar, tiny almost faded.

I continue with my story, Gloria is writing up notes as I go down memory lane, every detail matters and every detail will have an impact on my application. The abuse is going to be included in the hope that it will give us an earlier date. However, Gloria has mentioned that unless there are police reports, GP visits to show as a proof of evidence, abuse may not be considered in my case. Unfortunately, I did not ever report anything, because every time after an episode of Shona's dreadful abusive behaviour, I was threatened that if I did report anything then I would be accused as the perpetrator in front of the police, the one breaking in to her property and assaulting her. Meaning, that without a legal status and a formal connection to Tia, I could had been served an ultimatum, the locks changed and the accusations turned towards me. Shona had twisted stories locked in her box of cunning crafts. The police would have believed the biological mother, not me, as they highly rely on evidence which I of course did not have. I had just remained in that captivity of fear instead of putting little Tia through a scene with police, where Shona would put on a dramatic act and Tia witnessing the police probably removing me from the property. She would have been heartbroken, scared for her life and I had no courage to take that risk, not then. This is what had kept me from coming out, speaking up about the abuse I was going through. The length of the relationship had some positives as all the relationships do, but with the abuse, both emotional and physical, it could no longer survive. It is so true; parents try hard to stay in an unhappy relationship for the sake of their children, but it is short lived. I did it myself and eventually I could no longer take it, it drained me, it was slowly ruining *me*, the person I am. That worried me more than anything else as I didn't want my child to grow up seeing me unhappy, watching me suffer, listening to her parents argue and she wouldn't have thrived under these circumstances, the opposite, it would have harmed her overall development. The decision to break up was made, when many lines were overstepped by Shona, including threats with a knife, and such I could not take lightly. It terrified me to the level that I needed to sleep with Tia to protect us both, that was the period when things began to get worse, shortly before the night when the worst fight broke out, when I had nothing more left than finally end the toxic partnership. When I announced the breakup, I remained in the family home, until I felt that Shona calmed down, and could rationally think and accept my verdict. Firstly, I was adamant to not leave until we had a clear childcare arrangement in place, providing equal days with Tia. What made me feel good was the fact Tia was with me in my nursery setting, and she would only go back to Shona's for the evenings during the week, on the day when she would have her. The arrangement was not my idea solely, Shona was happy about Tia continuing in my nursery setting, and even suggested how beneficial that would be for her to continue with her routine, with the break up circumstances.

Interestingly, her attentiveness in what is best for Tia, was temporary, as she may have realised that I am no longer interested in amending our relationship and that I put my foot down, once and for all. Shona may have never thought that I could ever be brave enough to leave her. Tia was always my priority and Shona knew this, hence why she may have managed to manipulate and control me all these years. I didn't think I would ever have the courage to put an end to this. After the break up, I cried myself to sleep every night, as the partial detachment from Tia saddened me so deeply already. The fact that I would not be with her every morning when she would call my name after waking up or every evening when she goes to bed. It terrified me. Additionally, it was painful that her parents were on the verge of breaking up and she would need to divide between the two parents, until the age of eighteen. Although I tried to reassure myself that families do fall apart, however sad it is, the importance is the continuous love each parent can still provide, the care for the child, can make separation an easier process for the child.

So I remained until things calmed down, childcare was arranged and we both sat down with Tia to explain the family situation, after things had calmed. She was still very young and we had to talk in an age appropriate manner so she could try and understand the situation in her own way. She was sad and tearful as to her understanding, her parents were separating into two homes. I was leaving the family home, well one of us had to, but what reassured her was that every day of the week she would be with me, including weekends. Tia thrived from her routine, surrounded by people who love and care for her. Sadly, the handovers did not go so well, but she did not have the opportunity to adapt to the change. The handovers may have been the reason why Shona decided to cut Tia away from me. Shona may have hinted some inappropriate comments, that she could not allow Tia back with me, if she continues this behaviour. That was slightly worrying, but I didn't think she would ever do that, not to me, but to Tia. I stayed alert, and the thought to involve the court crossed my mind, but I was too focused on Tia settling into her new routine and trying to help to leave my side easier, so I did get pre-occupied. Shona may have never accepted my connection with Tia and for being the biological mother herself seeing the way Tia resented her, that she may have not easily come to terms with. I absolutely tried to keep the peace, help Tia during the handovers, and support Shona with how to use positive language to get Tia more comfortable to go with her. There were times when Tia ran back from her car, or shut the door on her refusing to leave. It was heart breaking. I was becoming concerned, and I had plans to get my legal recognition through the court, but I didn't want to scare Shona off too early. So, instead I suggested a mediator to look over our childcare agreement and make it more legal by witnessing it. However, she did not like that either, and that is when she had enough. That was when she cut my relationship with Tia via *the email*.

'Vivien, this is all fantastic, thank you for sharing these difficult events of your life. I have everything that I need for now and I will prepare the draft statement over the next couple of days. I need to attach relatable law clauses and sections, in support of your story. I will email it to you over the weekend and if you are happy with everything, we can send it off to the court as soon as early next week. What I need you to do in the meantime, is please send me over any sort of evidence that we can file in with your statement. Anything that you find relevant. There is no wrongdoing of such, as an unusual form of evidence, that the judge will appreciate to find, is better than no evidence at all.'

This is it; it has begun. What can go wrong, it is a strong application, the court will see how important I am in Tia's life and the time spent apart could only be causing her damage. I am leaving Gloria's office, feeling uplifted and speaking to a lawyer, seems somewhat therapeutic at the same time. As not only, Gloria listens to me every time, but has that legal affirmation to possibly bring on a favourable change. That has made me speak to her more comfortably, as it initially started off.

I am about to cross the road, to get into my car, when I notice a stationery shop just right next to the cafe on the opposite side. I shall begin sending the postcards to Tia, from today. The shop has quite a good selection of postcards, and the one with a Hippo wearing glasses, chilling on a rubber ring in the pool. That image makes me smile, and it will do the same to Tia. Great! I get a first-class stamp and walk out the shop. I write a message, without much of a thought *Hello my sweetheart. How are you, are the soft toys listening? :) I was passing by this shop, and I thought of you when I spotted this card. Love you, Mummy Vivien xxx.*

# Chapter 6

## Astonishment

'Strength is energy that is buried deep within you; channel it correctly and you will discover its capabilities.'

The day has arrived, the statement is ready to be filed, it has been a tough few days, editing the statement, adding every single detail, no filter, no ifs or buts, and everything has gone in, fair and square. Gloria spent her weekend drafting my statement and we exchanged a few emails, until the draft was one hundred percent ready to go. Little tweaks, and adjustments that I wished to add, were all appropriately drafted in. Gloria has outstanding expertise in converting a page long of my comments, into a legally required concise paragraph. Incredible! The judge who will open my case, will have no idea who I am. The statement had to be prepared to portray the best image of me as a person, as a mother, based on truth and honesty. To be frank, the evidence I managed to gather took me days to search for. From emails to messages, searching for anything where Tia or our living arrangement was mentioned. All day and into late nights since Friday, I searched and took screen shots. Including pictures from family gatherings and Tia's birth. Invoices from shopping deliveries, flights and holiday bookings. I sent everything to Gloria, who printed all the evidence. Apparently, at least fifty pages of various evidence material, all arranged from the most important to the smallest detail evidence. The judge, seeing this collection of true-life evidence, will have no doubt over my story presented in the statement. I literally satisfied each requirement in a very unconventional manner, through exploring every detail of my family life since Tia's birth, over four years ago. Can you imagine the amount of texts, emails, bookings, invoices, pictures, to go through? Almost endless! I will never give up the curious nature I have had ever since I was a child, and that grows with me, despite my adulthood and responsibilities. I have that child still in me, who will never stop exploring. I explored every single possible form of evidence for the application, as this is my only opportunity to find my way to Tia. Whether it will work, will depend highly on the judge, who will *open* my statement and study my file. It would be a great shame, if the judge would not bother to look through every piece of evidence of such a heavy case, but reject my application, based on lack of required information to the relationship with the claimant child. I had to try what I do the best, and that's never giving up. My desperation and pain will drive me to fight for our reunion, all the way. Gloria is the best match to represent me in front of a judge. Fingers and toes crossed, that my application is accepted!

    I can slowly feel my spiritual repair, deep inside, in the very core of my existence. I can feel each part of me that I lost in the past couple of years, slowly rising to the surface. Listening to my instinct has never been stronger and I will continue trusting it every step of the way. I will remain truthful and will not let anyone build hatred or place blame on me. I will not hold on to grudges, as those are negative feelings that I may not be able to use to re-energise. People come and go in our lives, some stay for a reason, some for a season, some will stay in our lives for a lifetime. I came across a person, whose past events, childhood trauma may have caused them to become the person they are today. Difficult to know for sure and Shona did not share much with me from her childhood, only that she experienced and observed physical mistreatment in her family home before the parents split up. Did she receive any support as a child growing up in these circumstances? Whatever the answer, some things must have shaped her character, and I cannot form an understanding from assumptions, so I leave this as an open page.

Shona hurt me badly where I hurt the most, my heart, she ripped my baby away from me! I will never forgive or forget what she has caused, but I will not poison my soul with hate, as that will lead me nowhere. Instead, hatred would eventually consume *me*. Changing me into a bitter person and that's not who I am or who I would ever allow myself to become. Tia wouldn't like to see her mummy in a form she never knew before. So, I will keep strong and grow spiritually to be a better person, ready for when she is back in my arms. I wish she could be part of my spiritual healing journey, but she is close, deep in my heart and that is my inspiration. With my heart I can see rightly, and I will hold on to this vision tight.

Now that the statement for child custody is filed, all I can do is wait and hope for the best outcome. I tie the laces on my trainers, put on my headphones and take on my usual running route. The sun is peeking through the dark clouds, but it is breezy this evening. Despite this, I love running outdoors and besides, this is the first time since *the email* that I am energetic enough to run wild. I am going to embrace this beautiful evening with my favourite playlist. I don't run to a usual running playlist, I run to music that is dramatic, dynamic, instrumental. that feeds my wandering mind as I run. Running not only fuels me with endorphins but it fuels my mind with inspiration and ideas. Many of my ideas were born during my runs. I run, I thrive. As I dodge pedestrians and dogs pulling on their leashes, I spot a card in a shop window, so take a sudden halt. The image of a heart made from fingers, a gesture we always used at goodbyes with Tia, it's the perfect next card I am going to send. I fill the card with my words *Hi darling, what a beautiful evening it is today. I am out running, come on, I race you! You can't catch me :) I love you, always.* Before I post the card, I take a picture on my phone and kiss it to send my loving vibes. I have had no response to my first card yet, and there is no doubt in my mind that Tia may never see my cards. That makes me just feel so sad, as Tia may think that I have just disappeared from her life, and I am no longer interested in being around. But I must believe that her strong little heart is filled with memories of us together and I have to hope that she is going to wait for me, no matter the length of time. I just want Tia to stay strong, strong like me, as strong as I have managed to raise her to be and trust that if any defamation of me as a person may take place in my absence, is false. She must trust in our connection, something that she may not be able to comprehend in her mind, but her soul is aware and will make her brave. I resume my run, rechannelling my breathing pattern and attempt to focus on exercise that is my current fix as it can decrease feelings of anxiety and stress. As I approach the final destination – my house – I receive a text message. Every time my phone rings or beeps, so does my heart, as I am in a constant waiting mode, for Shona's change of mind.

'Hi, how are you holding up lady? Any news from Shona? Boys have asked me about seeing Tia, so I have told them that we need to look into our diaries, to save some time. Want to go out tonight for a meal and some wine? I know it is very last minute, so no pressure.'

Oh, what I do need right now is the company of my dear friend. Bless the boys, they have played with Tia since they were born, especially the oldest one Jack, who is the same age as Tia. Madison and I go back many years, even before we had children, even before we both entered relationships. The days when we partied and met up for social events. Although mostly we do meet up together with the children, we do like our adult meet ups now and again. When we can, without the awareness of the children around, chat freely. Unless Madison minds, she could keep the children's friendship going, for their sake, but putting her anger and disappointment towards Shona's act aside, may be an impossible task. In fact, Madison was the last friend who visited our home for a meal with her whole family and witnessed the way Shona spoke to me. Besides, Madison already knew, even if briefly, about the issues that occurred in the relationship. So, her reaction to my breakup was concluded into one sentence *how she spoke to you the other week, in the presence of your friends and the relationship troubles that you shared with me? I am very saddened, but not surprised that you have ended it.* She nailed it!

'Hi Madison. Your timing couldn't be any better, I am very much in need of food and wine. I can meet you in about a couple of hours. Look forward to seeing you lady.'

Madison is fast paced, an active person who barely has a

chance to have those self-embracing 'nothing to do' moments in life. With two children and a thriving profession, finding time for a friend, can be often challenging, so, I do appreciate the spontaneous offer to meet, eat and chat. I only have a small circle of friends, but they are my loyal people, whom I really look forward seeing because time spent with them is filled with quality talks and laughter. Friendships of such value, in which everyone has that freedom of speech with a zero-judgement attitude, are remarkable treasures and need to be appreciated. With years, now as mothers, Madison and I, continue creating new memories. Tasty red wine accompanied by a set of delicious tapas dishes is very satisfying. I may have had a long monologue about the past events, but Madison has sat and listened intently, with tears in her violet green eyes. We eventually seize to the emotions, share a look that says it all, get up from our table and share a mother-to-mother hug. I am in such a need for hugs, and what's better than my people who will hug without asking, as they understand what I need, what I am like, and now especially, knowing what I am going through, something exceptionally painful, so tuning in with my needs matters to them more than ever. Madison cannot hide her anger about Shona's hurtful acts, as to how a mother can do this to her own child. She is outraged and shocked. However, Madison offers an idea, to attempt to text Shona and ask for a play date with Tia, in respect of her boys and Tia's friendship continuity. I reassure Madison that she is not at all obliged or asked to do anything that she is not comfortable doing. I place my hand on my chest and I feel a surge of adrenaline in my body causing a butterfly flutter effect on my chest. I am excited, as if my friends could continue seeing Tia while this horrendous ordeal lasts and give me updates on her life, would mean the world to me, as I would know how Tia is coping with the abrupt changes in her early life. Oh, I would appreciate that so much. Although, I doubt Shona will agree to any of that. It's not something I would ever ask of any of my friends but if they offer their attempt to try, I can't resist the chance to hear about Tia. Madison, releases from our long-lasting hug, lifts her arm to order some more wine and I try to divert the attention to her, so we move on to her life matters. Honestly, I am a listening ear to my friends at any time, and at the moment I do need that distraction, to just listen and discuss others' life matters.

The usual day at work, the nursery setting is filled with loud noises of playful children, but missing the voice of one child, that fills my whole universe. I am trying hard not to channel into my aching heart, as I have decided to feed into every bit of a distraction that my days may bring my way. With the focus on the now, as if I let myself go, I can lose everything, so I am putting my work mask on and just carrying on towards the unknown. So, I decide to walk down from the office floor, onto the toddler group floor, which has children's behaviour, more challenging than the older group on the first floor. Here, children require plenty of attention, and that is the distraction that I need. Besides, I shall monitor my additional staff, who I have trained for the early years practitioner role, and may require a review. Productivity and efficiency make my days go by quickly. I just need my work to be a place where I can hide away from my troubles.

As I finish the dance lesson, which I opted to teach, children move to prepare for outside play and I lift my phone and find Gloria's name displayed, eagerness to speak to her rushes through me. I run back upstairs to my office and return her call immediately.

'Vivien, are you ready for some good news? The court has accepted your application and has set a date for a hearing. The hearing will take place on 11th August. I know you have been expecting something to happen much faster, but I can reassure you, in the court world, this is an early date. What really does matter and is an amazing start to your journey in getting Tia back, is that the judge considered your provided evidence and believes in you being a mother. You have been given a chance to be heard.'

I have momentarily frozen, I can't yet level with Gloria's excitement as the thought of not having Tia back for over two months is unimaginable and worrying. I stressed the importance for an urgent hearing and what I naively expected was a matter of a couple of weeks at most, not months. This can't be, how can I possibly continue living, without any contact with my daughter and what does the hearing promise? This uncertain wait will feel longer than two months, it will freeze me in a world, where snails push the handle around the clock, making one hour seem long and two months like an eternity. Okay, now I have to up my game, build a stronger protective wall at work, refocus my free time with something that can distract my mind more than chatting can, otherwise the days ahead will become even more of an intolerable torture.

'That is fantastic, Gloria, thank you very much! I am super excited, but I cannot seem to handle the fact that I will not see Tia for another two months. It is unimaginable how much Tia could be getting more confused with time. Will the hearing be just a one off and then with the judge's permission, I will be able to see Tia again? May I hold on to this hope?'

'Unfortunately, I cannot promise you anything as we have to wait for the hearing, but I will do everything in my power to get you time with Tia. Shona will be served by the court and notified with the hearing date, but she will not be obliged to attend. However, her non-attendance will pose as an agreement with your statement, and the hearing will go in your favour. Shona will also receive a copy of your statement, including all the evidence that we filed in. If she still stands her ground to keep Tia away from you, she may file a response statement with her own supportive evidence, just as we did. Her response will have an impact on your statement, but we will stick to our plan, do not worry. Let's wait and see!'

On another note, it has got me thinking, could the thought of a court revert Shona's intentions and aid her realisation of her wrongful acts of snatching Tia away from me? I may get a call or an email from Shona indicating that she has changed her mind after her anger has subsided. May she ever realise that her mean, selfish and revengeful act has led us both into the court, where the truth will prevail, at some point anyway? The court hearing may hopefully motivate her towards wanting the best for Tia! I do wish for her senses to find the right place. How could Shona think for a second, that I will just sit by and give up on my daughter just because she may have successfully achieved making me legally invisible? This ruthless act has clawed me into this mess. I am to blame, and I am going to have to fix it myself. I am beginning to see the relationship from a different perspective now as I am disconnected from it. I shouldn't have been understanding of Shona's circumstances, my stupidity, my own failure but back then I trusted her, I believed in conceiving a baby together, and lived in that thought until I ran out of days to make my legal imprint in Tia's life. I had changed along the way, an absolute U-turn, when I realised that everything was a lie, that I lived everyday unconsciously in a lie. The only truth in the relationship that has ever existed is Tia, her purity and innocence, she should have no role in this dramatic ordeal. As the non-biological mother, I have not suffered from feeling left out in the union, or as the third wheel. I owned up to my mothering title, by actions, not only words. So, the only inequality was the legal recognition missing from my formal title. Why wasn't I allowed to have the legal privileges? I asked her, I demanded answers, but when Shona chose not to talk, I seemed to have always hit a brick wall. She may currently think that she can just act as I never existed, believe in her biological entitlement to Tia and cut me out of her life, but the judge may recognise that as an act of spite. Something of a disadvantage to Tia. Mothers, or in fact fathers too, may try to keep a child to themselves if their safety is questioned but I am not involved in drug taking, alcoholism, nor am I abusive or a criminal. I am a parent, a mother. I have spent every waking minute, hour and day with Tia since she was born and not purely from obligation, but from my heart and commitment. I have invested my whole self to support Tia's needs and that is why it is so painful for me to be apart, I miss a huge part of me – my baby. Separating a child from someone they formed an attachment with, could have prolonged neurological issues in the child's development later on, possibly causing anxiety issues, socialising difficulties, relationship challenges and possibly the inability to manage emotions in general. Tia had formed a secure attachment with me, despite of our non-blood relationship and being detached from me, may cause her harm. This is the fundamental reason for having my child back, it is not just an emotional need, but the worry over the potential damage this situation could cause Tia. I would do anything without a reason or doubt, regardless of not sharing the same flesh and blood, our relationship is living proof of a bond flourishing in an unique way. Many lesbian non-biological mothers or gay fathers I have met, deal with issues of bond, not being accepted by their children and question their own sense of belonging in the family union. I had not dealt with such issues, but that is only because I followed my mothering instinct, and never paid attention to social labelling. Societal expectations, that can put pressure on lives of so many people, especially LGBTQIA+ parents and families, who may not fit into a box of norms, and struggle being accepted by others. Two mothers, two fathers, single parent titles are still a lingering stigma, as people rather reject something different than seek understanding. I have followed the bond I felt with my daughter, introduced myself as a mother, stood proud of my family union with not a slightest focus on pleasing the society we live in or those who disagree. I will continue to convey my beliefs with confidence and courage in the hopes that society will learn to appreciate the diversity and uniqueness of each person.

Soon I will have to stand up in court, and prove this magnificent life we had shared with Tia until the day of our separation. I will only speak the truth, the whole truth, and nothing but the truth and keep my fingers crossed for the judge to believe me. Please, oh please let them speak to Tia, whatever way that is suitable for her age, but please listen to what she has to say about me, as our stories will match. I have read that young children are being more often listened to during the process of court hearings, especially custodial cases. Although the judge may listen to young children's opinions, their wishes may not be taken into serious consideration. Judiciary may view young children, slightly unreliable, as they are changeable and move their preferences of their two parents way too often. The generalisation of this concept may not apply to Tia, but it poses a slight worry. What that day will bring, is currently uncertain.

Discussing this news with Gloria is comforting, it provides me with a feeling of security and guidance. Hearing from her feels gratifying, because she is the one with the answers backed up with legal facts. Her support is essential formally, different from the support I receive from my friends. My friends' support is emotional and priceless, as they are looking out for me, increasing my sense of purpose. Frequently popping up to check on me, and that does not let me close away from the world and deal with my traumatic experience alone. I am a strong woman, but I admit that this time in my life, my family and friends are making me remember my strength as I will need to fight hard like I never fought before.

After a brief conversation with Gloria, we say goodbye and I drop my phone on the table. I slide down my office door until I feel the floor beneath me. I let my sadness flow freely, take over me. Two months is too long. I will drown in this ocean of torment.

The days are crawling by, but my work gives me professional satisfaction, so I have buried my head deep in the daily commitments. Working with children through participation opens up the world of play, which allows me to study their perspectives whilst immersing myself in the imaginary. I learn about the way they think and make choices, as everyday it's new knowledge and being part of this experience is rewarding. Tia has been part of this team and she is greatly missed. Client parents are starting to ask questions, as they have not seen Tia running around when the doors of the nursery open in the morning, but as it's my personal matter, I try to keep it private. I need to avoid additional emotional reactions, from people, who may not understand my story as much, sacrifice my protective wall at work, and possibly open my nursery doors to judgments. Work is my work, private life is mine to keep safe. When I shut the door after saying goodbye to all of the staff, at the end of the day, has felt so strange lately, as behind the closed door I stand alone. Tonight I need *me* time, to digest all the information, which I had no opportunity to do, while I worked within the walls of distraction. I cycled back home, and the thirty-minute ride has built up an appetite. So I serve myself some tasty chicken soup that my sister brought over last night, shut all the blinds, light my candles, and cover myself with my soft blanket and hit the on button on my television remote. I need something, nothing deep, nothing with a psychological twist. Yep, I have got it! *Orange is the New Black* has just recently released a new series, so I am going to catch up with that. At the same time, I spot the pile of study material on the dining table in the living room, which I seem to be behind with. Nope, not tonight. I cannot put my head around studying right now. Tonight, I do nothing, nothing at all.

Few days down the waiting line, panic fills my chest, as I search everywhere for my phone. I have had my anxious eyes locked on my phone like magnets, as I cannot afford a missed golden opportunity for a possible weak moment that Shona may have. This rush of hope is predictable, what else can I do in this situation other than hope? Two months, well less than two months now, is still too long. Even just one additional day would do my head in. I cannot for one minute believe that Shona wouldn't turn to someone, who would advise her of her wrongful acts. Someone who would open her eyes to allow her to see the impact her choices may have on others, including her own daughter. Someone, who could warn her, that at the court, if she agrees to attend, she will need to tell the truth. Someone, who could advise her to opt for mediation, to avoid the court, which would significantly reduce the harm that Tia may suffer. The additional two months are going to be just as difficult for Tia, and even worse, as she is only a four-year-old, who may be currently sad and confused.

I try to push the temptation to just leave my phone behind, it's okay, and nothing will change in a matter of an hour, as I am only cycling to the local supermarket. But the pull is stronger for some reason, so I take a U-turn on my bicycle and speed back down the road. I lower my bike in the grass by the gate, and run into the house. My phone is left there right on the curtail step, typical. As I press the home button, a faint image of Tia appears on the screen, but it is not delivered from Shona, but Carol. This was the pull, this was that force that I couldn't resist. I fling myself on the stairs, my heart pounding, hands sweaty, I open the message from Carol. She managed to take a picture of the girls just before the gymnastics lesson, last Saturday. I do not understand, as I did go to the community hall and waited around to catch a sight of Tia? The picture shows them giggling and holding hands. Tia has her soft teddy in her other hand. She seems all right in the picture. Oh, thankfully, Tia has resumed her favourite activity. I am so very relieved that Shona is offering her some sense of continuity, as that is important.

I don't know whether to cry or smile so both seem to happen at the same time. My beautiful baby, I miss her so very much! Seeing her in the picture makes my heart feel overwhelmed, almost causing it to ache. I place my fingers on the screen, and stroke her little face on the zoomed in image. Her ash blond locks are tied up in high pony tail that is looking certainly longer than the last time I brushed her hair. I zoom out the image, and realise that she has grown a tad taller as well, her face maturing as the weeks pass by. I just want to run to her and squeeze her, but I don't want to behave foolishly and jeopardise my hearing. I have to obey Gloria's rules as she knows what she is doing. After dealing with nasty child maintenance battles, every tip she passes on, she gathered from the mistakes many parents made. I will wait for the hearing, and follow her guidance in the interim. I trust this expert woman. I can't stop myself from bawling my eyes out, and teardrops smudge my phone screen, so I wipe them with my jumper sleeve. I just stare at her face, repeating *my baby.* I have one image, at least one. I want to just cherish this moment and hold on to it forever. Only her and me, through the means of technology, but yet it seems so surreal.

'Carol, thank you so much for thinking of me and managing to take a picture. It means the world to me, as it makes me so happy to see her, that she is safe and okay! How did she seem to you, was she all right? Also, I stopped by the community hall last Saturday to spot Tia, but there was – strangely to me at the time – a different mix of age groups exiting the lesson our girls attend?'

I cannot thank Carol enough, she is so wonderful for doing this for me, she feels my pain, and it's nice to see that she finds my story genuine. We barely know each other, only on the surface really. But what she probably sees, is a hurting mother, who is madly missing her child. Besides, she has kept her word, as to when she sees Tia, she would update me. Isn't she just so thoughtful and kind-hearted?

'Tia seemed all right to me, but I only met her for a few minutes before the lesson began. You know how the girls get when they see others, they just run around playing. When she walked in, she did cling on to her teddy, closely but straight ran towards Jackie. Shona didn't mention the separation, and I didn't ask about you, so I will keep it that way. We will be going to the park at some point, so will update you then. I am guessing you are not on the mailing list anymore, as the Gymnastics was an hour later that Saturday, but back to usual time the next week. However, sorry this may be saddening, Tia will not be attending lessons any longer. Shona said that she is not interested in doing Gymnastics. I found that curious, as Tia loves it. Anyway, I will keep you posted. Take care of yourself!'

I take in the response, and the only thought that can cross my mind right now, is that Carol will update me again, meaning that I will see more images of Tia and hear any kind of information about her. I cannot seem to care about Shona, or what she says, or not. Honestly, the Gymnastics discontinuity is not Tia's decision, but what can I do? Nothing. I lost a chance where I could catch Tia, even if from afar. To push the sadness away, I switch my focus back to being excited. I change my screen background to the image of Tia, and kiss her little face gently, sending her my loving vibes. I press the share button on my screen and add all the recipients who will be very glad to see Tia, even if just through an image.

I added a message to avoid confusion: *My friend took this picture before Tia's Gymnastics lesson,* and I press send. Never again will I leave my phone behind, I had an intuition and I followed it. The more I do this, the more I believe in it. This is the magic of my evolving empathic skills that I carry inside me. I pop the earphones into my ears, shut the door behind me and dial my sis, before I jump back on my bike.

'Sis, have you seen how much Tia has grown? So cute, isn't she?'

'Yes, aww it is nice to see her, even if not in the flesh. I am debating whether to show the picture to Charlie, may be better not to, as he will just get upset and will demand seeing her. That Carol is a gold mine to us right now! That's so kind of her.'

I can hear more messages arriving into my phone through the message tone peeping in my earphones. I bet everyone I have sent the image to, is pretty pleased! My feet seem to be peddling my bike to match the rhythm of my heart, so I am zooming down the main road with the speed of a light, if not faster. Tia's face is the boost that I need!

Two weeks have passed already, and Monday has come so quickly. I feel tired, even though I slept a lot over the weekend, even with some cat naps during the day. Sleeping is my safe place that creates dreams which take me to a different reality and each time I wake up, my brain takes some time to distinguish the dream from reality. Often I ask myself, whether the past weeks have just been a bad dream? However, once my brain is fully awake, it comes to terms with reality.

Today is going to be a good day as I have a burst of innovative ideas towards activities that I worked on over the weekend. I felt highly creative over the weekend, besides my sleepiness. I can feel my pain turning into renewable energy so I am going to take advantage of this, for Tia's and my own sake. There is lots of work to do in our house, such as decorating the walls and decluttering my stocked-up storage. I had some flat packs delivered over the weekend too, so I will get my girls in for some beers, and get some serious DIY into motion. Having a crafty mind, and having always been quite resourceful, DIY is not my strong suit. So teamwork, which means I do not need to do it myself, is a great idea, ha! Plus it is going to keep me busy for a while, and that is exactly what I need for the next few weeks ahead.

I am about to open my computer screen in my work office, and upload the activity sheets for the weeks ahead, I get distracted by an email that is delivered to my phone. I pull my phone out of my bag, the display message shows an email delivered from Gloria. I look at the clock that shows 9 a.m. that suddenly startles me, as that's an early email from a lawyer on a Monday morning. Although, Gloria often operates out of hours anyway.

'Vivien, this is Gloria, please open the attachment in your email as soon as possible and please call me once you have read through it!'

Oh blimey, this cannot be good!

# Chapter 7

## The Response

'To vilify my innocence, will make your lies more voracious.'

I cannot believe my eyes, I cannot believe the title of the subheadings, I cannot believe in the capabilities of this woman. Shona has indeed opted to respond to my court application statement, but what I didn't know is that she will add a twist to it. What a statement of utter bullshit, complete nonsense. This is a pile of lies! What lawyer has approved to represent someone, who is clearly fabricating allegations to just get back at me? To jeopardise my one and only chance! The judges will be swept by this horrendous case, puzzled by two sided allegations, who will they decide to believe and what if they take Shona's side? So, the fabricated story begins with Shona claiming that it was my aggressive and abusive behaviour to both Tia and her, that always left them both feeling scared. So the reason why Shona broke up with me, is because she found me no longer safe to be around, but I took the break badly, and continued harassing them. Adding that she has always been the one and only single parent to Tia. Atrocious cruelty! There is an *appendix* attached to the statement, so I quickly scroll down to the attachment, and find that the birth certificate is attached as evidence without my name printed on it and Shona's tenancy agreement, also without my name. Another lie, that I was a short-term partner to her, who Tia had become very fond of as I visited occasionally, but never lived in the family home. As I continue reading, I find that Shona claims that Tia may have, on some occasions visited me in the nursery setting, but was full time in her care, visiting other groups and recently starting school nursery where she is attending full time, since the separation . Aha, that is why I couldn't see Tia going in the time when I drove around at lunch time, as that was the start of the afternoon part time session. Okay, now it makes sense. What an appalling collection of allegations. I am portrayed as the perpetrator, whereas, none of the above is true. Shona is claiming that Tia has never formed an attachment with me, and that she is very happy, living her life, in her home where she has always resided, with her one parent. One parent? Whoa, I feel like something has whacked me in my face, and I have gone unconscious into a world where only evil exists. I am seriously disgusted by this response! On another note, how has Shona got herself a lawyer in a matter of just a couple of weeks, and has managed to respond to my statement, both in such a short period of time? Has she already hired a lawyer, to have on standby, as she may have caught on that after mediation, that I would be applying to the court. That is an assumption, my rational explanation. A sudden heavy feeling in my stomach leaves me stranded with my thoughts. I want to scream out of frustration, this dreadful misconception of me as a person, as a mother is outrageous. How am I going to stand the slightest chance in the court?

I quickly press Gloria's contact on my phone, and after a

few rings, I find myself with a voicemail, so in a shaky voice I leave a message – Hi Gloria, I have read the statement, and I am upset and worried about the content of it. Please call me as soon as you can. Thank you! – feeling frustrated as Gloria asked me to call her back, but then she is no longer available. Of course, she has other clients too, but currently I need to discuss these allegations with her. I guess I will have to wait.

Things are just getting worse, not better, not easier but harder to bear. I am speechless, so instead of a phone call I forward the email over to my sis. The anger is elevating fast from within! I am just shocked to my very core. I can't wait to speak to Gloria, discuss the response and take the next step, as I cannot leave her response just resting that peacefully without my self-defence. I didn't think that Shona would respond to the statement as she has ignored everything else since *the email* and her presence at the court hearing is not mandatory, so I assumed she would not show up there either. Little did I know that she will hit back this hard, out of silence, with bullets of lies targeted right at me. Her response is a description of an iniquitous person, and that's not me. How will the judge make sense of this messy situation? One person's statement, who has no legal papers to show of being a parent to the claimant child and the other person the biological mother's statement with all the legal documents in her hands. The judge will have to weigh up the risk factors in making a decision in Tia's best interest. With the judge's aim to look for evidence on the relationship between the parent claiming custody and the child, and how that parent who is seeking custody is able to provide emotional and physical support, a loving home for the child and offer parental guidance. Honestly, impressing the judge within these terms will not need reservation nor planning, I am true to my bond with Tia and speak for the truth. There is still time, and I still believe, that Tia should be interviewed before the court hearing. Tia's sense of belonging and her beliefs may have been manipulated over these past few weeks, but she will remember me always and stand by our relationship. Tia is the one and only, who could show the judge, which parent is the one telling the truth. I am hopeful but still slightly worried, that Shona may overpower Tia's innocent and honest mind before any interviews, as she did say in the text to Sis, that Tia is settling in a new life without me. Which makes me wonder, every minute of the day, what is Tia being told when she asks for me? I am not a friend who has just suddenly stopped visiting. Even if that was the case, Tia, if very fond of someone, will ask about them frequently. Who am I becoming in Tia's mind? An answer I will possibly have in a few weeks' time, after the hearing. What if my vision of her running into my arms in the courthouse, will not become reality? That alternative just terrifies me.

My phone rings, thankfully it is Gloria. A massive load of weight has just dropped off my shoulders, that relief! I have been so tense since reading Shona's response statement, and had the urge to hear some feedback from the person who has answers.

'Vivien, I am so sorry, but I was on an emergency call with another client, and the meeting went on longer than I initially planned. I gather that you have managed to read the response statement right?'

'That is all right, I understand. I am so upset, Gloria, as the whole response statement is based on lies and I am distraught. The hearing is just a few weeks away, and I cannot imagine what other obstacles may attempt to jeopardise my chances.'

'I understand how upsetting this is, Vivien, but I expected this to happen, if she was going to respond. Please try not to worry. Shona had to respond to your statement, as she disagrees with it. In terms of disagreement, she had to oppose what you are claiming. Now we know those may not be true, we will keep her response statement, right where it is. What we do not want to do is respond to her allegations, for now. The judges do not fancy the endless tick-tacking between parents and can simply postpone the hearing if the statements are an argument relief of the parents. We have registered Shona's response, and we will see her at the court. The judge will appreciate that!'

'Okay, thank you Gloria. I am finding this situation maddening, as Shona having the last words before our case is presented to the judge, is not reassuring, but I trust your strategy. Is there anything for me to do?'

'There is one thing you need to do, and that may help you to release some stress over the allegations, is to prepare a response to each of the allegations along with an explanation of why you disagree and attaching the relevant response evidence. Probably, aim to not repeat your existing statement material, but approach the responses from a different angle, if that makes sense. If you could send the material over to me, once you have finished, so I can study it before we go to the court.'

Whether that makes sense, is early to tell, but hopefully it will relieve some tension by letting my angry thoughts loose. Although, it is better to let things cool first, as I am way too upset and cannot think clearly right away. The day has taken a huge turn. I am upset, not because of the response statement, but more about how much one person can lie, but denying the truth does not change the facts. The person I chose to have a baby with over four years ago, is not the same person who I decided to break away from. This person has changed during the last few years, or she may have simply revealed her true colours, which were previously disguised. Please, let this ordeal end with one hearing. I do not desire anything out of the ordinary except for my child, whom I have always parented. Why would I be applying to the court, if I was not the true mother to the involved child? Hilarious! I mean who would do that? Who would fight for a child, other than their own, regardless of biology, or not? I've got to get back to work, and continue with my planning. This week is a busy one, as there are new children signed up to start, and the setting is also due an Ofsted inspection this week. Therefore, my attention must be on work, mind distracted, and response statement momentarily pushed to the back of mind.

    I attach the last pieces of the furniture and gaze at the final work in amazement. My sis came to the rescue this Saturday afternoon, as the drawers I bought seemed to have a guide that did not well match with the material provided in the flat pack. I put Tia's clothes and belongings into the drawer and step away to look at her room. I feel a great sense of satisfaction! The drawer is a nice addition to her room, filled with some of her clothes that will hopefully still fit her, and with some new ones I have recently bought, as she was due a wardrobe upgrade already. Everything else will stay like she remembers it, to provide her that feeling of comfort. I can sense her energy in her room. I often find myself sitting here on her bed, cuddling her soft animals, speechless, smiling at her pictures in the frame and her drawings framed on the wall. My happiest place is her room, where no tears are shed but memories treasured.

My sis shouts upstairs loudly, that the pizza has arrived. Pizza, anytime, the best food for a DIY day. I have been decorating the walls in Tia's room, since the morning, and I am absolutely knackered. But put that aside, I do enjoy decorating and refreshing the house a little. What I may not like as much, is gardening, and that also awaits, as the grass is as tall as Tia may be now. Frankly, I take on anything that comes in my way, as distraction is my way to survive this sad patch in my life. I may seem all right on the outside, but people that surround me, know that I am hurting inside, more with every day. That is not going away, with anything I try to do, but it is distracting me and keeping me sane. My little nephew Charlie is missing Tia. Every time he comes, he looks in her room, and asks me when she is coming back. Bless him! His presence fills my aching heart with affection, and his cuddles always come at the perfect time, just when I need them most. Watching him covered in tomato sauce as he munches on a pizza slice, is entertaining, putting a smile on my face.

After some delicious pizza, and catching up with Sis, whilst Charlie played with Tia's toys, I decide to take a seat at my desk, and bravely open the response statement for the second time. Getting my sister's perspective, in addition to Gloria's reassurance, has made me feel a little less worried. My attentive brain is evaluating each allegation carefully, and my hands are typing quicker than I can think with the focus on relevance. At this point, what detail could I simply deselect for its irrelevance and how can I predict what detail the judge will decide to accept as relevant. It is important to write down all my thoughts, let it all out, thereafter, narrow the thoughts down to a more concise version, leaving no room for further speculation at the court hearing as my response will be already laid out for Gloria, beforehand. This statement is the only response the judge will see from me but the initial statement is the primary document for them to rely on. I'll have to fight hard because I'm fighting for more than just custody; I'm fighting for respect as a mother and fighting against a false accusation that has just been lodged against me. This response statement is making me weak, it's very upsetting to read these odious lies against me, sentence after sentence. Taking an enormous hesitating breath, in between my snivels, I open up every single paragraph and begin the strenuous attempt to break down every microscopic fraction of these lies. How can someone think that they will be justified just because I am not on the birth certificate and my name is not on the tenancy agreement? Claiming that I have never parented Tia, whereas, I not only parented Tia but I was part of a decision to conceive Tia, I was part of choosing a donor and I was part of the nine-months pregnancy. Just the physical reality of being pregnant was the only distinction between two female partners expecting a baby because I was so emotionally active in the whole entire planning. It began with an extensive exploration, initially to be able to successfully conceive, besides finding a healthy sperm donor, who has never fathered before so we were not 100% assured whether it would work. The consideration into the amount of pre-pregnancy multivitamins and diet, to aid the conception success, was like a full time job. Dietary changes included foods rich in antioxidants and avoiding trans fats and refined carbs. Apart from the vitamins, I took part in the healthy diet and lifestyle, simply for support.

One thing that I didn't have to sacrifice was my naughty pleasure – caffeine but Shona never enjoyed that pleasure in life, as even just the smell of coffee put her off, so her caffeine substitute would always be tea. During conception I used to make a regular super beneficial green juice made with cucumbers, spinach, oranges and apples, ah not a pleasant taste, I still remember the taste. Conceiving a baby, for two women, requires a different kind of teamwork than naturally trying for a baby. Nonetheless, commitment and all the factors contribute not only towards conception, but also towards a healthy environment for the foetus to develop during the period of nine months. Conception vitamins and a particularly healthy diet became part of Gregory's daily routine too. He was devoted, and when it came to the ovulation days, he made himself free and available, so as to not miss out on one day of an opportunity window. Gregory was an absolute star! It was a blessing to have chosen someone who cares and so eagerly wants to help two women to have a child, outside of a clinical environment and on more friendly grounds. The home insemination is a much more relaxed way to conceive a child, the closest to a natural conception. Frankly all you need is an amazing known donor or a donor clinic who delivers on agreed scheduled days, sterile syringe and buckets of luck. The experience of handling a pot full of semen, that I had to keep warm in between my thighs as I drove, until it reached its destination to remain active, and that took about twenty minutes, so the pressure was on. Besides, this is not something that a lesbian ever dreams of ha-ha, but I felt like a super heroine who has the most precious jewel to keep safe and deliver to the fortress. I played an important part in the conception period, not as important as Shona's body, who had to work extremely hard to create an embryo. The principle is that we both had a significant input, even if not equal, and that counts! It had to be repeated for a few months, each month with the three ovulation days in a row, and to highlight, the dedication from Gregory was priceless. Month after month, the negative results were taking a toll on us all and then we all agreed to take a break, there was one more month left to try. Isn't it always that irony, when you just stop trying so hard, then miracles happen? That very last try, the one where we felt the most relaxed and almost prepared to break again, and have me take a turn to try and conceive, the pregnancy stick showed two lines side by side, meaning one thing only – we were pregnant! It was a truly triumphant moment, a moment when the two lines represented that equality between two parents. Papers and formalities are additional as they don't define a parent, the two lines do. Those two lines made me a mother forever.

Mothering Tia has been the most extravagant gift I have ever received. I didn't experience hormonal and appearance changes during the pregnancy or the contraction pains and the excruciating delivery agonies. Yes, very true, I didn't, but if it was me then I would have taken every part of that experience. I often regret that I thought about the financial outlook of having a family too much, and didn't just take the risk to get pregnant first out of the two of us. Life can never be too planned, but back then circumstances were just different. I didn't have much savings, so working was my only choice in order to support the family plans. Shona did not work back then, so the choice had to be made. What matters is the result, and that is the amazing Tia.

Anyway, I lived the pains together with Shona, even if not

as thoroughly. These pains are referred to as sympathy pains, and is a common discomfort when the pregnant partner is in the first and third trimester. I could certainly very often relate, especially when pains were compared to menstrual cramping or the level of oestrogen and progesterone increase during the months of menstruation that causes hormonal changes, similar to those experienced during early pregnancy. With respect to male partners, it is very common in men to feel these symptoms too, such as mood swings, weight gain, cravings, bloating, a condition known as couvade syndrome. As a female partner I may have been in a better position to appreciate and understand the difficulties and the beauties of a pregnancy. But the womb is where the magic happens, the period of nine months in which the embryo transforms into a human baby, is incredible, beyond breath taking. When the baby is born, the transformation is not complete, it continues the whole life time, both physically and emotionally. So after this fundamental life experience, I'm completely thunderstruck that I am accused of not being Tia's mother, just to rupture my relationship with her. Shona knows the truth, and that is why her response statement had to be a pile of fabricated material. As if she did agree to everything in my statement, then there wouldn't be a hearing. It is not only me who is a living proof to my parenting relationship, but family and friends who were part of our lives during conception, pregnancy and continued being part of Tia's life too, until the day of *the email*. Shall their opinions be considered by the court? I see no problem, why my friends wouldn't help me.

The tricky part is that Shona has no evidence of any abuse that she claims happened, and I have no evidence of the real abuse that did actually occur in the relationship. So, how will the judge make sense of it all? What the judge will find very difficult whilst considering all the allegations against me, is the section I cannot prove – the section where Shona responded to my statement, that the reason I am not stated on the birth certificate is because we didn't have the baby together and that she had always decided to be a single mother. Also, that the reason I am not named on the tenancy agreement because we never lived together. I am astounded! This added to my inner panic, knowing that I don't have a copy of the donor agreement, it's daunting for me as my statement could be potentially portrayed as fraudulent without any substantial evidence. I did drop a message to Gregory the other day to see how his search for the donor agreement was going, but he confirmed that he cannot find his copy. He is absolutely certain of never throwing it away but with two moves in between the past few years, he may have lost it. Although, he looked absolutely everywhere, even in places he would not look otherwise. There were only two copies, one for us and one for Gregory, signed by all three parties and the solicitors. I was so foolish to trust the agreement being in Shona's hands and I always believed the document was kept in a safe place with other important papers related to Tia's conception and birth. I completely got lost in the baby excitement and never had the reason to look for the agreement since the day all three of us signed it. Until the day when things began to get heated in the relationship and I wanted to get a copy of the only proof I had regarding the conception. Obviously Shona refused to disclose its location and may have it still locked away in the same place? Shona disputes the existence of the donor agreement in her response statement, which she is able to do because she did not see it added to the statement filed to the court, which contained all of the evidence we submitted. The donor agreement explicitly states the names of the parents, including my name as one of them, and that we are responsible for every aspect of Tia's life. With Gregory as the donor having no duties, financial commitments, parental responsibility or a say in medical and educational decisions. I am gutted, this agreement would have made everything easier, but as Gloria said, the hearing would still take place regardless of the donor arrangement. I needed this specifically explained, why such an important agreement would not make a big difference. I understand it now, however, it would be one of the strongest evidence attached to my statement but Gloria explained that I could have been with Shona when writing up the donor agreement but could have exited the plan rectifying the claims Shona is making, that she had Tia as a single mother without me. Evidently, the donor agreement would very much strengthen my case, backed up with the testimonies, including Gregory's, but I can fight for the truth, and I will win, without the donor agreement. So, I have a chance without it, and I can actually relieve the pressure of Gregory, who has been searching for it for so long. However, I will hold strong, with the truth in my hands, an outstanding lawyer, family and friends as witnesses by my side.

I must say it has been challenging but I have a great response draft to all the allegations, thanks to my sis who helped me to gain clarity over some events.

I enjoyed having them over. I close my laptop, as I have had enough of writing and mental exercise, I wouldn't be able to come up with another sentence.

Suddenly a text pops up on my screen *"white or red?"*. Oh crikey, Helen and her curry night. I completely forgot! So

I reply in a hurry *'white, please"* while rushing to quickly put on some jeans, blouse and add some light green eyeshadow to complement my chestnut brown curls and green eyes. I slam the door behind me and hurry to catch a bus, trusting I won't be too late because Helen has gone to great lengths to prepare a meal as a show of support. Luckily it is only a fifteen minutes bus ride so I am right on time. Helen pulls me in for a good old hug – Helen's immaculate strawberry blonde hair glows softly radiant, with her red cheeks, always so cheerful and smiley, this woman a strong rock who has been through a lot herself – and sits me down at her set table with chilled white wine awaiting. It's difficult to express how fortunate I am to be surrounded by such wonderful people. Helen's curry is just so flavoursome, so satisfying after the day I had, with barely finding the inspiration to eat properly, besides the couple slices of pizza. Pinching some of the naan bread that's left over and sipping my wine, I bring myself to ask Helen for her opinion on providing a testimony. I get an immediate response, with tears in her eyes *'absolutely, anything for you Vivien, we need to get Tia back to you as soon as possible'.* Helen is one of my dearest friends, she has been part of Tia's life since she was a baby, and we spent numerous occasions together. Helen witnessed the good and the bad sides of my relationship and she will be a strong witness. I am over the moon, I have one witness already, who is prepared to not only write a testimony, but also take the stand at the court, if necessary. On top of this great news, Helen offered to put her anger towards Shona to the side and request a meet up for the sake of the children, who had met often as her daughter Amber misses Tia greatly. Amber has been asking about Tia and Helen cannot say much more than she is with her other mum seeing some family away. That was only short lived as Amber doesn't accept this any longer and doubts that Tia is this long without me, such a smart mind these kids have nowadays. She can sense something doesn't add up, as I have been seeing Helen and Amber in between and always without Tia, that is suspicious to a six-year-old when they used to see a child with one mother, most of the time – me. To distract her little mind, I tickle her and offer a bedtime story read by me, which is happily accepted so I race her to the bedroom. Amber closes the book after the story and asks me sadly, *"What family is Tia with? She loves you and it's a long time, she must be very sad being away from you."* I force my tears back as this moment just triggers my emotional state, indeed, it has been so long and Amber doesn't have a clue of the situation but the two friends are so close that I am not surprised by her intuition. The saddest out of all is that there are more weeks to come, and it has already been so long for everyone who loves and cares for Tia. I tickle Amber again – something that works on children like magic – to cheer myself on and respond with a reassuring smile. *"Amber is missing everyone, she has never been away from me, especially for this long but she will be back soon."* Amber's little blue eyes sparkle with hope and trust in my words, requesting a sleep-over once she returns. I leave Helen with a massive thank you hug and hand her the printed statement and Shona's response statement to work with as she prepares her testimony. My only suggestion is to keep it optimistic as in line with my statement, focusing on explaining my character and my relationship with Tia from her viewpoints, and above all, to be honest. I have to hurry and meet with my other friends and ask them for the same favour. I am proud of this moment; each day makes me stronger; each day takes me closer to Tia; nevertheless, the pain of missing her continues to grow.

# Chapter 8

## Perseverance

'Just when you think you've got your life under control, you're torn down, but that's when you need to get straight back up.'

A ladybird with rainbow wings, like a shield. *Colourful, much like you, my love, one-of-a-kind.* There is a slight sense of hollowness as I drop the postcard into the deep letterbox, knowing that my messages are unlikely to reach Tia. Nevertheless, I would not give up because what if, she does see my cards but Shona does not encourage Tia to reply, or another possibility, Tia responds but it is never posted. These thoughts are causing me nothing but heartache. All of these possibilities could make a person insane, which is why I've got to come to a halt with my wandering thoughts right now. I feel like a stray dandelion, standing oddly in the middle of a grass-patch, lost for stimulus. Today, I don't feel like doing anything, nor visiting either of my family or friends or any work related chores. I just cannot seem to shake off this sadness, that is surfacing from the feeling of not belonging anywhere right now. I am a mother, but without my child the title serves no purpose. Within, I am aware that I cannot merely give up and succumb to this despair, but frankly the recent events have been emotionally exhausting and it is catching up with me. There is one thing I ought to do, and that is to call my mum. I pull my phone out of my jeans pocket, go to my contacts and press dial. She picks up straight away. It's the evening, so I can picture her sitting on the couch, watching her favourite television shows and snacking on a bag of salty peanuts. After a brief greeting and sum up, I ask her for once not to talk about how I feel, just for once, so my mum starts to chat away about her life and work gossip, this is perfect for my mind. She knows how hard it is to go through what I'm going through right now, but she still gives me hope, determination, and energy, as if mother to mother. Rachel interrupts the conversation with an incoming call, she usually doesn't call me after work, but this is out of the ordinary which alerts me to inform my mum that I will need to call her back as it seems important.

'Hi Vivien, I have been so sad about you, and I want to help you so much to get Tia back, everyone is missing her little bubbly face! Of course, the way you miss her is not comparable. Please let me testify for you and Tia on the stand, but I have sent you an email to describe you and your relationship with Tia. My input, whether you will consider using it or not, you have my permission. Anything I can do, just please let me know.'

Rachel is such a kind and sweet soul, still a child at heart, but extraordinarily mature for her age, juggling studies and work, whilst looking after her younger siblings and her beloved pets, with plenty of energy still left to spare. Everybody's interest in helping me is truly touching, and empowering. I cannot say no to absolutely anyone, as all the little pieces will collect and form a bigger picture about the person I am, when I stand in front of the judge, fairly soon.

'Rachel that is so kind, of course you can help, and thank you so much for offering. I will have a look at the email, but I will speak to you at work tomorrow morning anyway. Your testimony will have a considerable influence on my case, based on your loyal long term of employment history. I really appreciate it!'

As Rachel hangs up, I immediately open the email and take a look at the testimony she has written. What an honest description, I couldn't ask for anything more than sincerity. Rachel's statement is beautiful, she speaks of me as Tia's mother, our unique relationship, that is always apparent as it is natural. She has also highlighted the detachment impact that Tia may be experiencing, because she has never spent time away from me. She has described me as a professional, who is compassionate, imaginative, and patient, and as an employer, who is flexible, hardworking and understanding. Ending her testimony with a touching message: *Please, return this child to her mother where she belongs.* I can hear Rachel's sniffles between the lines, as she would get tearful every time she would mention Tia's name. A devoted staff member, that has remained in my nursery setting, employed for many years, and has known Tia since she was born. Including her testimony, even just in a written form, unless required otherwise, is valuable at this stage. I am astounded by the amount of support; I cannot thank everyone enough. Whatever life throws at us, not being alone, is one aspect that helps to keep us going, however lonely we may feel inside, the social web to rely on, keeps us in that healthy zone. Staying in that zone, stops us from sinking deeper and deeper into a sink hole of nothingness.

I dial my mum, and we continue with her monologue. Interestingly, she never forgets the rest of her story, and she continues where she left off. That does make me giggle a little.

The morning at work starts with a large hot caramel latte, delivered right into my hand after a huge hug from Rachel, who hands me her printed out testimony, seeming very buoyant. I am expecting the day to be bumpier today, as we have another group of younger toddlers starting. Settling in days are mostly a little more eventful and my mind is usually a lot more distracted by one-to-one interaction with those who need a lot more help getting to know the routine and seem a bit wary of others on the premises. As the door closes behind the last arriving child, my phone rings in my pocket. The display is showing an unknown landline number, so I casually pick up the phone with my usual greeting, assuming it may be one of the parents of the earlier dropped off children, who may be calling from their work phone. But the response startles me.

'Good morning. Is this Ms Vivien? This is police officer Mike, and I am calling you today about a harassment report filed against you by Ms Shona?'

I quickly duck my head into the toddler room and tell the staff to continue with the morning routine without me as I animatedly point to my phone glued to my ear. My voice is shaky, I can barely swallow, and the sudden anxiety hits my stomach

'Good morning. Yes, it is Vivien. What is this about, I don't understand?'

The Police officer explain that the report was made based on my constant harassment of Shona which apparently she reported has been stressful to her and Tia and wishes for it to stop. I am so shocked, what harassment? What is going on?

'Ms Vivien, you are not required to come down to the station at this stage, but if we hear further complaints from Ms Shona, we will have to ask you to come to the station so that we can take a formal statement from you, take this as a gentle warning. Please, stop visiting Ms Shona's apartment, emailing, texting and calling Ms Shona from now on.'

'Officer, I have had no contact with Shona for the past couple of months, since she stopped my access to our daughter. I hired a lawyer and we applied to the court for custody and will be attending a hearing on Monday, next week. I have not been visiting or contacting Shona as her report states. I have respected her wishes and I have been sending postcards to my daughter, twice a week as advised. Postcards have been my only contact, age appropriate and by all means kind.'

My heart is jumping all over the place, agitated, I begin to walk around, holding my head. Tears are slowly building in my eyes and beginning to affect my speech and I think the officer is changing his approach in response.

'I understand, Ms Vivien, it must be hard being apart from your child, but our job is to follow up on a report against you, and at this stage, given the circumstances you have no access to your daughter. I strongly advise you to wait for the court hearing to get to the bottom of this situation. From now on, please kindly stop all contact as previously mentioned and I have to ask you to stop sending postcards as well. If the judge at the court permits the postcards, please continue sending them after the hearing.'

This is unacceptable, another lie, and the police are once again taking that one side – the side of the biological parent who in their eyes is the only right one. What is Shona trying to do, just shortly before the hearing? It seems like she may be trying to get me into trouble. No way would the judge believe this report made to the police without collecting any evidence, such as phone records, emails etc. I informed the police officer that I am happy to provide my phone records to show no signs of harassment but they didn't require that from me. I am being framed, Shona will have a report to present at the court, just to confirm her allegations against me, that I am abusive and have continued to be so. The judge cannot possibly consider these fabrications, if there is no evidence. Anyone can file a report against anyone but without evidence, it will be just another paragraph added to Shona's statement and we will absolutely deny these lies as an attempt to blackmail me. I must say, I am scared and more worried, even more so since Shona's response statement. I look at the time on my watch, as I need to go back to work, but I decide to quickly call Gloria and update her. Luckily, she picks up straight away. I summarise the call from the police and Gloria is very saddened to hear that there are further wrongful allegations made against me but she advises me to respect the advice and not send any more postcards. Only to show that I am a respectful person, who has done nothing else but obeyed Shona's wishes since the very start of her decision to detach my daughter from me. Gloria reassures me that the postcards were innocent and for me to not be concerned about the report as that will be reconciled at the hearing and if necessary, will ask the judge to permit postcard contact with Tia. I am slightly bewildered by Gloria's comment, why would I be needing to extend the postcards after next week's hearing? Are we not preparing for us to be reunited? I cannot accept anything less, no way! No more waiting, no more postcards, no more pain. I need to have my baby back in my arms. I take a deep breath, and feel slightly more at ease regarding the report after speaking to Gloria, but I cannot stop feeling anger towards Shona and having slight doubts over her potential spiteful actions in the next few days. I just have to hope for no more nasty surprises!

As I walk back to the nursery floor, and about to place my phone into my safe place, I receive a message from Helen that says 'I attempted to reunite Amber and Tia with a playdate, but was unsuccessful because Shona believes it is better for Tia to not keep seeing people who remind her of you because she is settling in well into her new life and is making new friends, and it is best to keep it that way. I am sorry Vivien that I couldn't be much of a help, Amber is asking about Tia more each day and I feel as if Tia is probably asking about her little friends too. I am sorry, let's meet for a walk and coffee soon. Keep persevering Vivien, this has to be over soon, I can feel it.' I am speechless about Helen's actions, despite her resentful feelings, she did try to at least continue the relationship between our children, may that be with, or sadly without me. She can at least mirror the sorrow of being unexpectedly separated from one's own child as a mother. I cannot shake off the reality in which Tia is learning to live a life without me, this thought is like a dagger through my heart. Shona knows that this information is hurting me very deeply, she seemingly just wants me to continuously suffer. I am suffering, but with each and every one of her words and actions, I convert them into an external strength and into my desire to fight, and I will not give in. This is unlike anything I have ever faced, but I am going to fight like a lioness who will do anything in the wild to protect her cub, at heart, gentle, but tough and courageous in her actions. I respond to Helen, highlight my appreciation, but I cannot hide my disappointment. What a shame!

I speedily walk to the bathroom and refresh my face with a splash of cold water. Fix up gently, and look in the mirror saying to myself: You need to hold things together, all the little pieces, do not let any fall. It will be over soon, a few days, and your baby will be in your arms. I walk back into the loud play area, where children seem to be settling in well. Without causing any disruptions to my staff, I walk over to check the outdoor space, where everything seems to be just as settled. I step sideways into my observation corner, and take notes that will later turn into a settling in report, in addition to the staff's own interactive notes. However, going back to my office is not part of my protective wall and I would always make sure to share my interactions on all of the floors and office space equally. However, today especially, even if the settling in seems to be going well, I will remain on the toddler floor, where music and language time is going to take place, and I will be taking part, just for extra support. I have trained my staff well, for them to carry out the activities consistently and efficiently, and it boosts them with confidence that they are trusted to carry them out without my leadership. So if I take a lesson, or join in, it is only for observational and enjoyment reasons, as it motivates me to discuss further ideas with my staff. We are always innovative and adapt activities to please and challenge all the children in the nursery, so they can continually develop in a thriving environment.

A beautiful afterglow is covering the sky tonight, the best time for an end of a day run. I tie my trainers and place my earphones into my ears, clicking on the playlist most suitable for my exercise session today Armin van Buuren, starting with the first song "Sunny Days", perfect. As I run, breathless or not, I can always for some reason multitask, so I open my emails and scan through them. Depending on the urgency of the email, I would only stop my exercise if the reading required in-depth reading, otherwise I would risk some serious lamppost to face interaction. I notice the testimonies my friends have sent over to me. Oh wow, this is all so amazing! Gloria, exquisitely said no family as they may come across bias – no matter how truthful their testimony would be. I was told, up to two to three people maximum who know me as a person, as a mother, as a partner and as a professional. It wasn't a difficult decision to make, my closest people, who have known me the longest to satisfy each area of my testimony, are here with me and have not left my side. Gregory and Madison who have known me for over fifteen years, have been part of my life as a single person and as a mother to Tia, both have written up such beautiful testimonies, strong to the point, very much in line with my statement, both truthful and positive, with the focus on my relationship to Tia, although mentioning their adverse experiences with Shona too. Interestingly, without any of my input, they described Shona as being hostile, controlling and often anti-social. Highlighting that Tia would seem closer to me and more respondent to me in situations, that she would ask me for things, or would hold my leg at social gatherings when she was shy. They assumed to themselves that Tia, just as children can be, had a closer bond with me. They described the connection that is visible when I am with Tia and that they wish for us to reunite, as this is painful to watch, and hard to imagine how painful this must be to us both.

I am more than convinced that my friends found it emotionally difficult to write these statements and I will be forever grateful for their help. My darling friend Sofia, who is my longest friend who is now living abroad, she would stand strong beside me, but she is expecting a baby anytime soon and travelling for her to take the stand at the hearing if required, won't be possible. Sofia has reassured me that if necessary, she is happy to provide a written testimony at the last minute, or take the stand via video call, if that will be necessary and important. She witnessed my relationship with Shona and my relationship with Tia but only occasionally when we managed to travel to see each other. It is great to know that my friends are prepared to fight with me. It is my *army of honesty* and we will not be defeated. Sofia, bless her, she noticed the way I was treated in the relationship during her latest visit, before she got pregnant. She asked me how things are and I couldn't really say much, as I had no idea myself but as Sofia put it *you are losing your smile, you are not happy, this doesn't look good*. I was taken aback as I tried to put a smile on my face and be there for Tia, try and work the relationship as much as possible but Sofia, a person who knows me so deeply, saw beneath that smile. I didn't like feeling vulnerable as I thought I was doing all right, pushing myself, even if pulling the cart alone, just like my dad used to say. Sofia and I met when I first arrived in London, over 10 years ago. We spent days traveling and exploring London, sightseeing whilst getting terribly lost in this massive city that seemed like a labyrinth to us both back then. We loved the odd celebrity spotting. We were not best friends at first, but with time, we aligned and found each other's personalities interesting and had countless fun exploring London, our home away from home. Hence we risked everything and took on the chance to begin renting in one of the biggest and most expensive cities in the world. Together, we didn't fear! We had good and bad times, met great people and whenever we meet we cherish the past, and we continue building new memories as individuals and as parents. Honestly, I love every aspect of our friendship! A sad moment in our relationship was when we parted because Shona was not fond of my friendship with Sofia and the distance between us built when Sofia left the UK permanently, to move to France. I didn't know anything about her for a couple of years, only that she married and since had two beautiful children and that is thanks to social media. Thankfully, our friendship survived and the first few times spent together were awkward and emotionally hard to be honest, as there was a lot to talk about, a lot to move on from. It was not easy, but it was neither difficult, as our friendship still felt natural and we eventually picked up from where we left off, ignoring the negative gap and leaving it in the past. We went through a lot together in life, and Sofia found forgiveness in her heart. Forgiveness for my mistake in not listening to her, and estranging myself from her, to stupidly focus on my relationship. I am so very grateful! I only had realised, after my rose-tinted glasses cracked, that there is no such thing, as a choice between a relationship and a best friend, as both can work with compromise, and both can be playing a significant part in one's life. Unfortunately, Shona's jealousy and control shadowed my perception of what a healthy and committed relationship should be like and so I naively sacrificed my friendship with Sofia to appease Shona. I missed Sofia a lot when she left, there was not much I could do, and travelling to see her on my own was not supported by Shona, so I never went. It took me a while to brace myself to speak to Sofia again. I felt bad and ashamed. Luckily, Madison's wedding was where we first met after a long time, we had great chats together and cleared the air. It was not an immediate reconnection then, but our spark ignited within us both. The light has remained strong and bright, and with my wiser outlook on a healthy relationship, will not threaten any of my beautiful friendships. Why am I so certain? As I have my *me* back, and no one can touch that ever again!

Today, I regret my feelings but it's too late, as I cannot change the past. If it was today, I would never dare to have such thoughts, and would absolutely not sacrifice my friendships to satisfy one person but depart and await someone who would love me for who I am and accept the importance of friends in my life. I would rather stay single! I tried to explain the importance of the friends in my life, as they were more than just friends back then when I was all alone in this big city – coming from a small village, with only a few houses – I had no family so my friends became my one big family. Since Tia was born, I have again become, slowly, closer to most of my friends, especially to those who also had children. It was as if Tia's birth, freed me from the fantasy world Shona tricked me into, and I began to see things for how they really were. However, I found that the issues arose when I attempted to meet my friends after Tia was in bed, although I suggested Shona to join and get Rachel to babysit, but she was not supportive of any of my ideas. I never understood why socialising was such a big deal in my relationship. I was doubted about my commitment, and my seriousness about being in a relationship was questioned every time I tried to spread my attention to anyone else but Shona. Simply put, the relationship was fine when I followed her rules, but with time, I began to stand up for myself so the dynamics only got worse.

So much worse, that I am here in this unprecedented situation today. I have regrets but I cannot revert the past, cannot relive my life, instead I can learn from my mistakes, to never repeat them again, and appreciate what I have – Tia, my baby and the future ahead. What am I saying? I do not have Tia, not now, not yet, but she is on her way back. The present is a mess, a mess that I never thought I would be in for trusting someone with cruel intentions, but I was a fool and I will fix this just like I fixed everything else, because the people who are meant to be part of my life, are still in it.

I stop for a sip of water and rest on a bench, and continue reading through the testimony from Helen from a professional and friendship point of view. We formed a friendship after our babies were born, and they have not stopped playing together ever since. Helen and I have many things in common and have grown closer over time. We always enjoyed each other's company, and in her testimony she has confirmed the relationship I have with Tia is unique and one of a kind. Helen has stressed that the disruption is causing disparity to both, the mother and her child. Ending her statement with a message: *Please, serve justice and unite this child with her mother as soon as possible.* I feel a drop of a joyful tear roll down my warm cheek, all the way down, landing above my upper lip. These testimonies will serve as references to the judge in support of my truth telling. I wipe my cheek blotched with wetness and forward all the testimonies to Gloria. I chuckle to myself and imagine Gloria when she opens the documents and is faced with reams of text. Just like me, my friends are a chatty bunch. However lengthy and amazing they are, she will convert them into a summarised legally required version with hopefully a smile on her stoic lawyer face.

I slip my phone back into my running belt and continue with my remaining running route. The evening is turning a darker shade now, as the sky has absorbed the colours of the sun set. The lit street on the outskirts of the woods is quiet, but my mind is as loud as the bang of a Bonfire night firework display. Each rocket launching into the sky exploding in a multitude of colours is like the excitement I feel about my Monday hearing. I literally hear Tia's little footsteps in the near distance, picking up pace to run towards me. A powerful smile appears on my face urging my legs to speed up as an unexpected adrenaline rush enters my bloodstream. The wait is almost over, and the quest for justice will soon commence.

# Chapter 9

## The Battle

'Resistance shattered by disappointment.'

Squeezing through people on the busy London Underground, during the morning rush hour is an ultimate dodge game. People rushing past me from all different directions, some juggling their full to the brim take-away coffee and bags whilst casually reading a book and maintaining balance with every turn and jostle. Then there's me looking completely freaked out and out of my comfort zone. Some people bump into me with their rucksacks and coats and briefcases, some without even a 'sorry love'. People running for the train doors, which only stay open for a few seconds, it's like seeing bulls running towards the red cape of a Matador. On a daily basis, this must be an absolute nightmare, and if not necessary, I would not attempt to travel during the morning rush hour. No way, not in my high heels, pencil skirt and a delicate blouse – that has miraculously survived coffee spillage. I shall embrace this warm-up technique as, let's face it, I am about to start a battle. I search for Emilia in the crowds, as she could be taking the same train. I think to myself, working in the city, she does this every day, in and out. Her petite physique plays the dodge game each time, although no judgment on her size, she stands out from the crowd. I try to scan the crowds but I cannot see her. It would have been lovely to see her enthusiastic face, but to be honest, I am the one who refused the company of anyone who is close to me. I swore to do this alone because I am already feeling overwhelmed, powered by the anticipation of seeing my baby – which may happen today – and regardless of how the day ends, I become lost in my thoughts and shut down to shield myself. As a result, I wouldn't be good company and I would feel bad for my loved ones. This is just how I feel and what I need today is waiting for me in the court room. My sis insisted, and I understand how protective she is of me in these circumstances, knowing how excruciating my life is right now, she just wanted to fight with me. However strongly she wants Tia back, today, at the hearing I have to be by myself, only with my lawyer. Strange approach to such a big day in my life, but I am following my gut. I promised my sis and everyone else that I will provide them with regular updates during and after the hearing. One thing, well one of many things, that I love about my sis, she always respects my decisions.

    I have agreed to meet up with Gloria prior to the hearing as she wanted to run through the court proceedings with me. I am so nervous, I can barely stop my voice from shaking, and it's not the caffeine, I am so scared of the outcome as I want to see Tia and I can't imagine anything going wrong. Why would I be denied access? What if the judge will believe the biological mother, because she has the legal documents in place to show? Wait, what if I want to eagerly say something. I ought to share this piece of a prickly thought with Gloria. In response, Gloria flings a note pad at me with a smug grin on her face and the answer is more than clear. Note sharing, what a relief as whispering is something I cannot do with my husky voice, even when I think I am being discreet, I can be heard a mile away. I appreciate Gloria describing the process to me when the judge calls the parties to the stand, as honestly, I have nothing in my experience to compare it to. I do wish to be called to the stand, I desire the questions to be thrown at me, I want to answer the judge, and Shona's lawyer. Although, I trust Gloria with absolutely everything. I may have to hold myself from standing up and defending myself, hearing dishonest accusations thrown at me without being able to speak my mind in my own voice, it would awaken the lioness within me. Instead, Gloria will be my lioness today, a more tamed, legally accommodated kind. I finish the last of my latte and we begin to make our way to the court door, a chilly breeze hits my face as we leave the cafe, it refreshes my mind, that is feeling so overwhelmed with the endless what ifs and buts as I have left my protective wall behind. Today, I have to shine bright and stand up strong for my truth. I pass my belongings through a security check and follow the signs that lead us to our allocated floor. As we open the door, a corridor full of lawyers and their clients, partly fill the seated areas. Once we register our arrival, we are advised to take a seat and wait for a court usher who will provide us with further details of the hearing, such as the name of the judge and the one who will escort us to the hearing room once the judge is ready. Gloria has been to this very court often and she is familiar with many judges and knowing what judge will be allocated to the hearing could help her read up about their cases, character and approaches during hearings. Apparently, the time of my hearing may be delayed as the courtrooms are all busy with previous hearings, which are not yet over. I sense an unexpected wave of uneasiness, additionally to the existing nervous storm that has been brewing in my stomach. I reach for my water bottle and start sipping slowly, the day seems to be rolling over some rocks, indicating a bumpy ride ahead. I cannot seem to shake the sensation that something is going to be wrong. Argh! Me and my sensations, honestly they could give me a break. The longer I am going to stare at that clock on the wall, the stronger these feelings will grow. I am not entirely sure whether I am prepared for a storm, and the consequences it could leave behind.

After two hours of waiting, I can no longer sit or talk to Gloria, the anticipation is making me restless. I decide to take a look around the long entwining corridors, they're like a maze. I try not to pry as I pass time, but people watching seems inviting. I unintentionally notice a father that is anxiously rubbing his thighs, seemingly waiting to go into a hearing or possibly receiving a verdict, accompanied by his lawyer, who is walking around in circles in front of his seated space. But, as I am about to continue with my wandering, a door opens right in front of me so I gently step aside and a child, approximately age nine, runs out through the doors straight to the anxiously seated man. He jumps straight up and opens his arms to accept the running child into his arms. Tears fall down both of their faces as they fall into a tight embrace. I cannot help but hear the child saying how much they missed their dad. The moment is gratifying. To my surprise, another man follows through the door, seemingly not looking impressed by the reunion. Only, when the child refers to both men as *dad*, although the circumstances are unknown to me, seeing same sex couples in the court room, provides me with a boost of positive vibes. I begin to wonder what their situation is and whether it could be similar to my own. I assume the child may have been deprived from seeing the dad that was waiting anxiously, and the court may have granted him access, given the happy victory moment I had just witnessed. Oh, this feels warming, so promising! I am just about to continue on my little roam, when my phone receives a message from Gloria, saying that the court usher has announced our hearing and the judge will take the stand in the next fifteen minutes. I say to myself: *You've got this girl.*

As I arrive at our original waiting area, Gloria is still sitting down but this time, seemingly ready to leave, with files in her hand. As I collect my briefcase with some additional items – which in my opinion may become relevant at some point, such as pictures of Tia and me and drawings from Tia, which I have from every year of her life – I notice Shona arriving, and the thousands of uncomfortable feelings rush through me, making it hard for me to even look her way, I am so angry with her for what she is doing. I will not be affected by any negative influence, so I decide to look away and enter the courtroom instead. I find myself sitting alone at the table for some time, wondering where Gloria has disappeared to. I look around but there's no sign of her and I become self-conscious of how uncomfortable I must look. The only one in the room is the usher, Shona – whose presence I can feel without directly looking at her – and myself. Has Shona not got her lawyer here today? Is she representing herself? An unbearable energy fills the room and I begin to feel like I am suffocating, something doesn't feel right. I am desperate for someone to enter and say something in order to save me from my wandering thoughts and the unbearable intrusive gaze of Shona. Someone, please come and rescue me from this torture. Phew, just at the verge of my panic, Gloria enters the room.

*Finally*, I think to myself, and I let go of the breath I didn't even know I was holding. Gloria looks at me disconcertingly, leaving me feeling very uncomfortable as I have no idea what is happening. She asks me to collect my belongings as she strokes my upper arm – a sign of comfort that Gloria seems to use, so I oblige and follow her. I keep pleading on the way in a whispering voice, to tell me why we are leaving, she says nothing and a terrible feeling plays an off key tune in my stomach. I exchange a strange look with Shona's lawyer, whose face is contorted into a smirk, they both look sickeningly smug. I break eye contact and try to keep myself together. Something has gone wrong but to their advantage, I just know it! I can feel it! I follow behind Gloria as we exit the courtroom and move into a vacant room, the sound of the rain ferociously hammering against the windows, mirroring the storm that is taking place inside me. She stands behind a large table adorned with blank pieces of paper, pens and a clear jug of water. I take a seat on one of the wooden chairs, reminding me of the many times I was called into the Headteacher's office. I am so confused and wonder if anyone else will be joining us here. Finally, Gloria begins to talk.

'Vivien, I know you are going to be extremely disappointed after what I am about to tell you, but don't worry, this is very common, please just hear me out. The judge called Shona's lawyer and I to their chambers and informed us of their great delay today in the courtroom – there is an unforeseen emergency hearing that must go ahead, seemingly larger than what we are here for today. So instead of giving us a hearing today, the judge has requested for next steps to be taken based on the filed statements and has given us a date for a full hearing, where he will make a custodial decision. He has informed us that he will be requesting a Cafcass report, based on the allegations that now seem to be from both parents, due to the response statement, urging the judge to conclude his decision of shared custody with other professional's advice. Usually in custody trials they would advise the couples to try to mediate and then return to seek the judge's help, so we are ahead, and he was happy to see the attempt for mediation. So, that is great. Everything will be concluded, including the Cafcass report and their thorough statement examination of all the attached evidence. Due to the twelve week by-law time frame for Cafcass to carry out assessments, visits and providing the judge with a thorough report, means that the full hearing is set for November 20th. The judge has given written permission for you to safely continue sending Tia postcards, up to two cards a week, without risking harassment reports made against you. Also, in your favour, the judge found the police report malicious and it will not be considered as evidence, nor as character judgment or your suitability as parent. He is removing these from the allegations made against you. I have asked for permission to have some kind of supervised contact with Tia but the judge wouldn't allow such, without a complete report from Cafcass, and for the safety of the child, to avoid confusion and further emotional harm. The judge believes it is better to keep things the way they are right now in Tia's best interest. They would break the law to allow you any contact, as you could potentially be the perpetrator. Now, we do know that is not true, but sadly the judge cannot just trust us, they need evidence, based on necessary investigations. The judge would have probably made a very different, on the spot, decision if the response from Shona wasn't so negative and full of allegations against you. The judge doesn't state, they believe one or the other parent, but for now, they must keep the child with their primary caregiver – the biological parent, to where all the formal evidence currently leans. They are just following the legal steps.'

I wish to run away right now, to run through the heavy rain, to wake me up from this nightmare. Am I asleep and dreaming, has today not yet happened? No, no, no! Gloria takes my hand, asking if I am all right, as I am absolutely frozen in silence, staring at her in shock. Instead of words, tears answer her question. I just cannot stop myself, this the worst I could have expected. I freely let my cry flow, taking no consideration over being in the presence of my lawyer. Gloria pulls a chair towards mine, to face me, pulls my hands into her hands, gives them a gentle pat as a gesture of comfort and tells me to take my time to digest the information. I try to compose myself and slowly start discussing the information Gloria has shared, in a brief but heart breaking monologue.

I couldn't help but tell her that I cannot accept to not see Tia all the way until November, that's way too long, we need to see each other. I kept repeating, why the biological mother gets all the faith, it is the other way around, the perpetrator is not me. I begin to sob again in between. I have come today in the belief that I will be reunited with Tia and get some kind of custody over her, even if just a temporary arrangement which would have gradually built into a stable, steady agreement.

'Gloria, I cannot walk away from here today knowing that I will not see Tia until November, I will not survive this, and Tia surely can't wait until then, she is missing me, I know she is! She is certainly not getting my postcards, she thinks I am gone, that I left her! And months without me, could just redo her whole life, like a layer of new wallpaper covering the layers of existing wall paper beneath. We have an amazing connection but now, more than ever, I am terrified that without physical contact our relationship is under threat, everything that we had could be potentially damaged. She is being made to believe in a world without me, where I do not exist. Please, I am begging you, we need to do something.'

Gloria seems to understand my situation emotionally and, as a lawyer, she would turn tables for my case, but she verifies that there is nothing more that can be done right now. Adding, that six months, altogether, is still a quick proceeding time frame. Blimey, quick? I live in a world where quick is considered to be definitely shorter than the three months that have already passed. Gloria states that the postcards will need to be shown to Tia as the judge will ask about that at the hearing and the Cafcass officers will also mention the postcards at their interview, however, the judge didn't order, therefore it's not mandatory for Shona to show them to Tia. But, if she will show no proof of showing these to Tia or encouraging Tia to respond to you, the judge will certainly make a negative note of that. Therefore, as of until now and for the time ahead until the next hearing, I shall continue sending positive, loving and age-appropriate cards to Tia, up to twice a week as now permitted by the judge. Gloria insists that she did her utmost to convince the judge, but Shona's lawyer kept reminding the judge how scared Shona is of you and how harmful you could be to them both. So, the judge didn't take Shona's side, but has ordered an investigation to gain an understanding based on firm data collected by family court advisors. Of course, I stood up for you, stressed the critical points in your application and provided the judge with strong opinions regarding your detachment from Tia.

Apparently, this judge is one of the great ones, familiar with same-sex parents and who will also be allocated to my final hearing. Which is unusual, but very fortunate as they will personally read all of my evidence pages and testimonies and will be the same judge who will glue everything together. This is not a defeat, but the beginning of a torture that I am far too terrified to envision! I believed that the judge would rule, and Tia would run into my arms, but that seems like it had just been my magic hope to keep me sane and stable for the past three months. I am gutted! My heart has been shattered into many million pieces. The storm seems to have passed now, leaving me lying powerless in between all the debris and wreckage left behind. There is nothing left here to hope for. The law is complicated, and the court is not what I expected. I pick up my bag, Gloria following right behind me, and begin making my way through the corridors. I cannot accept today's verdict, so as we reach the entrance hall, I stop Gloria for a second and ask desperately

'Can we please appeal against the decision made on the supervised visits with my daughter? I need to see her. I can't go another day without her. She needs to know the truth, that I am working really hard on getting things sorted so she can come and stay with me again, just like before the detachment. Please tell me there is something more, than 'nothing' Gloria?'

'I understand your disappointment, I really do! There is always an option to appeal, and as your lawyer I will always provide you with all the circumstantial possibilities. Yes, we could appeal, and that would take me about a day or two to prepare, but the response can take up to twelve weeks, as other senior judges examine appeals and the grounds they are based on. Also, making an appeal could risk losing the amazing judge you have been allocated, and may also interfere with your existing date. I am afraid, however, that an appeal, will not get you to see Tia any sooner. There will be more loss than gain. That is my opinion, but I am happy to follow your wishes, but that would be in my disagreement as a professional. Take your time, sleep on it and let me know tomorrow?'

'Oh, no, I do not want to jeopardise my one and only hope, that has a plan with a set date. I just thought for a moment that I could appeal and change minds. This is just a mother thinking out of agony. Thank you for today.'

We part outside, Gloria feels deeply sorry for the way things went for me today because I didn't get what I wanted, but she confirmed that the hearing booked for us is apparently still an urgent date. The judge is one of the best ones on my case, the November hearing is going to go ahead, and it will give me what I want – my baby. I just ask, why me, why my case? Not fair, not at all! Gloria feels frustrated herself, because we didn't get the chance to fight in the court, but these things can happen, and often lawyers cannot do anything either. Shona may have responded to my statement, as advised by her lawyer, possibly planning on the fact that the hearing could be delayed because of her accusations. It seems like Shona wanted more time to get Tia used to her new life, to strengthen their dynamic and erase me further out of that picture. I approach Gloria for a friendly, but slightly more professional hug and thank her for everything she did for me today, however disappointed I am. I turn around on the pavement, sharing one sad glance at the court building and begin to walk towards the nearest underground station. I pull out my phone and give my sis a quick call, she picks up immediately, as she must have been waiting for news, any news. I quickly tell her that I don't want to talk over the phone, my voice begins to tremble as I say

'I don't have Tia back and I cannot see her until 'maybe' the final hearing on November 20th. I'm devastated, that I cannot find words to speak right now Sis. I will come over to you and will explain everything.'

'Oh Viv, no way! I am sorry! Yes come of course, I will pick you up from the station, let me know what time.'

It is a monsoon in London today. I decide to get a warm drink, and I expect the cafe to be buzzing with people and noise, music, whatever can shun the negative thoughts away. Today could not have been any worse, I feel like a flat tire abandoned on a deserted road, exhausted, irreparable. Interestingly, most customers grab their coffees and continue standing around in the cafe, chatting in groups. Probably it is the small table seating areas that have tiny round tables and one or two chairs, some have no chairs at all. I grab my opportunity to take the single chair table seating and place my caramel latte on the table in front of me and open my phone browser to search about Cafcass and what they actually do and how they carry out their reports during custody cases. Who are they? The search engine pops up a brief description, that they represent children in family court, who advise the judge about what is the best and safest for children experiencing parental separation. What catches my attention is that the children's needs, wishes and feelings bear fruit and that their voices are heard at the family courts. Cafcass is the official representation of what I want for Tia and what I believe children deserve, that's what Tia deserves. Cafcass to my rescue, I close my eyes to capture the tiny little shining ray of hope in my heart. I continue browsing and I find that they use different techniques and interview methods to listen to children's opinions, wishes, thoughts, depending on the age of children. The techniques are not specified, but given Tia's young age, based on my professional knowledge, drawings, toys, form of play may take place to gather information and match the outcomes with each of our statements. Based on how Tia has been affected, and to comment on the allegations made against me. Tia will speak the innocent truth and Cafcass will see how important I am to her, how close we are, who I am to her and our whole life together. What is Shona going to do after all her allegations, already denied by me, will not be rectified by Cafcass after they have interviewed Tia? I finish my caramel latte, I needed the sweetness, it satisfied my nerves, slightly. I feel as if I am slipping into the need of being alone, going against what Gloria thought would be best, what my sis feels the best to do. I am an independent individual who enjoys being alone, it's healthy and I am not afraid of being alone, not for a bit but I am going to do what's best and talk it all out, I shall not spend the time talking over the phone, personally it will be more comforting at this stage. I leave my seat, someone straight away takes my place – a lady in a peach beret, drenched from the rain that seems to be hammering down now. I leave the cafe behind and head towards the underground entrance, leading to the Piccadilly line that will take me to my sister's. As I shake off my umbrella, I notice a doughnut store on the opposite side of the road, I push my umbrella opens again and cross the road. I select a box of six various doughnuts, including caramel and chocolate glaze, jam and custard fillings and plain sugar glazed ones. My nephew Charlie loves doughnuts, and so does Tia. Everything, everywhere, reminds me of Tia, all the time, and looking at children, around me excitedly selecting their little treats. On the outside, it makes my face smile, but on the inside, the gnawing in my heart brings tears to my eyes. Today was supposed to bring about a positive shift in my case, but instead it intensified by possibly the worst outcome.

I have lost track of how many stops have passed; how many people got off and on the train, I just suddenly realise that my stop is coming up next. As the escalators elevate me from the underground, I regain reception again, I quickly check my missed calls that appeared on my phone. What am I so eagerly seeking? That call from Shona, coming to her senses after today's hearing and realising that she doesn't want to put Tia through this ordeal anymore? I might have to stop myself from creating these false hopes, that after such a while, and a court hearing, which put Shona at an advantage as she gets to have Tia for herself for months more, to get her used to a new life, she would just turn around and change her mind. No way! She is on her way home, to reunite with Tia, not me! She is the one to get to hold Tia, not me! The lioness is wide awake within, I will never lose my strength, I will find a way to get through this. I might have lost today's battle, but I'm going to win this war!

# Chapter 10

## The Aftermath

'New day, new possibilities.'

I open my eyes, the room all of a sudden seems unfamiliar, half asleep I wonder where I am, I look around, this is not my room, and the noisy traffic outside doesn't resemble my street. My brain is slowly making sense, of course it's not my room, I stayed over at my sister's last night. We stayed up chatting until the early hours. I was an emotional wreck after my defeat, by the time I arrived at my sister's house. We had doughnuts and various snacks, as breaking down yesterday's event took some philosophizing. I was and I am still distraught over one thing only, not having contact with Tia. When I left for the hearing yesterday, I had imagined that contact with Tia would be reinstated, instead what I have got is two postcards a week to Tia, that she may not see anyway. Disappointment reaches deep inside my heart as I think of today as a new day, and the almost hindered days ahead without Tia, I wipe my tears into the duvet. My sis was just as upset, we had every right to be. I spoke about feeling the fear of Tia estranging from me, as the time apart has already been more than three months already, she is young and her mind could be reshaped, her beliefs could be changed – what will I mean to her, will she still remember me? Will the judge ever grant me contact with Tia? What if the judge will see Tia settling fine into her new life without me and will see not much of a benefit for me to disrupt her routine? What if the judge will not feel the need for my existence in Tia's life? Absolutely not, not for all the world! Answers fly to rescue my thoughts, but these are my assumptions, perceptions and views, as I know what I mean to Tia, and probably what my absence is doing to her little soul. I have brought up my baby to be resilient, to never give up, to trust those who love her for who she is – a girl with the strength of a lion cub. She is smart, she knows how to build a wall, she is a fighter just like me, and she is finding ways to continue to live her life. But, in her heart, she is with me every day, she kisses me good night and good morning, she knows I am here and that I am coming for her. I feel it, she feels it, and we both know it. So I am going to transform the negative event into new energy again and use it for another three months, even if it will be a living nightmare. Once again, I am reset, to zero time, not looking back, not seeing the past time without Tia, but live my life on a day-to-day basis and never look back. However insane this tactic seems, it had worked in the past, as counting minutes without Tia was unimaginable for me before, so counting minutes into days and months is dangerous for my own welfare.

Sis asked me to show her the pictures of Tia and her drawings that I took with me to the hearing, which were photocopied and included in the evidence file sent to the judge, but I carried the originals with me anyway. We giggled awestruck over her baby photos, remembering times spent together, especially when visiting our mum, with Tia as well. My mum always says, still today, that she is an actress, creative, imaginative and talented, one of a kind. That's probably a biased view, but I have to agree. Tia has always stood out from the crowd, able to express her individualism and creativity. She brings joy to everyone with her cheeky personality. Making others laugh is her favourite. Seeing others sad it is her primary task to cheer them up. Her excitement, gets the whole world dancing and twirling in the around her. Tia has a magical vibe. One picture captures my attention, the one where she is dressed in her monkey onesie on holiday with a huge grimace on her face, doing the monkey bars for the first time. Other children watched in awe, given her young age. It was a moment to celebrate forever, she was ecstatic after she completed her challenge, she just couldn't believe it. Since then, she has mastered many monkey bars, and keeps her first-time achievement medal safe in her memories. I have thousands of pictures of Tia, but not one with a serious face, apart from her school photos, but why would she be serious, life is meant to be fun. Children are meant to live their life happily and that involves play, fun and learning naturally by exploring the world around them. It's a shame that sometimes we tend to lose this magic in adulthood. I wish for my darling to have a childhood in which she is happy, loved and able to explore her interests. All the pictures are so vibrant, full of her cheerful spirit, and looking at them, projects her life on the wall in front of me, my imagination putting it into motion like a movie of our life. I see Tia dancing, spinning around, cuddled up to me on the sofa, swimming, kicking the ball, dressed up and performing her ideas. These transformations will keep her loving vibes alive, as I am so scared to face the reality, even just for a moment. If I do, I will detach from myself, from my hopes, from my sanity, from my energy as another three months is a long time. Allowing myself to think of the amount of the months in total, my breathing gets all panicky. If the panic captures me, that is it, there is no way out, it will follow me around, and affect everything I have worked so hard on for this entire time. So I will brace myself, keep my head up, my heart strong filled with my treasure – my child – and time will reward my suffering. My late grandad used to say, *patience brings roses*, please may that be true because I have run out of patience and daily I am reaching my threshold.

I fell asleep last night cuddling her baby photo of when she was asleep on my chest after a long burping session. I embraced the moment of our closeness that night, and many nights. I remember an exhausted breath that let out a faint *I love you so much* sigh, and then I must have completely conked out.

I suddenly catch an awareness of the time, and jump up into a seated position on the sofa bed. Phew, what a relief, when my phone screen displays it's Saturday and I'm not late for work. I am about to tumble out from under the cosy cover when my nephew Charlie runs into the room, excited to see me there, he immediately jumps on me, expecting my usual alertness to catch him. My nephew is one of a kind as well, he is loud and slightly mischievous but leaning towards the entertaining side of things. He loves to be at the centre of attention, with his huge grin. The more laughter he gets in response, the more mischievous his behaviour becomes. Sort of a chain reaction, and Tia is totally up for it anytime. But she also has that influence on Charlie, when it is time to stop, at least most of the time. Tia and Charlie are very different, but they complement each other, and that is the way they love each other, just like a brother and sister would.

I tickle him all over his little body, and he lets out the largest shriek ever, but then he abruptly stops and asks me why Tia is not with me again. However happy Charlie is to see me, as we do spend some time together, he is becoming suspicious of not seeing Tia for a while now. His age is luckily still susceptible to the lack of time perception over the past few months and to what we tell him. I just need to remain evenly honest, so I tell him that Tia is with her other mum Shona and that she will hopefully be back soon. His little mind moves pretty fast, as he gets distracted by the Lego that lay beside the sofa bed in a box, and he pulls me to build a massive train station, so we begin. Why not, I have nowhere else to be, and this is my most favourite place after my own home. But my home is empty, it feels sad to be there without Tia, so being away right now, is beneficial. I need this time to just be distracted. Playing comes naturally to me, as I am in touch with my inner child, in my grown-up body, away from responsibilities, even just for some time. Life is too short, and there is no need to stop having fun, just because we have turned into adults. Life and fun can continue hand in hand, it needs that choice to grab the opportunity and go with it. I stroke Charlie's little warm cheeks, as I click the Lego pieces together, shaping up to be a small tower. Charlie says it looks like T for Tia. I am amazed, but because of Tia always going on about the letter T, he learnt it too. He then exclaims to name the station as Tia, the train station, and adds little Lego people to represent Tia and her family, so all of us, and to my surprise Charlie added Shona too. However upset I get at the sound of her name, Charlie understands that Tia is with her mum, and to him that is family. Charlie doesn't know the truth and he will not know how much Shona may be hurting Tia right now. He is too young to understand what is or could be happening. Tia will soon reunite with us, and seeing her again will be what Charlie needs and life will make sense again. I can smell coffee wafting from the kitchen, mmm I can't wait for my morning caffeine, and just then my brother-in-law David walks in balancing a tray in his hand with a cafetière, cups, sugar pot, milk jug and with a basket of something delicious by the looks of it. This guy is one amazing baker, he bakes goodies daily, and every time it works out to perfection. This morning he made some fresh brioche buns, to be served with butter and jam – my absolute favourite. He asks me how I am feeling, but Charlie interrupts my answer, asking for all the attention to play with Tia's train station, that we have been busily building. David spends a lot of time playing with Charlie, so gets down to the floor to join in, and offers me the coffee to enjoy peacefully with a smile on his face. David can tell how I'm feeling by reading my body language in response to his question, which had been interrupted by Charlie. To those in my close circle, often no words are necessary. They all acknowledge that loss is irreplaceable, and they feel there is really nothing they can do to get Tia back to me. All they can and continue to do is give me unconditional support. I try not to be sentimental around Charlie because the moment I do, his little face would mirror mine, his blue eyes would get tearful, his lips would quiver, and that's even more heart-rending, it would weaken me. He is immensely dear to my heart and to Tia's, and he can sense my pain of detachment, so I must shield him. I will not let sadness dominate my soul, I will not condone defeat! Doubt and guilt wash over my tender shores, but the negative attempt in my mind is saved by my sis, who barges into the living room, deeply falls into the sofa bed next to me, and squeezes my arm for a warm hug – my desired shot of comfort. In a sisterly manner, she orders for me to stay for another night, and any gentle opposition she senses from me, is greatly rejected. She pulls out a bag full of my belongings from my home. When did she disappear to do that? I couldn't say no, but I don't really want to say yes either. I actively encourage myself to be spoiled, I'm selfishly in desperate need of it. Charlie overhears that I'll be staying another night, so he runs through the Lego pieces laying on the floor and wraps his arms around my waist excitedly and shouts out loud, "*Yay! Vivien is staying, let's build a Tia train as well, that can bring her to you. Let's make a fast one, a very fast one because you miss her. Come on!*" Charlie has gathered that much! Suddenly, a poignant reminder of the passing of time strikes me in the chest, shattering the only remaining barrier that had kept my suffering hidden. All of the agony erupts, allowing all of it to fall into the sink hole that is currently my body. Yesterday's court loss hit me hard, it shattered months of hard mental work, and left me feeling like a failure. If I could, I would have pleaded to the judge on my knees, begging them to let me see Tia. Yet again, the law has failed me. I failed Tia, I failed myself.

I respond to Charlie with a smile, realizing that I need more of this, more happy moments, and that this may just be my survival kit. I must gather my shattered pieces, build back the protective walls, but now in need of a stronger foundation, to hold this tremendous pain. Allowing myself to acknowledge the disaster I am experiencing, but aware that I must keep my head focused, for Tia and for myself. I need me, I need the strong *me*, the positive *me*, otherwise I will lose the war, and that would implode my whole existence that may not ever recover to be the same again. That's not me, I am a fighter, I always stand up after falling, and hit back harder. I'm in disbelief where this wave of energy is already coming from, as all I feel is damage right now, but I love it!

We begin to build a fast train, with long tracks, that will safely arrive at the destination – where I will be waiting with my arms wide open. I enter the world of imagination, where everything is possible by playful manipulation of ideas and emotions. Let's do this. Let's visit Tia, and take her on a trip through our wild imaginary world.

It's already been a couple of weeks since the hearing, I'm powering through with work and feeling a little more positively puréed up, with my survival kit in constant use. Currently, my work mode serves as a dose of realism as I am driven by a hectic schedule. Particularly, in the next few weeks, I have to conduct development reports, something that is due every three months to monitor children's development and plan for their needs accordingly. Consequently followed by a parents' meeting, where my findings are reported, open for discussion and further planning drafts. I do everything I can to empower parents and share my experience so they can benefit their children, because the child's support system umbrella is an intense factor in achieving positive results for each and every individual. In addition, I offer apprenticeships to students pursuing childcare qualifications, by providing assignment assistance as well as practical experience in my nursery. Rachel began her childcare career in my setting, earned her certification, and is the only student that I approved for a full-time job as I was hiring at the time. Other students who finished their studies with me found jobs elsewhere, sadly, I was unable to accommodate everybody. That reminds me, Lily, my university pen pal, with whom I've grown close with lately because we have so much in common that we can chat for hours, is supposed to video call me tonight to discuss a subject for my own upcoming assignment. Lily has been following my court case with zeal and that has been so encouraging. We met on the day we both started University and started interacting on the online welcome forum. We have continued chatting since then. Lily is witty, charming, likeable, diplomatic, observant, bright, and extremely fast at typing; I can hardly keep up with her. Her profile picture was a scene she shot while traveling across Asia, it was breath taking, and I couldn't wait to learn more about her adventures. I am enthralled, as she seems like such an interesting individual, and we can barely stop talking, when we get a chance. We exchanged numbers and began talking in a more intimate forum after that, and we kept chatting with the same fervour as when we first met. Whenever Lily's name appears on my phone display, there is something that glues me to the screen with a huge grin whenever she texts or calls, and to my nice surprise, Lily felt the same way. Beginning of a wonderful friendship, something that life can throw your way, when you least expect it. Is she someone that has come into my life for a reason, a season or a lifetime? I genuinely wish for the latter.

  As I sit in my office chair, enjoying my well-deserved break, an email is delivered to my screen, so I take my last bite of my delicious tuna salad, I swiftly open the email. My eyes widen from excitement as I read that it's from Cafcass. I have been waiting for this letter. I hurriedly place my plate on the table and hastily begin reading through the email. I have been invited for an interview with a Cafcass officer who has been assigned to my custodial case and will be advising the judge of the assessment outcomes in a report, before the day of the hearing. My assessment interview is in three weeks' time. Wow, a date to look forward to, that is going to be a super boost for my bloodstream. I drop heavily into the chair, excitement is rapidly developing in my mind, causing a flash of heat to run through my body. This is it: the independent court advisory team that represents children in family court proceedings and advises the court on what is safe and best for them. Hurray! I have an appointment, I'll be consulted! Cafcass are the experts in assessing the relationships between children and their parents. The officer will conduct an interview with Tia and Shona on the same day and in the same place, according to the letter. Will Tia be there, when I am there? Will I be allowed to see her? Will the officer let us meet, even though just for a short while? All I need right now is a moment with Tia, we both need to see each other and be reassured that all is well and that we will be reunited soon. This is my chance to prove to her that I haven't left her, though I won't be able to tell her the whole truth, I will tell her that Mummy is taking care of a few things, and that's why I have stayed away, but that I miss her terribly every day. Perhaps I will bring her one of her favourite cuddly toys from home to console her and give her hope. I know exactly the toy to take with me, her monkey. And what if I get her a teddy, especially from me, that she can take home and cuddle up to because she would know it's from me? I would refer to it as the cuddle teddy. It could provide an additional sense of hope, comfort and safety knowing that I am here thinking of her incessantly and did not leave her behind. Tia is a sentimental soul; it would mean a lot to her. The enthusiasm is overwhelming; I can't resist reading the email repeatedly, as this is a pivotal moment, the Cafcass interview has the potential to change everything. A smile stretches across my entire face. I must inform Gloria. I can barely hold my excitement, as I dial.

'Hello Gloria. I'm so glad that you answered straight away. I have been invited to an interview with Cafcass, and I'm really looking forward to it. I cannot contain my excitement!'

Gloria simply lets out a giggle, clearly pleased with the progress, and asks for the letter so she can have a read of it and add the letter to her court files.

'Ah that's amazing! The interview is all about you and Tia. It is your time to shine, to prove your mothering relationship to Tia, the love for her and that you only want what's best for Tia. It's time to finally start to demonstrate, in deep honesty that you are innocent of the abuse allegations, but the Cafcass officer shall see that for themselves.'

Gloria sounds satisfied with how smoothly the process is going. From her experience, in some of her previous proceedings, she had to ask Cafcass to expedite the court application on behalf of her clients as court dates progressed, because without a response from Cafcass, the judge could adjourn, if not cancel, a trial.

'Gloria, do you think that I will be permitted to see Tia on the assessment day at the Cafcass office?'

'I am afraid that is very unlikely, best not to get excited about it, and see what the Cafcass officer will advise you on the day.'

As my work urges me to return, I thank Gloria and respectfully excuse myself and say goodbye. I ask myself; do I need to prepare for this interview? Absolutely not, not when

I am the one who holds the truth, I can only answer questions to their honest meaning, as described in my statement. I am not the one who needs preparing, neither is Tia. There is only one person who has to memorise the lies! What I wish for Tia, is the ability to speak to Cafcass privately, as I'm afraid she may be unable to talk about me in front of Shona. However, the hope is once again with the system. I quickly inform my sister and mum of the wonderful news. My mother's lengthy text full of motivational speeches and my sister's succinct yet to-the-point responses, are both equally valued.

Days seem to go by fast, but the evenings drag on and on, no matter how busy I try to be. I try and deceive myself but the emotional turmoil is fighting to be stronger than everything else I try. I am fearing the two week holiday I had already booked ahead of last year, but I will go ahead with it, as there is never a way back, only forward and I will embrace this free time away from work. Work is my protective wall, something I have held on to for that sense of sanity. One thing I know, I need to spend minimum time at home, as the emptiness will eat me up alive. Everything I look at, reminds me of Tia. I wish to squeeze her tight, and never let go. However much I have tried to avoid her bedroom; it has not been successful. As I am here again, in her room, sitting on her bed that still smells of her, with her soft toys still arranged the way she left them. As I lean against the wall, I notice something hanging just above her bedroom window. Looks like a bat, a very small one. Still not convinced, I put the soft teddy down back on the pillow and pull myself up to get a closer look. The light from the sky appears diffused, the sun is close to set, but the rays shine into the room just enough to see this mysterious hanging object. As I look closer, I realise that it is a very dry, brown coloured ivy leaf that hangs upside down creating a heart shape. I cannot understand where it has come from, as there isn't an ivy bush anywhere near the roof nor on the bricks of the house. It feels warming to see a heart shape, almost enchanting as it has appeared in Tia's window. A beep tone throws me out of my magical moment, my phone has delivered a message. It is from Carol, so I immediately unlock my phone to read it.

*Hi Vivien. How are you coping? I assume your hearing is still ongoing, as we bumped into Tia and Shona in the park during the week, but you were not mentioned. The girls had a little play, but Shona seemed in a rush, so I didn't manage to take a picture – I am sorry. Tia had a little school bag, you know girls started school on Monday, time flies. Tia seemed all right walking with her ice cream, she didn't say much though, which I thought was a little out of character Hope to see you soon, stay strong. Carol.*

Just as the last rays of light disappear behind the trees in the garden, a warm teardrop falls down my cheek, followed by another, and then the flood gates open. I was not there, I didn't hold my baby's hand when she crossed the school gates. I was supposed to be there for her, to give her those comfort cuddles to reassure her. My baby took a big step in her life, the school year has begun and I missed it. I still managed to receive the email about which school she got into, before our detachment and it was a great choice, so I at least know that she is in good hands. I can imagine her little face looking at the teacher, her eyes wide open observing the daily happenings. I have got to believe she is doing well, my job as a mother has prepared her for this journey. Tia is smart, has a strong heart, gets on well with a diverse mix of children, but may be a little shy and quiet at the start. But, once she gets comfortable, she is like a butterfly, spreading her wings to take flight, to explore her environment and make friends. My heart smiles, over the thought of her making sense of this new addition in her life, a place where she will spend more days in a week during term times, than at home. Apprehension befalls me, after the thought of her home. Tia's sense of belonging, after these past months, is most likely set in stone, her home with one mum, her new school, her new life and new friendships. This is all very likely, I cannot deny any of it. Children are adaptable, but that does not mean they accept the choices made for them! Hopefully, Tia does not have the full awareness of time perception, for months may seem like days. I assume that she is moving on with her life, as she has a parent to follow, to guide her, however controlling she may be .Tia knows that I am coming, but she is probably thinking where I have gone. Many days, bed times, and meals have passed since the last day I saw her. The very last day I saw her was the worst handover in our history. She kicked up a fuss, refused to leave my side, clung on to me like a monkey with her arms and legs. That very last day, she even ran back to me from Shona's car and shut the door behind her, saying that she doesn't want to live with her, only me. I withheld my cry, it was an extremely difficult time. Eventually, I managed to calm Tia down, and got her in to Shona's car. I knew how much the move between two homes was causing Tia distress, but I had to reassure and encourage her to adjust to her parents separation. Sadly, that last handover, I told her that in a few days she will be back and the days will go by quickly.

'Do you pinkie, Mummy?'

'I pinkie, sweetheart.'

Those days turned into months, and Tia had probably

passed the disappointment from the pinkie promise I made. She may be too young to link the events, but she is not too young to feel sad and let down by me. I had always been there for her, I had always kept my word, and I had not ever failed her. Until now, as now I am failing her, as I can't keep any of the promises I made. Fresh tears rapidly fill my eyes, this is the most unfair thing I had to ever be part of. *So* frustrated and angry, I feel a fire burn in my soul. My heart roars in agony, the lioness accepts the moment of weakness. I let out a massive howl, as I lay back on Tia's bed, pull the duvet over my aching body, and close my eyes to find peace in tonight's sleep. I will never lose hope, and it is my hope, not my pain that will shape what comes next.

# Chapter 11

## Awakening

'Vivien, live, laugh, set yourself free.'

I wheel my suitcase out through the door and onto the street that is still quiet from the night's slumber, the air slightly chilly and carrying the scent of fallen leaves, as autumn is beginning to set in. I pull my jacket tighter. There is something beautiful about dawn, when the sun is peeking over the horizon, it is a pleasure to behold the beauty of the sunrise. I take in a breath of crisp air as I walk towards the taxi that has just arrived. The trip to Kings Cross St Pancras should be fairly quick, as traffic in London has not yet had time to build long tails. I have made a decision to spend some days of my holiday, traveling, to visit two of my friends I miss dearly. This trip is my saviour, I need to escape this place, for a while at least. The timing couldn't be any better, as Gloria is taking annual leave and I will be back well before the Cafcass interview. There are no more statements to work on. The only remaining task is the wait and that's what I am struggling to withstand. The days seem to have slowed down, I often find myself feeling weaker, and experiencing the agony of being blamed for past mistakes. The mistake for trusting my worst nightmare. I am highly sociable, but I don't trust easily, nor express my emotions lightly –

hence my loyal circle of friends who are close to me and I have known them for quite some time. So, what went wrong with me? I am a strong, career driven, smart woman, yet someone so toxic managed to completely screw me over. Simply put, I believed Shona's story and the sincerity of it, which I of course highly doubt today. I had just happened to meet a pathological self-centred woman who may have been after a woman who is strong, has a lot to give, including my trust. My fantasy of being in a female relationship is bruised, shaken and in need of rebuilding. My interest in a female partner has not been affected, I am very confident in my sexual orientation. What I am more than certain about is the kind of personality traits to avoid, immediately, when those red flags show. I am only human, I made mistakes in my life, although never such harmful ones, as the one I am suffering from today, but I would always learn my lesson. I got up each time, however hard the circumstances may have hit me, and these mistakes helped me to become the person who I am today. Courageous, ambitious and persistent. My previous relationship has crumbled my entire existence because of my daughter, not the break up. Currently as a mother, as a woman, as a person, I am battered, but nonetheless I am not weak! Life's challenges and hardships have the potential to either break or empower us. I am opting for nothing less than the latter. My soul is on fire, I have an inner strength that has come to the surface from the pain I have experienced. I acknowledge my feelings, face them, cry if I need to, scream if I need to, curl up if I need to, but I am one hell of a woman and I will fight more than I ever had to before to get back on my steady feet. As a child I used to walk miles with bruised, bleeding knees after falling off my bike or a tree, far from home to get back to, without friends, with no one to help me. I was out exploring all day because it was safe, and it was fun. I explored the great unknown, without examining the possible risks. Was I ever scared or frightened? Yes, no doubt, especially the times when I was alone and being chased by a dog or getting lost in the woods. I found my way out, every time, even if that was with tears in my eyes, running manically to seek shelter. I remember seeing that light at the end of the tunnel. I had this immense urge and gut sensation that has led me home. My childhood experiences have contributed towards my resilience, towards the person I am now. This person may have been treated wrongfully, abused emotionally and treated unfairly. The one who witnessed her own mother being taken away from her and the one who today has had her daughter torn away from her. Nonetheless, what life brings our way, is impossible to predict, but we must not give in nor give up. I just want, what my heart is missing, what my soul is longing for – my baby girl. Without the missing piece in my life, I couldn't possibly live to my full potential. With Tia I was as a complete form of art – radiant, moving and bold – but now, tarnished through an intentional act of destruction. Soon enough, this spoiled piece will be replaced by one even more compelling, and it will proudly exist once again, with that missing piece reclaimed.

    I have finally arrived at the station, ready for my first trip to Paris. I cannot wait to see my dearest best friend Sofia, who is happily married with two beautiful children, living in the suburbs which I am so grateful for, as I don't fancy the buzz of the city. I haven't seen Sofia since her wedding, besides the fun we had until the early hours, that night she noticed that something was off in my relationship, which was not apparent to others, but was to Sofia – who knows me very well. What confirmed her worries on her wedding night, was my abandoned phone on the table, with thirty-six messages and four missed calls from only one person – Shona. Who decided to turn in early, expecting me to do the same. I respectfully disagreed, as it was my best friend's wedding. I joined her special day, to have fun and celebrate her love and union. It was not the time for an early night, and not the time for arguments either. Tia was sound asleep and I respected Shona's decision to turn in early despite the pre-arranged evening babysitting. As the night continued, I kept receiving phone calls and text messages from Shona about when I was planning to return to the hotel room. I gave a few simple clear answers at first reassuring her that I'd be up once the wedding party was over, I was confused why she seemed so bothered about my whereabouts when she knew exactly where I was. Feeling that she was appeased, I left my phone on the table, as the night turned into a non-stop dance craze. But the messages from Shona kept filling up my screen. She seemed to have got furious for no reason, it was not my fault that Shona did not want to join. What was so bad? I still remember Sofia, with her hair in a ponytail, still rocking her red after-midnight dress with a pair of trainers on, flashing my phone in my face and saying bluntly: *'You better sit down, and tell me what's going on, this is not okay!'* Looking rather upset, and as my best friend, she demanded some answers. Sofia had her doubts since before the wedding, especially when some drama unfolded and controlling concerns arose during her hen weekend in London. Shona didn't like the idea of me going out to celebrate with the girls or spend time with them in any sense, in fact she didn't like me spending time with anyone else at all. She even went as far as to threaten to change the locks on the doors. This was the first time I realised the situation I was in, although naïve to the extent, and despite her threat I decided to break from her restraint anyway and her threat was just that – a threat. However, it lingered on my mind and the months that were to follow became more abusive as I fought for my autonomy.

Anytime when my attention went elsewhere, other than to Shona – the centre of attention – that was when drama exploded. I explained the night to Sofia, but she couldn't understand what the problem was for me having a good time, she couldn't understand the frequent bombardment of texts and calls. Sofia reassured me, that with all respect to my relationship, it was not at all right. I agreed, as I was slowly beginning to see the person I was with already. Prior to the wedding, I proposed to Shona, to take time to herself for a couple of days, while I travelled with Tia to the wedding. She didn't seem interested in my friends, unless out of courtesy, but she didn't allow me to travel with Tia alone and insisted on accompanying me. I didn't want Shona to go somewhere, where she didn't want to be, but she insisted. I was not going to do as she ordered. Sofia's wedding bells struck the alarm bells in my relationship. Saddened by the events at the wedding, I realised it was unhealthy. All of the past events concluded at once, and it all made sense, I was in a controlling and abusive relationship, and the more I used my voice to stand up for myself and attempt a balanced lifestyle as an individual, a mother and a partner, the more it aggravated her. I may have become, for Tia's sake and for everyone's sake, obedient to Shona's rules, avoiding belligerence in order to sustain the peace. Everything was on her terms, it was one rule for her, and another for me. Decisions regarding Tia's needs and interests, slowly started to slip out of hand as we barely agreed. Becoming parents, involves having the same morals and values shared, as without this sync, an agreement can be awfully difficult to reach. When one believes in hitting other children as a way of protection or not sharing toys for example, were not the teachings I wanted for my child. It was endless disagreements and tiring arguments. Regarding Tia, if she met Shona's expectations and Shona was in the mood, the dynamic was great between the two. But if she didn't, Shona's patience would quickly run out, and she would approach Tia with hostility, leaving Tia in floods of tears. I often had to come to the rescue, and make amendments. She wouldn't physically harm Tia, I would never let her lay her hands on her, but the words she may have chosen to discipline Tia, could be rather mean and unkind, especially to such a young child. Those were the times, when I had to be the most skilful, to only tame the situation, but to guard Tia, to distract her from feeling those words. What do you do with a crying child, after being left confused? Cuddle them, calm them, tell them how much they are loved, but keep the parent in a positive light so the child is not scared of them or left resenting them. How much I was able to maintain the positive image that is hard to tell. But I was there, always there to guard Tia, who only needed understanding, guidance and loving responses to help her successfully pass the developing stages. Shona may have tried, but she may have lacked patience and that's one of the key approaches regarding children. In general, Shona would always attempt to try, but easily pass the turn to me, opting for the easier option. It may have felt like I was trying too hard to encourage something that appeared unnatural and tedious at times for her. I had to do a good portion of damage control in the family unit, often it felt exhausting, despite me believing that children mustn't be bubble wrapped, thinking that feeling angry, sad, upset is not an okay emotion to feel or show, but they need to learn how to gradually manage them. This positive lesson is the best achieved by firstly role modelling and secondly by verbal education. That has always been my parenting vision, and one can obviously just do their best. Aside from that, I imagined a different form of relationship, one in which I am treated with respect and dignity. Sadly, it was not always successful. Orchestrating a serene environment for Tia grew more difficult, as my parenting, as well as my energies, began to fail me. It all became too stressful, and I had enough of empty promises. Shona has not had much interest for the past few years, but is suddenly claiming all the four years of Tia's existence to herself, through some serious lies and allegations. Detaching Tia from my love, shielding and everything she had known since her birth, is concerning. The hearing date is still far away and Tia may be smiling on the outside, pushing through with her inner strength, but she may be feeling scared, abandoned or even misunderstood. I hope she is not ever criticised or made to feel unworthy or unwanted. This great unknown is not how our human brain is wired; we starve for answers. I am wired this way, when I don't know, I search, I read, I ask but there is nowhere to search or no one to ask, therefore my mind opts often for the wonderful journey of wonders, but that is a dangerous journey. When I feel the weakness, when I can hear my mind beginning the *what if journey*, I stop, and it takes a strong will to surrender without any possible answers as an alternative, but I must prevail.

This trip is necessary for me to leave my world, I need to

run away for a short while. Not to forget, but to reset and hideaway from the tragedy happening in my life right now. Breathe, just take few deep breaths, *one, two, three*. My eyes are on the verge of welling up, but I refrain from crumbling and attracting unwanted attention from the strangers occupying the seats near me. Ironically, a couple of weeks ago I started reading *The Girl on The Train,* as the story is captivating, distracting, and certainly very twisted. Can I relate to this fictional life story? Apart from the murder, absolutely. The controlling partner, the emotional abuse, it's all so close to home. The severity of the relationship issues sends shivers down my spine, but the story feeds into my interest to read, barely wanting to put the book down. I love connecting to what I read, and if time permits, I can read a book in a single sitting. My train ride to Paris, has allowed me to finish the book. What a twisted emotional torture this girl had gone through, so unaware until someone, just one person made it all clear, it ignited her memories, returned her sanity, made her strong again. Strong, ready to fight for her voice, stand up against her enemy, to the one who made her insane, a laughingstock. The one who made her feel ashamed, embarrassed for things she had never done. Having her entire existence gaslighted, by the one whom she trusted and loved the most. Meeting just one wrong person in life, can change you, but just one awakening can trigger enough to pull you out from where you have fallen too deep, because of that wrong person. There is always a way out, there is always a sign, it is whether we notice the signs, the choices we make, the decisions we take, will contour the way our life continues to unfold. One way or another, our life ends up the way we chose to live it. We can keep pushing away, taking wrong turns, making wrong decisions, but eventually, apart from losing precious time, life will try to bounce us back onto the correct path. It is up to us to accept it or to continue getting lost with all the wrong turns. What makes us happy inside, is the feeling of being worthy, loved and appreciated, it is what as an individual we must not ever forget to hold in our hands, and not letting anyone or anything make us feel anything less than that. Whether that be a friend or a partner, if anyone makes you feel this way, you have taken the wrong turn. Get back on the right road, however scary or unsure the circumstances may seem from thereafter. Once you have yourself back, you will find strength, you will find a way. Don't ever forget who you were before that first hand lay on you, before you lived your life frightened, before you stopped laughing, before you stopped going out, before you doubted yourself. That is not lost, it is only suppressed by someone, who has their own issues, their own reasons, and they are way too lost and avoiding taking the correct road to a better life. Don't take the same journey, take that risk, get out before it's too late. Children need safe journeys in life, take them on the correct one from the very start, as they can be lost just as well as you guide them to be. This vicious circle could have no end, but if you get yourself and your children back on the correct road, you can help them to become respectful and kind adults. I had made this decision; I saw the sign. I was scared, as I felt terrible and unsure of what life would bring but I was offered a way out, an escape from someone that made me feel unworthy. I sacrificed myself for far too long, to shield my daughter, to offer her the best life that she deserves. But when I felt that I no longer could continue to do that, I had to put a stop to the bad, for Tia and for myself. Saying the words "It is over" is hard. To break up with someone is easier when children are not involved. I couldn't help myself, nor could I have helped Tia in the relationship, that was just worsening with time. I had to leave and make amends from outside, regain my strength and feel *me* again. My non-biological status and my non-formal existence didn't allow me to take Tia with me, so I had to be smart, very smart to agree on childcare arrangements. I had a plan to continue keeping Tia safe and connecting with the courts for protection and guardian rights, but that diverged. I do not regret my decision, I made the right choice, and I am more than certain. I couldn't obtain my legal ties to Tia, and I couldn't take any more threats from Shona. I have to cope with the suffering, and that was not part of my plan, but it seems like the only way to get my legal rights put into place. I just didn't think that Shona would hurt Tia this way, but she may have wanted to cause me pain for leaving her, and the only way she knew it may hurt me the most, is through Tia. If that could provide someone with some peace, very well, but don't use a child's heart, that is just a careless and selfish act. Shona made up so many lies and allegations against me, as she may know that regardless of my non-biological status, I can gain my visibility as a mother in the eyes of the law. I can and I will! She may believe that giving birth to a child bestows a tag, and simply claiming to be one, may give her all the rights. Which sadly, has so far been justified to Shona, but Cafcass and the courts believe in what's best for the child, and that may not necessarily be the birth mother primarily. Since Tia's conception, she has had two mothers, and this only changed when Shona cut off my contact with her. Nonetheless, the two parents are still there, and one of them cannot be easily erased, especially if their desire to be a parent is so profound. I have applied to the court to gain my legal visibility and an equal shared care arrangement for Tia. I may have some reservations about Shona's parenting approach as proved in the past, but Tia would thrive in life from the support of both parents. Shona may be claiming her biological mothering rights now only to get rid of me. But where was she before all of this? Why wasn't she the mother she ought to be, the one who she could be before we separated? The answer is easy, she may have had the status tag already and I did the hard work. She may be showing what amazing job she has done to have raised Tia. There were some pleasant times in her parenting, but Shona avoided any challenges or behavioural problems that Tia presented. I often left her alone to give her the chance to tackle difficulties alone, but she asked me to return and assist her. As a result, she fled the scene. She did mention before that the young age stage is not for her, and could see enjoying parenting at the later stage, such as primary school age. This comment has always baffled me, parents cannot choose when or where to be parents, in my opinion, it is a full time commitment from day one. I guess Shona had a choice, and that was me, as I never stopped being a parent and I didn't want to, I loved it. I still love it, and will resume my responsibilities, once this mess is dealt with. Children observe the family dynamics, and they learn to understand who is there to meet their needs, unconditionally, not only when they are happy. That may be the reason why Tia was so distressed at having to leave me behind at handovers, as she was used to have me by her side. Apart from her biology, Tia has a big part of me in her and I am certain that it will be visible to all of the professionals who have never met us, as to those who do know us, recognise the resemblance very much. I have naturally earned the *mother* title, thanks to my connection with Tia, I proudly and rightfully claimed it by simply being one.

After a couple of hours, that I filled by reminiscing and reading, I arrived in *La Ville–Lumière* – Paris. I head from the platform at Gare du Nord, one of the busiest stations in Europe, into the main area, the station décor is breath taking, but the station buzz distracts my wonder with hearing *excusez-moi* repeatedly, as people whoosh by me, some bumping the wheels of my suitcase so I decide to quickly exit the station. I review the detailed travel instructions from Sofia and search for the bus to begin the start of my journey to Saint-Cloud. It's a rainy day in Paris, people running towards shelter holding a newspaper above their heads or flicking an umbrella open, the rain must have started to pour down all of sudden, by the looks of it. The rain has thwarted my plans to do some sightseeing before going over to Sofia's, but no matter, it can be done on my return day. I take a glimpse of the Eiffel Tower, the symbol of Paris – the iron tower, that stands strong looking but rather dull in the daylight, especially under the grey rain clouds which gathered in a matter of minutes, bringing on even heavier rain.

I get off at the, supposedly correct bus stop, pop my umbrella open and walk the streets, following my phone map with directions to Sofia's place. It seems like forever to figure out which way the numbers on the buildings flow but I successfully arrive at Sofia's building, *finally*. As I reach to ring the doorbell, someone creeps up and scares me from behind, but my fright immediately turns to relief as Sofia jumps in front of me, swinging a bottle of Prosecco in her hand, exclaiming that her partner took the children to his mother's, and we have the whole day and evening to ourselves. Although I have been looking forward to seeing Sofia's girls,

I am dying for some one-on-one time with my best friend, who I don't get to see as much as I wish to. We hug for a long while, jumping around on the spot at the same time, clearly both very excited. We soon find ourselves on the large corner sofa, Prosecco in hand and our fingers dipping in and out of the various bowls of snacks she so kindly prepared. Sofia has clearly made an effort, I always feel comfortable and welcomed in her house. After an update on her family life, she takes my hand and asks me to tell her everything I have been through, despite being briefly aware of the events already. Sofia tries hard to disguise her anger, but I can see right through her. I take her hand, and explain how right she was, at the very start of my relationship and admit my naivety, wishing to have listened to her warnings about Shona not being right for me. Sofia and I may have passed the apology stages by now, but it feels like good timing, to reassure her all over again. She worries about my status as the non-biological mother, but truly believes in justice that the courts will trust in the true mother I am to Tia. She asked her family friend, who happens to be a divorce lawyer, for advice, but the law is different in France, although the story is common when couples break up. The mother often deprives the father of their children, but the father always has that biological status, even if not listed with parental responsibility, or in some cases not named on the birth certificate, but their parenthood can be easily proven. What remains for a judge to determine is the relationship with their children, and that's how they set the custody arrangements. However modern the law is becoming, same sex couples and custody cases, are not common and he hasn't yet experienced anything like it. As a family lawyer, he briefly understands the story line, and is certain, based on the law in England, that the judge will take my relationship with Tia into account, regardless of the non-existent legal paperwork. The advice continues towards being patient, as apparently court cases can last months to a year long from his experience, and the time frame that has been allocated to my case, seems very reasonable, however painful the wait may be. French or not, the advice is precious and much appreciated. It does seem, as my court hearing period in total including the November date, is indeed fortunate. I must not open that can of worms, but embrace this fracture of positiveness.

Sofia is fuming, as a mother, she can only imagine how my torment feels, as she wouldn't be able to spend months without her children. What I truly admire, is that my friends and family, see me as a mother, regardless of who gave birth to Tia. That has always been the case. I am thankful for Sofia's loyal friendship, despite the past gap in our friendship, when we didn't know anything about each other. We genuinely reconnected when our children were born, as such news couldn't be deprived from either of us and we haven't stopped being in touch ever since, and we both strongly believe that we never will. I will not make the same mistake twice.

To ease up on the long hours of deep emotional talk, we bring on the nostalgic discussions, that's always such fun, as our past is certainly colourful. We can laugh for hours, and it seems like it was only yesterday when we look at photos that bring back many memories. It feels so nice to be holding printed photographs rather than swiping through images on our screens. We only had pictures taken if we had our film camera with us. No camera, no pictures. Most of our memories are saved in our minds and are there to be told and remembered. Tia enjoys listening to my life before she was born, obviously age appropriately, but sharing memories is a beautiful way to bond with your children. Sharing our past, from the life before the birth of our children, opens the great doors to our personality, as children want to know their parents beyond the family life. The older children get, the more of the parent's personality unlocks. Relate to your children's feelings with your own childhood or early life experiences, and you are equipped with the greatest guidance you could ever provide. As our stories offer possibilities, that may not provide an influence, but may aid children in making their own choices. Equally, to help them comprehend all of the events and adventures you went through to become the person and parent you are today. Sofia and I, we feel the same inside, we are still those young girls in the photos, only now with more wrinkles on our faces. That simply adds character and value to our long term friendship, with more adventures and wrinkles to follow.

The next morning I wake up to the sound of traffic coming from the main road outside, and the sound of giggling children on the other side of the guest room door. It must be the girls, already back from their grandmother's house and awake at such an early hour, something I am used to anyway, so I decide that the sleep I had was enough and it's time to wake up. The smell of fresh croissants, eggs and smoked salmon fills the entire apartment. The giggles continue, as the girls pull me right past the dining table, and I just manage to say good morning to Sofia as they sit me down in the middle of scattered toys, and hand me a Barbie doll to play with. The TV is playing some cartoons in English, Sofia wants the girls to learn both languages, so she puts on English cartoons or plays English music so they can enjoy the learning in a fun way, until they start school and begin learning in a more formal manner.

Francesca, the oldest – the same age as Tia – hands me a comb for the Barbie's hair and asks me why Tia is not with me. I dread these questions from the children who know Tia, and have only ever seen me with her. It is so hard, but I have to keep things very simple and answer all of Tia's friends honestly – with her other mum. Francesca's little face goes still and she continues combing Barbie's hair, saying that she wanted to show Tia some toys and play her favourite board game. I threw in a gentle smile and confirmed that Tia would have loved that, and offered that I will share pictures with Tia when I see her next. Sofia spoke from the kitchen to join her for some coffee, so I excuse myself from playing and bow like a princess on the way out of the lounge. I take a sip from my cup and purely take in Sofia's morning vibe. Juggling breakfast preparation, coffee making and unloading the dishwasher. I miss it. My home is very quiet in the mornings at the moment, only juggling putting on the kettle and managing my thoughts. Sofia explains that the girls were apparently jumping on the sofa when they heard that I am here although they thought Tia was too. Sofia didn't know how to explain it, so she explained Tia could not come this time and left the rest to me. To be honest, that's the best she could have done, as what's worse is contradicting stories, as those are the ones that could make children very suspicious or left confused. As we clear the breakfast table of empty plates, Sofia offers to visit a park, only a short walk from the flat. Why not, the day is looking sunny, although a warm coat and hat is now necessary as autumn hits with low temperatures. So we all get kitted up, with thousands of items packed into two backpacks. Once you go out with children, it is not just a phone and your small bag, but a large bag, that never seems big enough.

The girls scoot on the smooth paths of the gardens, it's beautifully green and enchanting. I feel so calm here, taking each step slowly, talking to Sofia, it's a place that can easily capture every soul, with its image of freedom. The girls scoot towards this magnificent playground, full of cheerful children. Tia would love this magical place and I can't wait to bring her here with me next time. There will be a next time. I sit down on the nearby bench, near the exit to the playground gates to watch the girls take on the climbing areas, as Sofia grabs us both a coffee from the cafe. I decide to enter the playground, and chase the girls up the climbing frames and whizz them down the slides, Charlotte the younger one, a small version of Sofia – cheeky, free-spirited, independent and does and says whatever she feels like – needs more support, so she is loving my little fun input. I miss playgrounds, playing with Tia, and I have so far successfully avoided play areas, and that's because hearing children's laughter and watching them play, hurts me to watch. But today is different, it is unavoidable, if I am visiting my friend who has children and I cannot stop my natural connection to the playful world. Playing with my little nephew and with children of my dearest friends, fills that void with joy, and as I realised when I was with my nephew, laughter is my survival kit and I think it is fulfilling its purpose. I sit back down on the bench, letting the girls play on the playground that seems to have gotten busier since our arrival.

'Hello, do you speak French or English?'

A girl, aged about twelve or thirteen, sits down next to me, removing the hood from her head, and places her scooter next to the bench. I feel a little uneasy, as children shouldn't speak to strangers. Is Paris more relaxed? I don't want to seem rude, but I keep my distance and speak simply.

'English.'

'I am waiting for my mummy, she is getting a coffee from the cafe, is it okay if I sit next to you?

'Yes, sure.'

'You seem sad, do you miss someone?'

Despite my smile and friendly attitude, she managed to somehow pick on a different energy. A little empath I think to myself.

'Yes, I do.'

'They miss you too, I am sure.'

Then she picks up her scooter, as her mother approaches from the distance, she hops on her scooter and waves bye to me. The most bizarre conversation I have ever experienced, not because she was a child, but her skills to read people at such a young age was impressive. I do not think I look sad. Do I? Is it so visible? I feel completely baffled by what has just happened and decide to treat it as a sign from the universe. Sofia comes back with our coffee and apologises for the long wait as the cafe was rammed with customers. The park does seem busy, I even opted to skip the que to the gift shop. I wanted to get a postcard to Tia, and send it directly from France using a funky postage stamp.

As we people watch, I somehow cannot stop myself from becoming frustrated, by examining happy families all over the place. Okay, so no people watching, especially not in a park. I inhale the coffee aroma, which has proven to be relaxing and allow Sofia to indulge me with her life in Paris. I know that she made new friends, but settling in was not easy after fifteen years spent in the UK, and it took her some time to adapt. Now, she loves it back in her home country, where she has reconnected with her roots, enabling them to reach deeper into the grounds. Maybe if she fell in love with a person, who resided in the UK, Sofia may have stayed in London or elsewhere in the country. That could have been super amazing, but I am happy for her and that's what matters. Sofia is the news bearer, as she always updates me about people we used to know, and she still knows of. Many have families, some divorced, and some still stuck at the partying stage, but all mostly left the UK. It seems like Madison and I are the only ones left from the gang. Oh, the old crazy times!

After a lovely meal cooked by Rick, Sofia's husband – a spicy but flavoursome green curry with sticky rice – I am close to complete a rather colourful unicorn puzzle with the girls, on their gorgeous huge balcony terrace overlooking the surrounding suburbs. We have stayed seated outside, appreciating some fine red wine and the stunning views. Rick is great company, he is a man who enjoys female company and gets involved in rich conversations with an open mind. Although, he likes to touch up on any opportunity to discuss business or politics. I am open to any topics, but drag on with the finance and politics talk and you have lost me. I humorously think to myself. I stay on the balcony after they all retire to their bedrooms, with a blanket and the heater that is still warming the whole terrace space. I cannot get enough of this moment, feeling far away from everything that is hurtful. I close my eyes and switch off, completely shutting down my brain. Thank you Sofia, *merci* Paris!

Today, it is unusually sunny again and call it lucky, a very pleasant for a last day of sightseeing. I decide to leave my luggage at the train station locker, and we all book a tour bus that will take us to every point of interest in this gorgeous city. I can't get enough of this cultural satisfaction, seeing Notre-

Dame Cathedral, this magical place, where I could picture Quasimodo and Esmeralda dancing behind the walls of the beauty of this Gothic architecture. The delicious luxurious pastries at **Ladurée**, transport me to a land of sugar with every bite. What a moment of serenity. I feel somehow more peaceful, relaxed, even if very fragile in my soul, which confirms that my travel technique has worked so far. I am retaining my strength and it is helping me to persevere. Crumbling up into small pieces, curling into my bed, shutting the blinds, locking away from the outside world is probably what I had felt to do after my lost battle. That is not how my baby Tia knows me, and it's not how I know myself. I push ahead with an energy that comes from beyond the deepest part of me, where I have not unlocked before. Somehow, I feel as if my depth is limitless, and with time will expand that ocean of strength that I may need for the next two months, or for another event in life. Life is so extremely unpredictable, and that is what makes us feel alive. Alive does not always mean stress free, it means life and that that is an oblivious umbrella we hide under.

After visiting the Louvre Pyramid, I could barely feel my legs, what a beautiful selection of art, especially the famous Mona Lisa painting, but the queue was at least an hour. I did take a look at the Moulin Rouge, and the surrounding markets, but sightseeing aside, it was enough for me. I highly appreciate the conversations with Sofia while the girls are occupied with Rick, who is graciously allowing us to chat. He loves Sofia so much, they are just such a wonderful couple, and he treats her well. Of course, they have their differences, who doesn't, but they respect one another and love each other for who they are. Sofia is loyal, but free to do what makes her happy and she is not threatened, nor made to feel emotionally battered for it. They met in London, during a party, and Sofia and I still giggle at the thought of their first encounter. Tracksuit bottoms and pizza slice in her hand, while catching Rick smiling at her. They have not stopped smiling at each other ever since. Sofia had a long term relationship behind her, where she was not happy, so Rick rescued her like prince charming. Whilst cheesy, these stories of the way people meet, do in fact exist. My family life has failed, but I will repair everything and create a family unit of me and Tia, one filled with love, freedom to speak and act as we like, respect for each other and where we could grow together as well as individuals. I notice a stand with postcards, and find one that has the Eiffel Tower on it. That is the one, for my baby, she will love it. I add a simple message *You're always with me, no matter where I go. I love you.*

We all feel exhausted after walking and travelling around the city and we decide to end my stay with pizza and beers. Not very French, but who cares? It doesn't have to be about onion soup and snails when you visit France. Anyway, that's not me, and Sofia and Rick feel the same to be honest. I tried the onion soup, which is delicious actually, but I will never go anywhere near snails. I adore snails, and can spend hours watching them in the nature, examining their movements and their shell home they so proudly carry on their backs. I like stability in life, but my home wherever I go, will always be Tia's home, as she will find a home wherever I am. So after some delicious food, it is time for me to say my goodbyes. Sofia hugs me encouragingly, listen *next time, you are here with Tia* and throws her huge smile my way.

I collect my luggage, and head over to the airport to catch

my flight to Barcelona, to visit another of my dearest friends, Jess. After a quick departure, I feel the aeroplane lift off the ground. Air bound, is a feeling that leaves me out of control, not something I practically take lightly. So I place my headphones in my ears, tilt my head against the window seat rest, and gaze out of the small window. I shall let my body relax into the beautiful sunset that is taking place above the clouds, with the sun setting right ahead of me from this very point of view. The orange shade seems to be the only colour that is apparent in the skies tonight. I can feel my eyes closing slowly, sleepiness has come over me.

Barcelona is such a vibrant city and as I have visited before, sightseeing is not needed, simply the company of Jess is what I am after. Long talks, Sangria, Mojitos and some delicious Tapas. Jess relocated to Barcelona a few years ago, and I have missed her greatly. She hasn't changed at all, only her hair got longer, curlier but her lively character has remained. She is such a lovely person, easy to talk to, and fun to be around. We used to be clubbing buddies and actually met through Sofia when she lived in a shared house in London. The clubbing relationship turned into a friendship that has reached just over fifteen years now. It is difficult when really close friends leave the country, but the distance changes nothing and besides we can always visit each other. Since I had Tia, I haven't had the chance to visit her in Barcelona but we stayed in touch. What I fancy revisiting, is Park Güell, a stylish artistic park with colourful stone and mosaic structures and amazing buildings. Where I am absolutely charmed is the twisting rock pillars that grow out of the ground like tree trunks – it blows my mind, that's beyond creative. I'm much more drawn to magical places, I can sense a magnet inside attracting me to enchanted creations. Every moment restores my identity, I am regaining *me* and acquiring new particles to build upon it. Visiting this place with Jess is pleasurable, we just spend the time walking around and talking. Jess is clearly heartbroken from my experience, and she is disappointed as she thought I was living a happy family life in London. She pulls the zip up on her leather jacket and exclaims, *'Breakups are sad and can be disturbing, trust me I know, but never throw children in the middle of it, it is not fair on them.'*

Having not long ago experienced a breakup herself, we rocked in the same boat, she discovered that lies filled hers. Drinking a take-away Sangria – how amazing right? – Jess and I both felt the breeze in our leather jackets, so we opted for a night at this well-known tapas place, Bar del Pla, we are not only hungry for food, but also for more needed conversation. What I need, is Jess telling me about her life, experiences, work, dating, so I can just get lost in the Spanish vibes – Reggaeton music is playing softly in the background as we enjoy our stay, and delivers satisfaction through my veins. I find it still difficult to talk about not having Tia in my life, I feel my lips shaking, holding back my tears, every time, but soon it will be in the past. I show pictures of Tia to Jess, well the latest ones, as she had seen some that I shared since Tia was born. *The cheeks and the cheeky smile is just like yours, despite biology, she does look a lot like you.* I enjoy hearing these comments, as I had heard them before. It is psychology – the person that listens to the infant, addresses their needs, and interacts with them from an early age; enables babies to mirror that person's expressions, whether their relationship is biological or non-biological. Babies are intelligent; they communicate with movements and body language from an early age, and they form bonds with those who pay attention and respond to their needs. That's what happened instinctively between Tia and me, and it's a bond we'll both forever share. Regardless of the new dynamic she may be creating with Shona, our relationship cannot be disrupted.

I wake to the scented wafts of fried eggs and sausages; it fills the entire space in the small spare room. We are spending the day in Jess' apartment – stylish and colour-coordinated with a large balcony that connects all the rooms of the apartment. I take part in my morning ritual, hugging my hot cup of coffee and offer Jess my assistance with breakfast, but she seems to have it all under control. 90's music plays in the background, which is just perfect. After a relaxing day in her cosy apartment, Jess suggests that we go to a club that performs the best songs with live music. Years have passed since I last felt the dance floor under my feet. So, why not!

When we enter the club, which is packed with people dancing, chatting, and drinking, the beat of the music strikes me in the chest. The glittering chandeliers suspended from the ceiling reflect the crisscross laser lights illuminating the entire dance floor. I am in no need of a drink, I am getting lost with the beats, swaying to the rhythm, and I am going to dance my sadness away tonight. I can feel tears run down my cheeks, I let them run free, let my soul run wild.

I enjoy the few days with Jess, and I can't wait for her to visit London and see Tia again. Pulling out a bunch of postcards from my bag, I choose one with the mosaic lizard – Gaudi's Dragon. Tia loves lizards, and I fill the card with a message about who I visited, and the things I got up to. I always ask a lot of questions about school and what she's been up to, but I never get a response, so I have to hope she sees my interesting postcards, even though the messages are most likely not read to her. Jess and I share a tight hug, never knowing when we will see each other again.

I land in a cold and rainy London and breathe in the crisp air, *home* I think to myself, where Tia – my whole world – exists. When I switch my phone back on, emails and text messages appear in a row – lined up like soldiers awaiting my next order. I enthusiastically scroll through the received items, looking for one name primarily – *the* name that keeps me hostage in my own prison, filled with torture and despair – Shona. I would always search my phone screen for that name, hoping for any details about Tia and, even more desperately, for her to reconsider her decision to keep my daughter away from me.

I had dreaded the flight times without internet connection, as I just couldn't bear the fact that I could miss out on a significant update. Sadly, nothing from Shona. The anticipation had worn off as soon as I reached the bottom of the list on my phone display. Again, as I have done so far, I need to accept the things that I cannot change. However difficult that may be! Breathe, hope and wait! My recent travels distracted my mind by diverting my thoughts in strange places, and it worked, on the surface at least. I covered up my pain, for the sake of my own sanity. Now, only a couple of weeks to go until I see the Cafcass officer, and I may get a glimpse of Tia, even if that will only be short lived. Gloria did say that the officer may or may not permit contact with Tia, it would depend on their opinion on the court statements received from both of us. I could only just hope, but the response statement from Shona only worries me, as what will the Cafcass officer make of it all – will they be in a place to tell the truth from the lies? I guess that day will tell. At least, a short countdown, that breaks down the dreadful wait for the November court hearing, which is still seven weeks away. I am about to board the train to the airport terminals when my phone peeps – a tone of a message – I immediately pull my phone out, with my eyes wide open – but the message is from my mum. She's just taken some time off work and booked a flight to London to spend a few days with me. Mother to mother, from heart to heart, from pain to pain, her comfort is one-of-a-kind.

# Chapter 12

## The Resemblance

'The temptation to surrender, to despair, to fill the void of sadness, intensely fires through me.'

With my eyes closed, I open the door and like a creepy crawly, I slowly cross over the doorstep wishing for the hallway floor to be littered by at least one postcard. I have sent so many cards and the judge advised Shona to show the cards to Tia and encourage her to respond to me, in Tia's best interest. Was it an order? No, it wasn't! Shona has a choice, not an order to disobey. However, Gloria reassured me that if the judge sees no action regarding the postcards, they may not be impressed and on that note the favour may sway in my direction. In all honesty, from the bottom of my heart, wishing for nothing more than the best outcome at the hearing in November. But receiving a card from Tia, on the other hand, would mean the world to me, just as seeing her photo from Carol did. That would melt all the pain that has been frozen around me like a heavy armour, that I need to carry around everywhere with me, as its part of me. Settling with accepting how things are, is not an easy process to go through. I need to live with my mistakes, reflect on them, convert them into a new energy, strength and move forward. Why do I keep torturing myself, just because I am waiting for the presumably impossible? Yet, I still search through the pile of post on my floor, flipping through flyers of local businesses just in case, but besides the usual bills, I have nothing else. No postcard, not one. *My baby, I am so sorry, the days I pinkied to see you next, have turned into weeks, in fact months. I am so sorry!* I place my back on the wall and slide slowly down into a seated position, flinging the recycling to the side and placing my head in my hands, with my fingers slipping into my hair, tapping my feet, in an attempt to calm my soul. I am not going to fall deeper. I have got this. I rub my hands up and down my face, to get over yet another disappointment. This is seemingly the story of my life, and lowering my expectations is becoming a big part of it. Tia feels me getting closer and closer with each day. She can feel my loving thoughts with every single beat of her heart, hear my voice with every breath she takes, and see my smile with every sight she sees. Our bond reaches beyond the need for physical and tangible justification. Oh god, I do miss her so much. I will not deny the way I feel not to anyone, not ever. I have never felt so devastated in my life. The pain of losing a child is the worst imaginable pain a human can imagine to live through. That force of the everyday, wanting to be there when she wakes up, make pancakes with syrup, watch the cartoons she loves, going on our outdoor adventures, tuck her into a peaceful night sleep, but most of all making her feel loved and safe. The need for a life, a life known for over four years, the pulls are hard to resist. Once a child enters the heart, the journey of life takes a different shape, that is moulded around the child, to offer the best opportunities they deserve. This is a life I choose to have, and did not choose to ever let go. Without Tia, my journey is troubled, full of stalls and an unclear vision of the destination. But I will not detour, and leave my journey, I do not know whether the six months wait period, will be the very last. Nothing is set in stone. Trusting Gloria, does not mean the equal trust that I have in the court proceedings. What may come as a surprise again, is frightfully beyond me. I suddenly remember the amount of time that has passed and lately every time that happens it immediately makes my chest heavy. I get hold of my amethyst and rub it gently with the tip of my fingers and I slowly begin to feel focused and clear. I place it back on my chest while keeping my hand flat on top of its rough edges. This calming exercise has been effective, alongside my saviour toolkit, and that is spending time with people who remind me how to smile and laugh. I cannot forget, only distract my mind, work on my inner self recovery and survive this ordeal. It will be remembered forever; it will become part of my personal history, no tears will be shed, but memories embraced and be passed onto future generations. Tia will be right at the centre, hearing our story and passing the story on to her future family, just like my mum did with me. Obstacles can only be avoided if a different path is sought, driven by diligence and persistence. Honoured, I will treasure every day of my emotional anguish in order to be formally defined as a mother, a battle I was unprepared for, but fought with my most powerful weapon, my heart.

 I slowly pull myself up from the floor. Each day is like an emotional ambush, but the sadder I feel, the more I miss Tia, and somehow the stronger I get. There are just some things we cannot tell ourselves to stop doing and that's to stop feeling. I feel heartbroken, resentful and exasperated from what Shona has done to me, but to find a way to convert these feelings into a new form of energy that will aid towards my goal. There is no doubt that these feelings don't get stronger with each passing day, as they do and often I feel that I could easily fall into their trap. But to find the way out from being captured by negativity, would jeopardise my custodial chances. So, every day is a new mental fight my end goal being the light at the end of the dark tunnel.

The next day has arrived and my mum is coming. Sis and I are on the way to collect her from the airport. Too early for Charlie to rise, so he is not joining us but he will have a pleasant surprise when he awakes. Sis is ranting on about her work drama, she is certainly wide awake, so I just listen and respond when necessary. My close people know not to tiptoe around me because of what I am going through right now, instead they know what I need is the sense of normality and that even includes any stress-related conversations. I want to hear them all, as in my world of family and friendships, support goes both ways, no matter what situation the other may be in. We all need to talk things out and the time should not be conditioned to what we may be going through in life. It is my greatest satisfaction to be able to support my loved ones, despite my sad situation. Early morning sunlight is shining through tall trees and fog spread over fields, setting a scene for the dull motorway filled with speeding vehicles. It is looking like a lovely day ahead, in fact the next few days of Mum's stay is forecasted to be pleasant for an outside stroll which she adores. Although, British people know not to fully trust the weather, spontaneity has become my motto whatever the weather. My mum loves the exceptionally warm days in England as she gets to enjoy her favourite parks with a coffee or ice-cream in hand and observe the buzzing city surrounding her. Surprisingly, she may be in a luck, as usually the wet cloudy weather hits UK around this time of the year, but I shall keep those wellies on standby. Anyhow, I cannot wait for her hugs, our face-to-face chats and snacking at midnight while watching our favourite movies together. We get to the arrivals zone, finally, and watch people exiting through the hall. Poking my head above and in between the crowds awaiting their family and friends, I instinctively know our mother will be the last to exit. Suddenly I spot a silver blonde head, placed atop a bright red padded coat and hear the sound of click-clacking heels drawing closer – my mother. Sis and I wave to capture her attention and her face lights up in response. We share a massive hug that lets the zillion different feelings transfer, instead of words, into actual meaningful actions. I suddenly feel the weakness of my mum's physique, but not paying too much attention to it, I lift her bags and we walk out of the airport and towards the car. As Mum breaks down every tiny bit of her travel experience, every complexity, the whole journey back home, somehow I keep looking at her reflection in the rear view mirror, something is different, something is not right. She notices my intensely thoughtful look in the mirror, so I smile back in response, so as not to worry her. Although, knowing my mum, she could probably sense my investigating eyes. After beating the early morning London traffic, we finally arrive at my sister's house, where my mum will be staying. The second we step in through the entry hall, Charlie jumps into his grandmother's arms, and excitedly begins to twirl in delight and whirling around like leaves in the wind. He is so excited to see his grandmother, and so would Tia if she were here. Bless her, if she only knew that she is in town. I pause for a split second.

'Sis, what if Mum texted Shona, to ask to see Tia, on her

own, without any of us? She is used to public transport in London and would be willing to travel to any place to see Tia, even just for a little bit?'

An innocent idea, but would this act belong under the harassment umbrella? I quickly text Gloria to shed a light on the doubts. Interestingly, to my surprise, a quick response follows, 'Vivien, there is no harm in trying, but it will need to be the grandmother texting only. Harassment is not a worry in your mother's case as she has every right to see Tia. Let me know what you hear back, if you will.'

My mum speaks English to her best abilities and she has no problem forming a simple text, in her own words, even if that is with errors. It must be authentic without any modifications. My mum would do anything in her power, and that is certainly tons more than just a text. However, everyone, including my mum who is just another lioness protecting her lion cub, must obey Gloria's recommendations.

*Hi Shona, I'm in London. I would like to see little darling Tia? I come on my own. Only little minutes. Thank you. Katarina.*

The message has been sent over to Shona, but I settle myself with no expectations. However, another, yet hopeful wait begins. One hour later, no response. Another hour, and hours later, still no text. The day moves on with taking mum and Charlie to the park for a play and a late lunch at the park cafe terrace. The sun is shining, people are sitting outside basking in the beauty of an unusually warm and sunny day. Charlie is over the moon for spending the day with us both, as Sis has to work and I don't think he has so far taken a single casual step. All the movements he seems to be taking are skips and jumps, holding onto to each of our hands, with a goal in his head and that is to reach the café. All that Charlie can think and talk about, is whether the café will have hot chocolate with marshmallows and whether it will be too hot to drink straight away. The mind of a three year old, honestly I am jealous of that right now. I observe my mother's face and can see the reflection of her complex intellect activity behind the excitement from spending time with Charlie and answering a barrage of questions. Tears well up in my eyes, trying to avoid being noticed, I wipe the tears away and scoop my nephew from under his arms and swing him around on the grass, faster and faster we spin around synchronised. Laughter and screams fill the air, until the dizziness takes over. Phew, I place Charlie down and take a few seconds to myself to regain my balance. Only then do I notice, Mum is already sitting at the café table, pulling a blanket neatly over her legs, seeming breathless and tired. Given the fact that she only rested a little this morning, I accept the travel to be the reason for it as my mum is an active type, and she would normally play with both of her grandchildren in the park, simultaneously, regardless of any inner troubles. Charlie and I walk over to the café building and a friendly gentleman opens the window, politely greets us both and asks for our order. Starting with Charlie, who is finally able to find answers to his hot chocolate ambiguity. Charlie is happy and he cannot wait to tell his grandmother. Running between the tables, he finds a way to get to her and jumps right in to her lap. Luckily, as I watch intently, Mum has just managed to grab him with a somehow weaker than usual catch. My mum just seems unusually exhausted, although, she denied my presumptions and refused the chance to rest after our arrival to my sister's. She is clearly pushing her limit. It could be the current situation, witnessing my disparity and worrying for Tia and me. So far, no response from Shona, so my mum decides to write up the postcard she has brought with her, as she initially planned to post Tia a card during her visit in London. There are many things she would like to say but keeping it simple is important right now. Every contact serves as a reminder of all of us to Tia and that is what I need to maintain until the court hearing. I think of Tia and what is best for her, which requires self-sacrifice and resistance. The postcard is an image of funny ice cream faces with humorous facial expressions, that Tia would find amusing and seeing her grandmother's kisses signed on the card following the words *Grandmother loves her little darling,* would be enough for her to know. Charlie overhears us mentioning Tia, and that has not been part of my plan. Oh no, we have got to be more careful, since every time I need to answer a question, I am out of answers. Charlie asks me if he could draw a picture for Tia, so he can send it to her as well, he wants to draw them playing in the park with grandmother. That is doable. Sadly, I doubt the picture will land in Tia's hands but what we can all do is try. I clutch my mum's card and watch Charlie's little, skilled hand move quickly across the page, forming and image from his mind. His kind deed is tainted with frustration because he wants the picture to be perfect, he's just like my sister in that regard - a perfectionist. Finally, the picture is acceptable in his eyes and he insists on taking his drawing to Tia himself since he misses her. Think quick. Get creative.

'Charlie, don't you want Tia's picture to come to her in the post by a delivery truck? That red Royal Mail truck that you have as a toy, Tia would like it.'

'Yes, yes, yes! In a big truck.'

Charlie runs off to get the truck from his room, and gets

playing in the hallway, making loud *vroom vroom* noises. Bingo! Diversion and distraction complete. I doubt that Shona will encourage Tia to draw a picture and post it to Charlie, after all, I have not received a response. She may still respond to my mum's text and we wouldn't like the postcard and the picture to cross those chances, so we hold off from sending them. Although it is a naïve possibility, as Shona claimed in her statement that Tia only has one grandmother and that's not my mother, but hers. Another lie, Tia absolutely adores my mum and calls her *grandmother,* and their relationship is beautiful. My mum had regularly flown to London a few times a year, to see Tia, since the day she was born. Tia is close to my whole family, and I hope she will be asked about them at her Cafcass interview, to tear apart those lies in Shona's response statement. My family has always been Tia's family, they accepted Tia as my daughter, no matter the non-biological status. I absolutely adore how everyone in my family has treated Tia, as the first grandchild, the first niece and cousin and it has been blissful to witness how much affection they have all showed her over the years. It was a nerve wrecking day when I chose to tell my family about the change in my sexual orientation. Their reaction followed the same pattern – shock, moment of silence and then the questions. The questions of how I came to feel this way or how am I so sure? The answers were simple – obviously to avoid any awkwardness – *I have always felt the attraction towards women but I never understood why or what to do with the feelings, until then.* Then I realised, that is very clear who I fancy and what sex I feel attracted to. My family was very supportive, as to them what mattered and what will always matter, is that I am happy. My brother is not a man of many words, apart from the *okay that's great* and making jokes to ease his reaction, such as *finally I have someone to talk about ladies with*. I couldn't have asked for more positive responses! When I planned to tell my family, I desired no weirdness or awkwardness and I was thankful it didn't end up this way. My family accepted me, and additionally understood me, and that went way above my expectations. I love them for who they are, and they love me for who I am, whatever the differences, we all stand united. However, my dad is sadly not so understanding and has struggled with my life choices, but hopefully with time his mind will adapt to my life, as he has always been proud of me as a person, and that person is the same today. Hopefully, he will learn to see things from a different angle than the heterosexual vision of a family. As his strong beliefs are blocking his open-mindedness, he is missing out on my life experiences. Parents who resent their children for becoming other than their own expectations, will only push their children far away from them. What children feel is what makes them happy and the life they choose to live, is their own choice, not a choice that shall make parents happy. Parents should instead feel pride in their children in having the strength to freely express themselves, the ability to live life as they wished to and not to thrive to fit society's expectations. My dad has one belief, a woman marrying a man and having children, end of. He was unable to accept my sexuality and cannot wrap his head around the situation I am in right now. My naivety in trusting another woman, fighting for a child I did not even bear is out of his capacity to understand. So, he is even more so disheartened. I put so much energy into trying to get him to understand my life that frankly I eventually decided to leave him out of it all. My dad has my respect, but that is all

I can offer him, but I cannot change the man he wants to be. The rest of my family is fully supportive and that is enough. Family that has survived a lot in the past. We are fighters and we don't give up. Therefore, I am not giving up and neither is Tia. She is part of this family, and we will be together once again and there won't be an empty seat around the table anymore.

The third day into my mum's stay, and still no response from Shona. We finished the evening with movies and snacks, as we always do, after an eventful outing into the city. It has been a day, just for us two, Mum and me. We rode the tube into the city and did some shopping, something my mother loves to do, especially with me. After a long morning, in and out of various shops, I treated her to an afternoon tea which was classy and very delicious. Mum is the type to be easily pleased, but she does love to be *fancy* occasionally, so she can dress up and feel elegant. Most of her visits to London require trainers, tracksuit bottoms that she can wear to the park with the kids. So, our day out was different, we could dive into deeper discussions without the fear of Charlie overhearing anything that he shouldn't. We talked about the court hearing, the statements, and the response from Shona as through the phone it is not the same. My mum wanted to know everything in detail. The protective lioness has come out in my mother too, wishing just to be able to go over and talk to Shona, to make her understand that what she is doing is very wrong, harmful and damaging to Tia and everyone that loves her. Mum is saddened by the abusive background of the relationship, and feels upset for me not sharing the concerns with her, so she could have helped me or at least be there for me. She is not the type to intrude on her children's relationships, but she would have liked to know what I was going through. Back then, I don't think I even knew fully. I just didn't want her to worry, as I did not know what to do without risking losing Tia. She understands why the escape was eventually essential, and why taking the risk was my only choice. Mum is not the oblivious type; she has her opinions regarding my mistakes and she does not shy away from expressing them. But she is non-judgemental, and I appreciate that. I am taking responsibility for my mistakes, and hearing the truth, just aids my resilience. Mum expressed that break ups are common, and when children are involved, they can be nasty. In my instance, one parent has remained positive and supportive, while the other has taken the opposite route namely, keeping the child to themselves as a selfish and revengeful act. I told my mum, that Amber – Helen's daughter – is now mentioning the length of time without seeing Tia and she no longer believes anyone who tells her that Tia is with her other mum. I share my worries with Mum, because if Tia is also beginning to be aware of the time length, that could potentially mean that the effects on her caused by our detachment could be worse than I initially thought. Amber is a few months older, so the situation from her point of view could be different, and I am choosing to hold on to that belief. The phase of disparity, Tia's anger towards me for not ever coming, may have already passed. Nonetheless, from a psychological point of view, later Tia could face insecurities, low self-esteem and separation issues. Hopefully, shortly after we reunite, we can work things out and we can continue where we left off. I can then help Tia to settle back to what she has always known and if any issue may arise in the future, as the consequences of our separation, I will be there for her, to guide her every step of the way. My mother couldn't hide her anger, but she reassured me, that whatever the time spent apart, Tia will never forget who I am – ever – and she will be waiting for me, regardless. Soon it will all be over and we will continue with our life, together. Unavoidably, I express my fears to Mum, over losing my legal visibility and potentially losing my right to have custody of Tia, and never see Tia again. The latter is not acceptable, but I cannot rule it out, every aspect of the law so far has protected the biological legal parent. My mum experienced the worst herself, many years ago when she lost her own children, so the feelings, doubts and worries she confirmed are normal and as I am coming closer to the end of the wait, scenarios keep crossing my mind and they trigger different emotions. She still finds it hard talking about her past, it was dreadful, the courts and the social system all corroborated against her. Although, here in the UK things are different. It is a rocky ride down the law lane, but at least it follows the legal path. It is inexplicable how history can repeat itself and that I came across the same person as my dad was back then. Who is punishing me for leaving her by causing me the biggest pain, by taking my baby away from me, with the belief that if I am not by her side, then Tia shall no longer be mine, only hers. The same motive that my father had when my mother left him, he couldn't bear it and revenge was all that drove him after his ego was hurt so he deprived us all from the person we needed in our lives – our mother. However, we stood up for ourselves once we had the confidence to face our father, but by that time we missed out on some years of not having our mother to rely on. I still remember the feeling today, that reunion with my mum, it was like coming home, where the truth was told about our past, as everyone in my dad's circle just lied to protect his image. I also remember feeling very angry with my dad for daring to do such a terrible thing to our mum who we deserved to have in our lives. I missed her so much, so many times I needed her, and that is who my big sister has always been to me for many years, a replacement for my mother. My support whom I curled up to at night when scared of thunder or the darkness. I had moved on with my life, adapted to the routine and continued going to school but without that mothering love, it was not complete. I wouldn't like that to ever happen to Tia, although she does have her mum, but the mother I have been to her is where she feels at home. Home where love resides, memories are built, and laughter never ends. I know Tia feels very confused, lonely at times and let down, just like I did when I was detached from my mum, but hopefully in a few weeks I will explain everything to her, to soothe her soul. My mum hugged me around my waist as we walked to the underground station, at the end of our day out in the city, and she whispered into my ear, *'You are an exceptional mother and everyone at the court and the Cafcass officer will see this too, just keep up the strength, you have always shone the light on everything challenging in life, and you've got this.'*

One thing that my poor mum did not have, and I have so much of, is support. She was all alone, her own father turned on her – my own grandfather, and if my grandmother was still alive back then, she wouldn't have let anything bad happen to us all. She was without money and a job and barely had a roof above her head. Some family and friends offered a place for her to live in until she got back on her feet. Everything was taken away from her and how she was portrayed at the court by my dad, she stood no chance to convince the judges of the ability of looking after three children. Whereas my dad, he was affluent, he had it all, including the support of his parents – both fit and prepared to help my dad to look after us. My mum had some weekend visitations ordered by the court, but to be honest I do not remember one taking place, and I only found out much later that my dad always made us unavailable. Again, that was all brushed under the carpet by the authorities. Apparently, when she reported it to the judges, it was fed back to my dad who had a connection in his support web, and no one followed up on the complaint. Mum had no more money to take the case further, above the district court, and no one back in those days had that amount of funds. Most of the people just about survived and covered their own living costs, and she didn't know anyone more well-off. I respect my dad as he taught me a lot, but he will not ever be forgiven for what he did to us all. I squeezed my mother back around her waist, she smiled back in response, and that moment no words were needed. Her sorrow, that pain she had to live through has been buried deep down in her existence. Once reunited with her children, my mother's sorrow disappeared. She loves us all, including her grandchildren, more than her own life and she would do anything to help us when seeing us hurting. The lioness in my mum is graceful, brave, determined and if anything is to threaten her children, she will become fierce. Mum has recently told me that we are always going to be her babies, no matter the age, and she will always be here to welcome us in her arms, to cry on her shoulders and her protection will live beyond her existence. She recalled peeking at our lives from around the corners of places where no one could see her, school assembly performances watched from a far distance or spotting us walking with our friends, Mum was not allowed to talk to us directly without our dad's presence. I remember seeing her hide in plain sight, her face sad yet full of hope and affection as her sad eyes caught a fleeting glimpse of me, happily playing and enjoying my life. That was from her perspective – parents can never see what really goes on inside a child's mind. As a child I obeyed my dad's rules, stayed loyal to him but not because I wanted to, but because I was too young to do anything else. Inside, I often cried for my mum as I have always been sentimentally natured and lacked that emotional connection with her. Our grandparents provided for our essential needs, offered their care and we always had everything they thought we needed. Our dad was not so good with emotions and he was not around much with the excuse of having to work to provide for us all. He may have never got to fully know us nor understand either of our choices. In his view, none of his three children have met his high expectations, therefore his is unhappy and feels betrayed. On the other hand, aware of our mum's deep presence in our lives, dad is paying for his past actions as we have somewhat naturally disconnected from him over the years. What goes around, comes back around. Back then, if I told my Dad about seeing my mum, it could have jeopardised other beautiful opportunities for me to see her, for her to see me, so I remained silent and cherished the moments, however brief they were. I knew, somewhere, even if I was still young, that my mum was aware of me seeing her too, an intuition that I kept focusing on. I envisioned her being there with me, every time I played outside, stood on the stage performing or faced challenging moments. I felt her protective aura guiding me. I was eleven years old when we were reunited, I told my mum about the way I felt and how I experienced her brief presence while absent from my life. She broke into tears, as that is what she wanted, with each brief encounter she was sending me vibes that she was there and coming for me and my siblings. Parents breaking up is a painful experience for a child, but after separation, what a child needs is love, affection, support and understanding from both parents, in their own special way. A child can only benefit from the experiences both parents can provide, as each memory stores in their mind and has purpose in identity and character construction. We grew up deprived of all the possible experiences, so decided to stick together in a sibling gang, side by side, we curled up in a single bed when we needed to, we talked into late hours if we had to, and we always stood up for each other in everything. When we reached secondary school age, we got the courage to stand up against our father and he could no longer physically stop us from seeing our mother, ever again. Ultimately, I made up my own mind, put my early years past behind me, and began to focus on the future with my mum by my side. No matter whether it is a female or male figure, a child can connect to both, one or the other, sometimes even neither. Who can make a child feel loved, safe and understood, is the one thing a child will seek at all times. Tia has not seen me for a few months now, and what she seeks and gets in return, is unknown. Ah, it seems like a lifetime for me without Tia, the most heart breaking period of my lived years, as I lived through the pain of a child losing her mother and now I am living through the pain of losing a child as a mother. I worked hard to overcome the adversity of my childhood, but I was older than Tia is now, and I remembered way too many details. Tia is young, but hopefully she also knows, just as I knew when I was a child, that I am there with her, everywhere she goes and whatever she does. I will be able to fix everything and catch up with her, just as my mum has done with me, and our separation was not months, but years. I must not forget about our bond, the protective aura and that will not ever be touched by any acts in the physical world.

Mum had no other choice but to post the card and settle with the fact that she will not be seeing Tia during her visit either. Tears filled her eyes, as she let the card drop into the letter box.

Running my usual six miles seems extraordinarily energetic today, I feel like I could run for another ten! I have had such a wonderful break, surrounded by lovely people. To my biggest surprise, the arrival of my mum made my break literally perfect. I have needed my mum and she has known that. As I look down to the ground still running at quite a moderate pace, I suddenly stop and take a few steps back when I capture a shadow of a leaf on the pavement in the form of a heart. That familiar feeling of warmth washes over me again. Interesting, I think to myself. Is this some kind of a message? I pull out my phone to take a photo. Straight after, a name pops up on my screen that immediately makes me smile – Lily. When Lily messages me, the words cover my whole screen, she always has so much to say, so much of what interests me, and so my replies resemble the same length. I read her message, and at the end she has put a cheeky smile emoji – I can't help but have a cheeky grin on my face in response. I close her message and take a mental note to respond to her later, after my run. I can't wait to talk to her, Lily has been so lovely and supportive regarding Tia and everything else. I can see the chatting going on until at least midnight again. First, I need to say goodbye to my mum, she is flying back this afternoon so I better hurry because she is cooking lunch and it is something delicious from my childhood favourites – dumplings, lamb slices and sauté, yum. Tomorrow is a work day, back to the tough reality. Eight more days until my

Cafcass interview and I will count down the days. I am super anxious, but finally it is time for me to shine as a mother. The judge has granted me with this chance, and I have to demonstrate to the officer that what I claim is who I truly am to Tia.

## Chapter 13

## The Voice

'The power of my voice is beginning to shine through.'

The day has finally arrived. Leading up to it, I have never been so aware of the twenty-four hours in a single day and how they can drag on so dismally. It felt as if I was an astronaut floating through the dark, endless void of outer space where time seems to be distorted and elongated. This infinite space, beyond the clouds, the great Universe, filled with stars, galaxies, dust, light and a multitude of observable planets. Tia and I often marvel at the night sky while lying on the ground, imagining the mysteries of the Universe beyond our own planet. Tia would often ask about human existence, and explore her understanding of Earth, and that has helped her to appreciate how special our planet is. Preserving it for future generations is crucial. So, Tia has shown an interest in recycling and ways to look after the environment from an early age, via various videos, that accommodated a more animated and fun version of learning. We would always watch the sky, feeling grounded – calm, stable and consciously present – Tia laying close to me, awaiting the clouds to appear in our sight. Spotting the odd shapes and describing the resemblance, would every time offer us joy and laughter. Interestingly, it would inspire Tia's brain with curiosity, and the topics of our discussions, could be immensely diverse. She has an imagination that is bright, colourful and inventive, with a mind that works in mysterious ways, and she has found her match in her mother, me. We travel on the same wavelength, we get each other, we see things through the same lens, even if in different colours. We may both be inspired on a different level, but we see the beauty in everything around us. They trigger the talks of our existence, fear of death, sadness or happiness. My mothering mission would always be to teach her how to see life, to recognise and accept any negative forces, and guide her towards tuning the feelings to maintain a healthy mind for that self-protection. Tia is still very young, but forming these habits from a young age is an important steppingstone process towards a healthy adulthood.

Our endless talks about clouds, how their formation is influenced by different factors and how they come in all different shapes, sizes and shades. It could be compared to humans. We belong to one species and that is Homo sapiens, and that is how we all unify! Our formation too, is influenced by various factors, we vary in size, shape and colour, but we are still the same, human. The mission for us all individuals on Earth is to survive, but that is a given innate skill, potentially achievable to all of us. However, we have evolved tremendously towards the 21st century – based on the Gregorian calendar – and we no longer only thrive for survival, we thrive to satisfy the materialistic opportunities that the world is offering us. We want more and more, but do we need more? The most important mission for humans is to find happiness, to connect with their inner selves and learn to express those traits in various ways. May those be through hobbies, love, careers or other forms. Having that feeling of passion, is the key to everything we aim to achieve. The enjoyment in what we do allows us to grow, learn, to thrive, and not only, simply survive. But that may not be through satisfying the society we live in, or impressing others, but to please ourselves, to show ourselves our worth and believe in ourselves. Only then can we learn to love ourselves, once we accept ourselves for who we are, what we want and how we choose to live our lives. Happiness is not a single term, it needs discovery and doesn't come without mistakes made. Without mistakes, we cannot possibly be able to compare and make a difference between right and wrong. Exploring, is a huge part of our human traits, and we do it every day, consciously or unconsciously. We are a fascinatingly intelligent species and everything else that our physical world has achieved is how the human brain has expanded and adapted over time, it is in constant motion, thinking of new ideas. The same theory applies to the core of who we are inside. Our interests change, and we constantly adapt to how the world is changing around us. But, the way we express our inner beauty has swept society from under its feet, as we have been not only adapting, but also questioning the norms and beliefs of many others that formed the society we live in today. We are all free to say *I love you* to whoever we feel to say those precious words to. Own it, treasure it, it is yours! Taking on the world is a big mission, start with you first and everything else will follow. You and your *me* matter and do not let that treasure out of your hands. Strength, confidence and resilience come from within you and when life throws you challenges, you may feel lost, hurt, but something from deep inside will provide you with strength that will make the struggles less mighty. That may be scary, it may make you feel like giving up or feel defeated by the negative forces but then, you will get stronger than any other force. I have become *me*, and it has been a bumpy process, filled with challenges, joy and impatience. I am not stopping the process, we naturally cannot stop it *that* grows with us as we mature with age. The *me* transforms and mutates, it gets greater every day with the qualities of life. I am in a process of facing one of my greatest challenges, and that is channelling my disparity and the heart breaking period of my life, into a new energy, with one aim that keeps the flame alive and that is getting my daughter back, so we can lay side by side on the grass, looking up at the sky once again. Believe it or not, Tia, age appropriately adjusted, tuned in to such talks with me.

I long to continue our talks. As she gets older, she will have more questions, curiosities and wonders that can determine many aspects of her life ahead. I want to be part of it all, and not miss out on any time when she may need me. I have had a child for over four years, and to never see her again is sadly in the cards. I feel as if *me* is crumbling just over the thought of it. I will never be the same without my daughter. I may as well declare myself purposeless and soulless. My fight will not ever come to an end, the judge may not favour me, I may lose the war, I shall continue until the day someone is able to deliver justice to a mother who has everything, but the formal papers stating so. Can they open their eyes wide and see that a non-biological mother or a parent deserves recognition that can be just as equal as the biological traits that have existed? Society needs an awakening, and adapting to the new lives many families choose to live in. Biology itself is no longer the only definition of a primary caregiver.

    Today is the day when I can finally validate my

truthfulness as a mother. Today I have a chance to demonstrate who I have been to Tia all her life and shine a light on Shona's deceptive story telling. My only worry is, what Tia will remember, how she may have been influenced or directed towards different ideologies about who I am to her. Shona mentioned in her response statement that she has always been a single parent to Tia, and that I was only a short-term partner who Tia grew fond of but only saw on rare occasions. This statement not only concerns me, but it also terrifies me. The Cafcass officer has by now read both of our statements, and however experienced she is, to make sense from which person is honest and which is the culprit in this scenario will be a difficult job to convey. The investigation will need to be detail orientated in order to capture my traits through body language and facial expressions, to determine whether what I assert matches my statement. Skills which I am confident this officer will put in great use in determining my mothering relationship to Tia. How they will proceed, is far beyond my knowledge.

I press the number four button and stand patiently as the doors slowly close and takes me at a swift pace to the required floor. The doors open to a corridor that resembles a day care centre but in the middle of an office space, filled with play equipment, books and children sized furniture. My heart races as the lioness tries to free herself from within me in search of her cub. I stretch my eyes down a corridor containing few closed doors labelled vacant or occupied. Is Tia in any of those rooms, on this floor, right now? The invitation letter from the Cafcass officer stated that the same interview will be carried out with Tia too, on the very same day. She must be here. I look around, seeming quite tense. The receptionist captures my restless body language and asks for my name and details to locate the booked appointment. The interview is shortly about to take place and she informs me that the officer is already here and will collect me from the waiting lobby shortly. I take a seat on a teal blue armchair, still looking around to see whether I can capture Tia's little face, whilst I try and look through some leaflets about parent separation, support guidance and about Cafcass as an organisation. I bring the palms of my hands to my face and bury my inside them to release this tension within me, tension that is not to do with my interview, but the tension from trying to hold back my tears. Tears, from feeling the disappointment from my relationship, how I did not predict that I'd meet a person who would end up hurting me so badly, that it would eventually not only break the family union, but my life with Tia too. A broken family is part of my history, and it will always be Tia's too. That makes me feel very sad as it was something I'd always promised myself to not repeat in my own life, but the decision to finally escape from abuse will not ever be regretted, nor will I ever blame myself for my actions. The unhealthy relationship is the one to blame, and it would have eventually reached into *me,* and the negative captivating force of abusive behaviour would have eventually ruined my mental health. A female partner as an abuser was something that hugely surprised me and led me to read articles, forums and different research findings to try and acquire evidence of why women abuse other women, in intimate relationships. Aren't we women supposed to stick together and protect each other? I found that women abusers have similar motives to male abusers, and that is to maintain control over their partners. The control is greater if the perpetrators have anything they can use as their motive. For instance, threatening the partner to report false claims that would jeopardise their child custody, legal or immigration status. In my case, it was all about child custody, I feared that my legal status as a mother would be jeopardised by being reported to the police if I would have ever shared the abusive experience myself, hence my invisibility today. The story would have been turned against me with a possibility of a criminal record, if the police would have believed the dramatic story from the legal biological mother. Absolutely, I would have not stood a chance and may have never had my application for custody ever approved. Further, the violent behaviour worsens when the perpetrators notice the effects of their behaviour in their partners reactions, and they begin to fear losing their 'loved one'. I question, whether what they feel is love or an insecurity. That fear aggravates them more, as the anticipation of loss and abandonment becomes more likely a reality. Many people may have experienced or witnessed abuse growing up, and without the ability to seek help and heal from these events, the risks of repeating these behavioural patterns could be much higher. Something, that I would have forever regretted, is such behaviour growing with Tia as well, and potentially becoming the perpetrator in her future intimate relationships. To avoid all of this, an end had to be put to this negative role modelling. My endless efforts to stop and divert the abusive outlets were only partly ever successful. There were many times I received a blow to the head by a thrown object that ranged from tins to a vacuum, to a fist. Therapy may work for some, but unless completely invested and committed it can only postpone, not change, a person and only for a short amount of time. Therapy takes time and persistence and the will to look at every part of yourself and dissect it. Shona believed she didn't need it. To fight back, is not sensible, that only makes things worse and becoming a fearful trapped being, is not the way to live happily. There is a saying that relationships are not supposed to be hard, but they can become very jaded and the two people, who form the relationship, would need to work together. Would it make the relationship tougher or weaker, that is hard to predict. But do we have to try? Hell yeah! Try and try and try harder. But when we hit the bottom of the lowest, there is nothing left to try. I tried and tried, but when Tia could have been potentially hurt, that was it, I was done. I began to feel scared for her and my life. To this very day, I remember the night, that very last terrible fight, those eyes dripping in spite, nostrils flared, lips thinner, signalling one thing *I am going to hurt you*. Tia was in my arms, wrapped around my neck, begging for it all to stop. Heart-breaking, those tears, that innocent voice. The lioness reached out to protect us both. I found an inner strength that night that helped me to physically resist being pushed, shouted into my face and find safety in a room where I could lock the door. The lioness guarded the door, the whole night! My baby fell asleep in my arms, feeling safe and content. That night will forever linger, my protective mothering instinct had never been stronger before. We were not hurt that night, but Shona's fury in her eyes frightened me more than ever before. I could hear her walking up and down the hallway, trying to open the bedroom door. Finally, after couple of hours, silence dropped on the other side of the door. I left the room for the bathroom, with Tia fast asleep. Sadly, the anger still prevailed, more in a verbal manner, but I stood strong against all the threats. I had texted my sis by then, who was prepared to get us both out of the flat. I was ready to leave, as my sis couldn't get to the flat door, unless buzzed in. There was no way to the front or back of the property for me to throw keys down to her. Shona detected some kind of a plan in place and arrogantly threatened me that if I go anywhere with Tia, she will report that immediately as an abduction to the police. Shona had a recited story to add to her report, which would have put me in the worst possible situation. I never contacted the police, for this reason, as without any paperwork to prove my relationship with Tia, and Shona's staged dramatic scene portraying me as some kind of an intruder and abuser. I could have been taken away and Shona could have filed a restraining order against me. So, I said nothing. I tried to calm storms when they occurred before that night, in order to convince Shona to add my name to the birth certificate and save time to search for the donor agreement where my name resides. I found absolutely no traces of any documents in the flat. Then the information hit the fan that night, and I heard from Shona that the documents are in a safe place, inaccessible by me. That fear of my invisibility in the eye of the law, trapped me again. I couldn't leave with Tia, and I couldn't leave my baby alone that night. So, I stayed, but not for long. I stayed to protect Tia, while things calmed, and the next day went to work with Tia as usual. I remember Tia's clingy behaviour that day in the nursery, I could barely leave her side. That day, office work didn't matter, I provided her with the support she needed. After a few days, Tia bounced back, and when Shona was ready to talk peacefully, we agreed on going separate ways, and agreeing on a fair childcare arrangement. There was no way back, no more forgiveness, no more pretending in front of Tia or to the world. It was over, the relationship was far over. Eventually, we motioned towards a shared care routine, handing Tia over between two homes. I did plan to seal the deal legally and apply to the courts for that yearning visibility that I was deprived of, intentionally by Shona. Little did I know, that the child care agreement would abruptly come to an end, when Shona realised that I was no longer considering reconciling the relationship when I suggested a mediation meeting with a solicitor. I exhausted every single speck of those tries, there was nothing left in that dead relationship, but Tia.

Suddenly I'm startled from out of my memories, a woman approaches and reaches out her hand towards me, introducing herself as Nicole – the Cafcass officer that has been allocated to my case. I jump up from the sofa, straightening my posture and introduce myself with a polite smile in return. Nicole guides me towards the narrow corridor lined with doors, which I already spotted earlier in the hopes of spotting Tia. I am guessing that behind those doors are the rooms, where interviews take place. Again, the thought of Tia being in one of those rooms right now, re-enters my mind. I peek carefully through the small squared viewing windows of the doors as we pass through the corridor, but the rooms seem vacant. Finally, we arrive at an open door that leads into a small room, different from the day-care set up rooms we had passed, and Nicole asks me to take a seat at this round table in the middle of the room. The room has some toys and posters across the walls. I take a seat, and place my bag next to the chair, with a teddy bear I got for Tia, poking out. This funky and colourful teddy has a personalised message written on it, as it has been intended for Tia, *I love you and I will always be in your heart,* just in case I will be permitted to see her and gift her this teddy. I sit facing Nicole on the opposite side of the round table, a social worker with a smart appearance and a friendly radiance. I am waiting patiently, as she attentively reads through the extensive file in front of her, but far enough to prevent me from seeing what's written on the pages. But this is unlike high school in the 1990's, when we as pupils, could hurriedly peek through the teachers notes when unprepared for a subject topic presentation. This was an anxious, but fun experience and required a lot of effort to place the puzzle pieces together to make some kind of a sense, almost somewhat of an art. Today, it is nothing of a presentation, nor a need for peeking and more about an inquisitive mind in a search for notes from Tia's interview. I feel slightly ambivalent, but beyond doubt ready to start. Nicole begins by telling me that she met Tia, this wonderful little girl just over four years old and that she was a delight to speak to. My eyes immediately begin to collect tears of joy, and my body jumps from the excitement whilst I manage to remain seated. Nicole can see my genuine reaction and offers a smile in response, but has taken an eye note of the moment, and remained professional as she has to convey the interview process. I grab a tissue from the box near me, just in case. I play gently with my spinning ring, which helps me to tame myself as all I want to hear is how Tia is doing and how the interview went, but I guess that is not the officer's immediate agenda.

Nicole politely thanks me for coming today and begins in a gentle tone.

'Could you describe Tia as a character, please?'

'She can be a little shy at first, but with the people she feels comfortable with, can become playful quite quickly. With time, you may see her cheerful, chatty and cheeky nature. Tia is a social gem, absolutely loves being around other children and adults who show interest in interreacting with her.

She is active, loves running around and climbing, but at the same time, she loves relaxing in a den with her soft teddies and colour or paint. If she shares cuddles at the end of meeting a new person, that is a sign that Tia has had a good time.'

My heart is beating so fast, I feel like I could talk for hours and hours, just about Tia. The elevation is vibrating through my words, I feel as if my voice is not only going to be heard, but taken seriously, for once. The officer smiles and writes down notes with a thank you added note. She looks up at me and continues her interview process.

'Could you roughly try and describe to me Tia's possible behaviour, in this room and with me today?'

'Tia may have come in a little quiet and unsure, but I think seeing the toys in the room and given your seemingly friendly warm approach, she opened up after a short playful period. Looking at that corner over there, she may have chosen the doll house to play with as she adores small figurines and any sort of bits and bobs toys. Then she may have bought some over to you and initiated some kind of role play – mostly she likes the swimming pool, beach or jungle. She may also explore all the toys around after a while, by trying them out in order to select the ones to keep for playing. Tia may have asked, who you are and why there are no other children, like in the nursery as to her toys and play is connected to other children.'

My answers come to me quicker than words can express. Knowing Tia from her everyday interactions makes it easy, it all very much depends on whether she has hugely changed in the past months. There is a small chance for any fundamental changes to her individual traits, such as lack of confidence and insecurity, but it is mind-twisting to try and figure that out right now. I have known Tia for over four years, her entire life, and I doubt there have been major changes in her behaviour, even if partially in light of our detachment and possibly alienation, my statement should be in line with Tia's true personality. So far, the officer has only responded in pleasant facial expressions, and again says nothing else but a thank you and continues, to what it seems like another explorative question.

'Did Tia possibly have anything with her today, like a comfort item, if she has got one?'

'Hmm, Tia doesn't have one item that she would attach to really, as she never got used to carrying around the same item, but there are some favourites. She loves all of her soft toys, and every time we would visit attractions or days out, she would want a soft toy. I think, a shop could be opened with the amount of soft toys she owns. However, Tia would not give away any of them and would remember each from where she got it from, or who may have gifted her one. From the last time I was with her, it could have been Teddy, as that has a small zip pocket where she would stuff in little toys to the very top and struggle to close it with her little fingers. If she did have that recent bear, then she may have told you its name and showed you every little toy from the stuffed zip pocket and allocated you ones to play with?'

Nicole giggles gently, shaking her head to what it seems like out of utter astonishment. Have I been right all this time, have I passed the test? I think to myself. I know my daughter, and even if I am not incorrect regarding specific items, but the character description should be what the officer shall focus on.

'Vivien, thank you so much for your thorough description. I must say, that in my long years of experience, only one person can possibly know such an in-depth detail about a child, and that's a primary caregiver. The scene you have just narrated, fits little Tia precisely. We did indeed have a short play with the small toys, and it was her teddy that she brought along, and noted that the teddy is from you. The latter truly caught me when I interviewed Tia, as she was unaware of the interview reason and your name was not mentioned. It is very clear to me, that you have been a parent, matter of fact, a mother to Tia until the day of the detachment.'

I fight so hard to hold back my tears of joy, but I can't fully stop my voice from shaking. I apologise to Nicole, as I have missed Tia so much, that sharing anything about her life is making me feel ecstatic yet so sad and desperate. She seems like a compassionate person, given her profession, and reassures me to not worry as she completely understands. I wipe my eyes dry with the tissue I prepared earlier, gather myself and continue listening to further questions.

'If you are all right to continue, could you recount to me what activities Tia enjoys?'

'Oh, that must be the wide world of imagination, setting up scenes and giving roles to everybody involved. Dressing up, such as animal costumes or dresses, is certainly part of her every day. She loves drawing, arts and crafts and moulding material in general. I can see some play doh on that small table, she most likely played with that too. Regarding games, she loves hide and seek, playgrounds and great open spaces to run around playing ball games. One of a kind, who does actually like the rain, and jumping through puddles. Tia is a busy little body, barely able to be out of ideas.'

Nicole has been constantly recording on the sheet in front of her, smiling at me in between for that reassurance. I feel relaxed, the interview is flowing so naturally, it doesn't feel as formal as the process I had imagined before entering this room. Nicole delves deeper, but seemingly more just out of curiosity to probably match what Shona may have said too. I can sense that she may not need much more proof to decide the kind of relationship I have with Tia, but more to gather evidence to back her assessment outcomes. She continues discussing books that Tia would have been curios to read, and she places an array of books on the table. The officer sits back and crosses her legs, with a pleasant smirk on her face. I bet she is expecting me to pick the books that Tia laid her hands on. So, no pressure there I think to myself, but when I look at the pile of books, I do not recognise them all, as Tia loves reading books, but to my recollection, she is only familiar with *The Very Hungry Caterpillar* and *Beautiful Oops!* I take a guess based on the nature of books Tia would choose in a book shop or the library. My hands immediately reach out to pull out *The Very Hungry Caterpillar, Beautiful Oops! First Day at Bug School* and *The Owl Who Was Afraid of the Dark*. Nicole unwraps her legs, and writes down her notes, but this time combining with words:

'Tia did pick up few books, but when she noticed *Beautiful Oops!* she quickly added it to her selection pile, and we did manage to go through the book, briefly. She also mentioned something else regarding this book…'

I quickly answer for her '… Did she mention that the book is from her friend Max?'

'Yes, she did! Indeed, she knows her belongings very well. Tia was keen to take me through this particular book.'

We exchange pleasant humorous laughter, and chat a little about how Tia likes picking books for her bedtime, and one is never simply enough. I am truly blessed to have been allocated such a wonderful person, although, even if she wasn't so nice, I would have answered the very same, in the same manner. Our open chat has led her to ask a question.

'How would Tia respond when feeling worried?'

'She would need that immediate body contact, so mostly lifting up her arms, wrapping her arms around my neck, or my legs if not lifted, and she would look directly in the direction of what worried her, intensely awaiting further action. Tia wouldn't really let go until content enough to reconnect with the surroundings. Depending on the level of worry, she would settle back if she sensed from me that it is okay and safe to do so. That sense of encouragement, and talking about what worries her, that reassurance, is crucial every time.'

Nicole shares a concerned look with me, but opts to take notes, instead of saying anything to me in response to my answer. I do wonder why she asked me that question. Was Tia worried or seemed distressed? In my opinion, the officer needs to analyse, based on Tia's character, how she possibly handled today's situation, if that was the case. The officer is educated and trained to understand young children's behaviour and so am I. But at this moment, with focus only on Tia individually. Although, Tia may not have had the same approach from Shona, and she could have had behaved and responded differently. I am almost certain, that my description is still accurate, as it has been months, but the short length of time cannot drastically change a child. Could it be that Tia's worries were not entirely comforted, and the officer clicked on a moment where Tia seemed to have been missing something that was not offered to her from Shona. Shona, by now, must have reconciled an affectionate relationship with Tia to some extent. What agitates me, is thinking of how Shona has handled Tia's questions about my whereabouts or any of her emotional outbursts? Feeling a little tense over the fact that Tia even had to go through this interview, however well she felt or enjoyed the one-on-one play with Nicole. She shouldn't have been here and assessed. This all for the false allegations filed against me, in that terrible response statement. It ruined everything, but there is nothing more to do now, but to stay focused, as only a few more weeks are left of the great wait.

Further into the discussion, the officer confirms that Tia indeed reached out to the dollhouse, and that they had a lovely little play and that was when Tia picked little toys to represent everybody from my family, starting with me, her grandmother – my mum, Charlie – her cousin, my sis – her aunt and placed them in the dollhouse. Apparently, Tia said that we don't come to the house anymore and that she misses us a lot and asked the officer when she could see us all again. 'Tia hugged me close during our play, and told me that she is missing you very much, but she can't talk about you and that makes her feel sad.'

The latter is heart breaking! Tia is sad! My baby, she cannot even talk about me, meaning, that her wonders, questions and worries are probably all suppressed. What a mean act towards a young child, she must be feeling so lost, confused and mislead. My chest tightens in response, and my breathing is shallow, I can feel the panic coming over me. I can't stop myself from the tears, as the second they appear in my eyes, the same moment they run down my cheeks. My baby girl misses me and everybody who loves her dearly, she is probably feeling so alone in her newly designed world without the people she has always known. Furious waves enter my system, I squeeze my spinning ring intensely. My child, she must feel so deceived, shut off from the world she knows, and forced to live in an artificial one, suddenly designed to fit Shona's vision. I take a deep breath, and continue to fidget with my spinning ring and I ask the officer if Tia is still in the interview department. To my disappointment she is no longer here but to my deepest sorrow, the officer planned for us two to meet in a room under her supervision, for her to see our interaction together and let us connect after a long time of not seeing each other. But, sadly, after Shona's disapproval prior to the assessment interviews allocated to today, Nicole had to reschedule their interview into a different time slot, to avoid a drastic collision by randomly bumping into each other. My chest has ripped apart into tiny pieces, the pain of hearing that it was planned for us two to meet, is agonising. Distress urges to the surface, as I know my little sweetheart hoped for the very same after she was free to express herself about me to the officer. Shona may still just be actively against me gaining custodial rights, so she may not ever permit such contact, if that was up to her consent. The law that currently still stands, is on the side of the biological parent, and that has been incredibly infuriating. The officer responds in agreement with my disappointment and reassures me that she has to follow the rules and regulations at all times, despite what she believes is right for the child in that moment, but the parent who has the legal right of the child, is the one who calls the shots, until the judge states otherwise.

More questions follow, so I try and calm down and pull myself together, and prepare myself for further investigation. Honestly, I wish to stay here for hours if necessary, as this is my one and only time to share everything that connects me to Tia, with a professional who has been in charge to assess me as a parent and person.

'Could you tell me little about your work?'

'My work has always been my passion, as I love working with children, and that is the reason behind establishing my very own nursery business, not far from our home. I enjoy following the way children grow and develop during their daily nursery visits. I am in charge of the activities planning and designing a positive environment to ensure that children's needs and interests are met in every aspect. I support the idea that not one child is ever the same, and that is reflected across the curriculum. Bringing out the strengths to face each child's weaknesses is presented through activities and team work. Tia has attended the nursery since she was very young, and has made many friends who do miss her dearly.'

The officer smiles and comments on Tia talking about the nursery and her friends, especially Amber who she used to play with every day. It is visibly clear how our stories match and I hope from the bottom of my heart that the officer can see that the allegations made against me are malicious, and I am truly significant in Tia's life. I beg her not to disregard the past, and settle with the fact that Tia is used to a different life now, as that cannot be good in the long run. She is in need of me, for her life to be complete.

The officer continues about the break up details and the abuse described in my statement. I provide accurate information of the past events, exactly as stated in my application to the court, and present my disagreement towards Shona's response statement accusations. There is only one thing to do, and that is to confirm my truth.

Clearly, the relationship and the causes for the break up were important, as the officer may have noted down any changes in the story line. Sincerely, I could not have made a mistake, so I am not worried!

'Thank you, Vivien for everything, I will conclude my findings and you will receive my report in the next couple of weeks, in time for the hearing scheduled for November 20th. I was also requested to attend the hearing, so I will be there.'

That is such great news today, as it seems like Gloria won't have to chase the report this time and the officer's presence at the court will be absolutely amazing. Often officers cannot take the stand if their caseload is too busy and they would only provide the written report to the judge to read. Meaning, that she can answer any additional questions, which I hope will benefit my case.

The interview has come to an end, I collect my belongings ready to leave the room and say my goodbyes. The officer offers her hand to wish me good luck, adding, 'It has been an absolute pleasure to meet you today, Vivien, and thank you for finding the time for coming all this way. I must say, that it's impressive how much you know about Tia and you are a great parent who is missed and I can see how much you miss Tia too. I am afraid I cannot share more at the moment, but one thing I can tell you now, and that is my opinion about your ongoing importance in Tia's life. I hope that your reunion will happen soon and I am sorry that I could not make that happen today as I understand how much it would have meant to you both. I will see you in court, Vivien. Take care!'

What a triumphant moment this is, the Cafcass officer has just given me the title of a parent and highlighted my status in Tia's life. My heart is shooting fireworks, the interview couldn't have gone any better. I have just taken a massive leap towards my victory! I also thank the officer for her time and for attempting, even if unsuccessfully, to organise a brief reunion that would have helped Tia's well-being and my sanity. My feet wish to dance their way to the elevator. I press the button for the ground floor, standing in front of the door looking highly satisfied, but inside I am on a mountain, high up, screaming loud out of my lungs with my arms wide open to let out all my frustration and allow happiness to flow through my veins right into my aching heart. Almost missing the opening of the doors of the lift, that have been open for a while, as they are just about to shut, I quickly slide through the open gap. The lift has lowered me back down to ground, yet spiritually, I am still way up high. I inhale and focus on Tia's energy being in the same space today, to capture her previous presence and exhale in excitement. My baby, she hasn't forgotten me, she misses me and everyone else. My statement has been justified, and I cannot wait to read the full report from the Cafcass officer. I step out of the building thanking every single staff member for today's opportunity, and as I walk down the stairs I see a stain on the concrete, old chewing gum by the looks of it, in the shape of a heart – the same feeling of warmth rushes through me. I am going to deviate some time to understand these hearts that keep popping out to me randomly. Earlier this morning I saw foam in my coffee shaped as a heart, but I was too preoccupied with my interview thoughts, to pay too much attention to it, but I registered that warm feeling.

    I immediately pull my phone out of my bag and call Gloria. She can tell from my exciting monologue, that the interview went really well. I am jumping and swaying on the inside, but I am convinced by the look on the faces of passers-by, that my feelings have made their way onto the outside. Gloria confirms that the officer's report will not only conclude her findings but will also advise the judge about what in her opinion, based on findings, is the best for Tia. From what I read; judges mostly do take on Cafcass advice before they make their final decision at the hearing. To deviate from Cafcass recommendations, comes with their opinions disagreeing. After Gloria satisfyingly comes off the phone, I instantly dial my sis and my mum in a group call and tell them about the meeting with Cafcass. Both are clearly very happy about the verdict, and cheer at the fact that the wait is not long now. The court hearing is just around the corner, and I trust in the judge making the right decision. Fingers crossed, the judge will see the same in me as the Cafcass officer did today. To attract positive forces into my current situation, is a possible saviour. I feel blissful!

I decide to send out a group message to everybody who has been so supportive, and has taken their time to write their testimonies, and are expecting my update from the interview. At the same time, a message from Lily arrives, it stops me in the middle of the pavement, something fascinating about this woman that just captures me pleasantly every time she texts me. Her intuition, caring instinct and her interest in my life, it makes me smile every time.

I jump on the train, swing onto the seat and listen to the sound of the underground with a massive grin on my face! I am a mother who will soon fill a space that no one will ever be able to take away from her. I am a woman who is fierce and strong, who will never let anyone harm her, ever again!

# Chapter 14

## The Symbol

'Does one's eyes see what one's heart wants to see?'

The smell of toasted bread diffuses from the toaster and spreads out through the air that surrounds me. I can feel my brain cells at once jump into an activity. The smell mingles in my memories, and takes me right back to my childhood, as I grew up on fresh home-baked bread and other goods. I can feel the knife cracking its way through the chunky crispy loaf, cutting away a thick slice, right in front of my eyes. As a child, I watched my grandmother punch and knead the dough until it was elastic and smooth – I often chipped in with that process, the sensory feeling of the dough, a feeling of satisfaction so indescribable and a feeling I still enjoy today, although I do not bake as much as I would like to – and patiently watched the sheet covering the fermentation process underneath until the moment it was proved to perfection. I followed my grandmother's steps, in every way. The wait in front of the hot stone oven was long, but the smell rising into the air with heat, was the smell I can recognise today. Scientists refer to this phenomenon as *odour cued memories* – our olfactory system is linked to our brain's memory and emotion centres, which allows certain smells to trigger powerful memories and emotions and transport us to specific points in our lives. It is comforting in times of difficulty, and the scent and taste of a fresh, soft, crispy-edged slice of bread is something I crave in times of distress. On the other hand, my grandmother also made delicious homemade butter that tasted rather sour and was not to my liking. I smile to myself in the memory of the face I pulled when I first tasted it, like the face that babies pull when trying lemon for the first time. Bless, my grandmother was somewhat of a goddess of homemade production. What I also loved was the homemade strawberry jam, made from the picked strawberries that grew in her garden, an absolute delight. I sigh sadly, rest in peace grandmother, your memory will live on with me! I become teary very quickly lately, this current ordeal of losing my daughter, has made me more sensitive than I usually would be.

    I reach for the butter dish and take a chunk out of the salted butter block that spreads fast and evenly on the warm slice of bread. Topping the bread with some strawberry jam to add that final touch to my grand vision of how I like to indulge in my morning toast. I am about to take a bite from my craved delight, when I notice that the heat that erupted from the bread formed a heart shape in the jam spread. These little hearts everywhere, I am absolutely mesmerised by the sensation that I experience when I see them. I finish the last bite of my toast, reach for my phone, and open the internet search. All I have to do is type in *heart shapes appearing around me* and hundreds and hundreds of results open with various interpretations from religious, psychic and scientific points of view. What captures my attention is that for ancient Egyptians the heart, more than the brain, linked all the body parts together and was the source of human intelligence, memories and emotions. For this reason, it was the only organ left in the body during mummification, so the deceased can have it back in the afterlife. The heart was wrapped in a protective scroll to not use the heart's memories and emotions against the deceased. Whilst I indulge in different interpretations, I cannot stop my brain from shaping its own perspective. The heart symbolises the meaning of love, unity, femininity, sensuality, sacred and mirror reflection, from what I gather. Every individual experiences something different with the symbol's appearance. In my case it seems to symbolise strength, as the moment when I spot the heart symbol, warmth washes across my body, I feel somewhat enchanted and that gives me such a positive boost, it empowers me. I feel as if I see the reflection of Tia's little heart embedded in the heart shape symbols, as if it was her in a nonphysical form, showing herself to me. I feel her love and joy radiating from the shape that is how I interpret the warmth that I feel. In the very moment, when I capture the heart symbol, all the pain seems to momentarily freeze in time. It unites us, in that frozen moment, beyond this physical realm. My translation is what matters to me, how I read the symbol is what will guide me through. Overall, I have never seen any symbols until the heart shape, and I am ready to embrace the feelings, whenever they appear.

I look out through the front window, take a deep breath and think to myself, how much more uplifted I feel since my interview with Cafcass. It was so encouraging, I keep re-enacting it in my head, every time analysing every detail more in depth and searching for answers. The anticipation of the interview outcomes are rather ambiguous, and I ponder on what the officer is going to conclude based on her findings she gathered from meeting all three of us. From what I gathered from the officer on the interview day, was that two people's stories match, but one person's story might not add up. I flick open my emails on my phone but there's no email notification from the Cafcass officer, so the wait continues. Yes she did say a few weeks, but that may not always be accurate. Anyhow I better get ready as work is calling, and the time is running fast. Time has indeed been running somewhat faster since last week's dreadful wait. Maybe the next few weeks will just slip through my fingers. Wearing my bright colours today, it just expresses how uplifted I feel inside – my yellow shirt, light blue tapered trousers and my funky red trainers – yes, bring on the day!

I jump on my bike and begin to ride at a moderate pace, listening to the morning talk show on Radio 1 and ready for work with Tia in the forefront of my mind. I may not need as much of a distraction or the protective wall at work. The energy rushing through me will lead me all the way to the hearing day. Not much time to go! The wind is blowing strong in my face, as I push through its force. I worry slightly as the dark rain clouds gather above and head straight right towards me. A cloud that resembles an angry grizzly bear, hopefully not planning to absolutely soak me while I ride my bike. Just as I finish that thought, I feel the first rain drop on my warm cheeks. I speed up the pedalling, but the rain begins to suddenly pour down from the grizzly bear cloud, too late for me to turn around and opt for the car instead. Ah bugger, not a red traffic light and too many pedestrians. Great. Moaning will not help me in this case, so I just let the rain drops cover me entirely. With a careless attitude, I continue on my journey, and I finally arrive at work, completely drenched! No change of clothes, so I will need to dry off with time, I guess. I walk through the office to check on all the children in the nursery, everyone should have arrived by now. I place my professional hat on, take a deep breath as looking after other children without having my own has been emotionally challenging, but I have made it this far, I do not even know how really. I always picture Tia in every corner of the setting, playing, running around and sitting as close as she could possibly sit to me during floor play or circle activities, when fairly reasonable and not inequal to other children. Tia and I, we had great teamwork. She learned to understand that Mummy at work treats all the children equally and has to spread her attention all across the setting. That healthy detachment in the nursery setting was beneficial for her resilience and self-esteem to be able to turn to adults when in need and seek assistance from other children to create social connections, just like all the other children did. My team and I specialise in highlighting everyone's individual strengths and work those well into their weaknesses, via group activities which enable children to learn about each other and discover their own hidden skills. Every day is a new dance, we get inspired by anything that the day brings on, including children's ideas or items they may bring in, and we implement these in the daily planned schedule. Children, just as adults, find something special in various things, and not one child would offer the same perspective. To respect that choice, they make to show us something they wish to share, listening to what they have to say about it and describing it in their own way, is what runs like a vein through this setting. If a child wants to touch a worm, we say *go ahead but be mindful as it's a living creature* or if a child wants to climb, we say *go ahead but are you aware of how you may need to get back down.* Children explore, it is the way they see how the world around them works, how to resolve problems and how to measure the risks to stay safe. My darling Tia has always been part of this team, and Rachel – who has been a loyal employee for many years – would often mention how much she misses Tia, she often talks about her during her lunch hour and ask me about how things are going. I find that hard as I try to focus on work that has been my professional mask to shelter me from my despair, but I can't possibly control what others say or ask. Lately, that is including other staff members who have met Tia and had become fond of her, but vaguely know the story of her absence as I prefer to remain as private about my personal life as possible. Also, clients who have had their children in their nursery since Tia joined in, ask about the case update. I have managed to overcome the trembling sensation from wanting to cry when speaking of Tia – it still makes me shaky in my voice, but it has made me stronger, easier to talk about with time. I have managed to face my situation, by looking into the mirror and often repeating to myself *don't speak of Tia as if you have lost her, you didn't lose her! You are her mother, and she is your daughter, awaiting a sheet of paper that will not serve your entitlement but present you with the legal voice. She is right here, holding my hand and I am going to speak of her in a way of beauty, the beauty that she is. The situation, you are in, is because you let yourself get into this mess. Naively trusting the wrong person, that unintentionally, cost you to become legally silenced. You do not let others make you feel weak, speak of your situation with confidence. You have come so far, convinced the court to consider your parenthood, and a successful interview with the Caffcas officer and the court hearing that is nearing, will bring you the fruit from the seeds you planted. All your wait will be worth it and when you hold Tia in your arms, the time will take you back where you left off. She has only aged a little, but she has not distanced from you. Own your situation, express your willpower, that courage and perseverance! You are brave and nothing can stop you in getting your life back on track. You have your magic back and it shines through you brighter than ever before.*

Children curiously touch my soaked trousers, and the questions begin coming at me, and that is how the morning is seemingly looking to be. The children run off to put on wellies and head outside to explore the rain. As I will be attending to matters from my office for most of today, I will only be leading the art lesson. I will prompt children to indulge in some paint to express how the rain impacts their mind and activate those five senses. I look forward to the spontaneous day ahead!

Sitting in front of my computer, after an active art session on the floor with the children, is not a satisfying aspect of my work, but an important business aspect and something that I daily need to dedicate some time to. I am about to open the staff rota spreadsheet when my phone delivers a message. I immediately catapult from my office chair and reach for my phone, pulling it vigorously from the charging cable. Is it the Cafcass report that I have been waiting for? Although the possibilities are endless, my mind is set on one thing. Please be it, please, please. As my eyes fix on the screen, the excitement drops like a heavy ball on the ground, leaving my chest feeling the pressure of that thud. A message, not from the Cafcass officer but from my brother *Mum is sick and she is now in the hospital. Viv, call me as soon as you can!* My brother hardly contacts me, he's more of a special occasion type, but the words in his message, however concise, set my heart on fire. When my mum visited, I had this feeling that something was not all right, but she reassured me and blamed it on the seasonal weather change and the travel, which was not new with her. I wasn't worried then, but I am worried now!

I immediately call my brother and he answers straight away. He has a similar deep voice to me, more masculine though, and he is known in the family for his humorous remarks. This time however, his voice is firm and sad, I have not yet heard him speak like this. *"Mum has a critical night behind her and she has been in recovery since this morning, but it will be a slow healing journey and whether she will ever fully recover, is currently hard to say."*

I am so shocked, saddened, and furious at the same time, to find out that my sis and I, were not notified when my brother called an ambulance that took Mum into the intensive care unit. Bro insisted to let us know but Mum asked him not to as she didn't want us to worry, given the far distance and besides what I am going through is enough to handle right now. Regardless, we should have been notified, no matter what! Bro sounds sad, anxious and shaken from my mother's state. The nurse warned him to keep his phone close by at night, as there was a chance that she may have not survived the night. I nearly drop on the floor as I almost miss the chair. I cannot lose my mother, no she cannot leave us, this is not her end, and she has to fight. Death? No, not my mum! The doctors still do not know what is happening and what is causing her condition, they are literally just keeping her alive. She is completely paralysed and cannot talk, and barely spends a few minutes awake. I am emotionally collapsing after each word my brother lets out. What is happening to my mum? Apart from the usual cold and flu, she had not ever had any serious illnesses. I am terrified, lost for words. Tears drop in between the keyboard buttons, barely capable of remaining on the phone. I need to call my sister and we need to discuss travel, at least one of us needs to go, to support our mum. She has always been there for us, now it is our turn. I hang up the call with my brother, but before I can make another call, I have to let my cry flow free. My mother is hurting, possibly dying! How much is there for a single person to bear? How can I possibly not fall apart right now? A sense of fear, agony and panic are riding on an emotional rollercoaster inside me, that seems to have unrealistic twists and loops. I suddenly feel sick. I attempt to gather myself, slowly cover my face in my hands and inhale deep and exhale slowly – an action that seems to be helping and lightens the weight of the panic for now. Sis beats me to it and calls me first. Sounding panicky and tearful, just like I am, confirming that she already knows about Mum. We decide to meet after work and group call our brother, as he will hopefully have an update from the test results by then, and we will aim to orchestrate a support bubble plan. The email from Cafcass has left my mind, the excitement from the anticipation, has been replaced by this unprecedented terrible news. I still cannot wait to receive the report, but my pain has diverted towards the pain my mother is feeling right now, lying in the hospital bed, powerless, motionless, speechless, and terrified for life. What broke this woman that is hard as a rock? I must go and see her, she needs my energy, she needs me. I have had an excessive amount of energy lately, that hasn't gone away with the amount of exercise I do. The purpose is becoming clear now, it is for my mother, and I need to transfer my energy onto her. She always said that I am an empath, like her, but even more impactful. There is this magnetic force that's pulling me towards her. I must go before it is too late!

Finally, my work has come to an end! I have already made some arrangements for the next couple of days and appointed my assistant manager to take charge of the nursery duties in my absence. I manage to book a flight for tomorrow early morning, and I will arrive just in time for the visitation hours permitted in the intensive care unit. Sis has offered to pick me up from work, as the rain has not stopped tipping it down the whole entire day, and riding my bike home would be brutal. I run out my office, and greet my sis with a very tight hug, that expresses my deep worries. What if our mother has given up after all she has survived in her life? We need to first understand her condition and then we can help her. It is too early to have this discussion as we do not yet know what the hospital results will show, hence why our bro hasn't called yet, the results will probably not be in before tomorrow anyway. Oh god, just please let her live, let her live the night! My mother cannot leave us just like this, from one day to another! Sis is keeping her cool, however stressful the situation may be, she analyses things more inside her head, she's more of an introvert, whereas I analyse every detail out loud. Sharing thoughts is the key to processing information, enabling the brain to make sense of things that life throws our way. Often, the brain is like a maze. There are many pathways the brain chooses to venture down and each direction teaches a lesson to either take another solution or continue with the chosen direction, to get to the epicentre of the brain, where the solution is hidden. Currently the maze has no clear directions, it is absolutely chaotic there. We know nothing! When the sushi that I ordered arrives, my sis kisses me on my cheeks and wishes me a safe trip and orders me an early night. She would have loved to stay, but everything has just happened too suddenly, and she needs to be home for Charlie, as David's night shift soon begins. Having hardly any appetite, the taste of rice, mildly sweet and sour raw fish and veggie wrapped rolls covered in soya sauce served with pickled ginger, is going down well. I am going to pack and have an early night, as I am mentally exhausted and will need to set off in the early hours of tomorrow morning. After receiving a text message from my bro, that there is no change, and mum seems stable, although still weak and sleeping all the time, is a tiny bit more reassuring. Also, that the doctor is awaiting on some extra test results but will have everything ready tomorrow. Sleep is the solution for the night, so I can unconsciously skip time and be on my way to my mum tomorrow.

My brother welcomes me at the airport, after a flight filled with several bouts of turbulence, but thankfully it was only a three hour flight. I kept sipping coffee and read two newspapers. I have missed my little brother, and I hardly get to see him, as he does not like to fly so that limits his possibilities. Thanks to social media, I have some kind of an idea what his life is like, otherwise he'd be a lost man in the mist. His dapper look, complimenting the perfectly styled gelled hair style with matching jewellery is the look that defines my brother. We do look alike, a lot more than I do with my sis, but I must admit, all three of us are a mixed blend of Mum and Dad. Bro looks shattered, he seems emotionally taken by our mum's illness. The results will be reported to us directly from the doctor at the visit, so we are heading straight to the hospital. A ride in the car is more luxurious in comparison to the flight, so I relax gently into the seat, close my eyes again, to speed through time unconsciously.

When I open my eyes, I realise that I have slept throughout the journey from the airport, even if it wasn't a long drive. I apologise to my bro and offer a catch up after we have visited Mum. I feel so claustrophobic right now that I cannot bear the enclosed space of this aged hospital elevator that is creaking on the way down, so I take the flight of stairs to the sixth floor and enter a lobby with a security intercom entry system. My bro walks into the elevator, and we agree to meet on the sixth floor. Lazy man, despite his fitness regime, opts for an ill functioning elevator. Ha! I pass each level faster than the lift. I press the bell, there is a slight wait, finally my bro arrives with an embarrassed smile on his face. I pat his shoulder and we lightly laugh. After few minutes a nurse comes to the door and lets us in, based on our name and the reason for our visit today. Without any delay, the doctor is conveniently in the waiting area, ready to talk to us. He was made aware of my travel and has made sure to attend to me. We all take a seat, and he begins telling us that all results came back fine, all organs are functioning normally. The condition our mum is experiencing is referred to as *tetany* and explains that it is caused by calcium deficiency in the body that in mum's case caused an involuntary contraction of muscles and affected her central nervous system, leaving her almost paralysed. He continues, that the recovery depends entirely on her, how she is able to push herself to re-train her muscles, get her lips moving to talk, and her jaws to move to eat. He puts it easily – our mother has to introduce basic life skills to her own body and it can take something between one to three years, which includes therapy, physio and medication. A nervous breakdown, mother and her life events crossed paths and crashed. The doctor instructs us to visit her only one by one, as they in most cases do not even permit anyone entering the critical cases unit. Obviously, making an exception for my travel all the way from United Kingdom, has allowed an exception for the period of my stay. I take the first visit and follow the doctor through the wide doors that open to his ID card only. I look around and spot Mum lying in the bed, motionless with her eyes closed. Tears gather in my eyes as an immediate reaction to seeing her in this state – she had lost at least twenty kilos and looks terrifyingly small. I lift my mother's skinny hand, give it a gentle squeeze and whisper into her ears; *I am here, take all the energy you need, Tia's love is here with me too. We all love you so much. Sleep, thrive and allow my energy to pump through your veins.* Mum opens her eyes, just a little bit, she can probably just about see me, but I am positive that she has heard everything I said. She attempts to talk, but the weak muscles don't allow the signal from the brain to put her lips into action. I can't bare seeing her this way, so heart breaking! I can see the hope in her half-awake eyes, twinkling like the night stars. I can see deep inside our mother, who beneath the weakened body, is still strong as a rock and she will not surrender to an illness. She gently squeezes my hands in response. I stroke her pale cheeks, tell her that we are all here for her, and to take her time to recover. We look at each other for a long while, holding hands as words are not required for us to exchange thoughts. My mother can sense my worries, so attempts to smile, even if the muscles do not operate in their usual way, the smile is visible to me. I hand her the cup of water and put the straw in her mouth to encourage her to take some sips, as she has been refusing to drink. I get in few drops by wetting her lips, as there is always another way. Mum lifts her hand heavily, to indicate her sleepiness, and the second her arm drops, she slips into a sleep. I kiss her forehand, leaving a wet mark from my tears that fully covered my face, so I wipe the wetness with my sleeve and whisper bye. I am asked to leave shortly after, as the time allowed to see her is very limited, due to the fact that it is not even permitted. I thank the doctor and share my appreciation for his help and ask him to call me as soon as anything changes. I walk back out into the waiting room, absolutely petrified! I feel as if I was chased by a wild dog, my chest feels a weight that is hard to carry, triggering the floodgates to open wide. Tears uncontrollably run down my face again! The shock of seeing my mother in such a state has sparked the feelings that I have tried to keep under control, and everything is suddenly turning bleak. I bury my face in my hands and let the sob fest run wild and in this moment I feel as if everything I am going through has won over me. I can sense the sink hole as I am falling straight through it, into its depth. Life can be so cruel, so unfair. Bro welcomes me into his warm hug, and we walk out through the lobby and the security door. He will need to see my mother next time but has seen her before and can visit her more often after my flight back to London. I catch the despair in the nurse's eyes as she holds the door open to us, and it unsettles me. The afternoon and the night ahead can still become critical. Terrifying! I fear the worst!

# Chapter 15

## The Entitlement

'Life can be a colourful rainbow if you choose to see it.'

Probably the hardest visiting trip I have ever had to conquer. Witnessing my mum close to death has threatened my resistance – something that has been supported by temporary, but solid walls to protect me from completely losing my sanity. Mum's illness, the suddenness of it has traumatised me. I have spent the rest of the afternoon researching and contacting medical professionals in the UK, who could have any knowledge into understanding this horrid tetany condition. The reasons of this condition are individual and vary in every person, and treatment is hard to determine. What my research and what other professionals confirmed, is that balancing the minerals missing from the body with physiotherapy is the way forward, followed by talk therapy as having gone through such a severe tetany attack, will have an effect on the person's mental well-being greatly. Besides, Mum will need to learn to use her muscles to form eating habits, speech and laughter movements. The latter is because the muscle construction collapsed, and that caused a massive impact on the bone structure, therefore, the body may find it extremely hard to recover to a good state of functioning once again. The sight of the effects in real life, are close to unbearable, and seeing my mother, her small frame fallen into the bed, makes me break into tears every time picturing that scene. What will affect my mum the most is that she will not be able to enjoy her favourite things in her life – eating, talking, laughing and playing with her grandchildren! She needs to understand that medication and supplements will kick in along with the exercise and therapy and things will get better, but time and effort are utmost important. Apparently, the psychological state of mind determines the length of the recovery. When I speak to my rock, all I see is a fragile human being, all I get is an attempt to smile, slurred speech and two large chestnut brown eyes widely staring at me saying *please get me out this misery, I cannot lay here so powerless any longer.* Only, a hand squeeze of a response that transforms my energies into her bloodstream, can truly carry the depth of my support, more than words can compose. I know, it will be okay, Mum! You can get through this, and you will, I promise!

I only have another day left before I need to head back to London, so I decide to call the hospital and request a visit before the night falls. Unfortunately, that is not permitted, but I am advised to head to the hospital first thing in the morning, around six. Flicking through TV channels makes my eyes tired, so I set an alarm for 5:00 a.m. and try to sleep. The residential street outside is quiet, only the sound of few barking dogs echo in the empty space surrounding my mum's flat. It is a small space, filled with trinkets that she adores with family picture frames placed on the shelves in the living room. I have chosen to sleep here because I feel comfort in this space, her room is small, and it would feel as the walls would want to swallow me.

Drinking a cup of fresh coffee after the early sound of the alarm, feels refreshing. This morning, it is only me who is going to visit my mum at the hospital. I take the bus, and stop off to get a bunch of pink roses to take to Mum. It will make her feel looked after and cared for. When I take the flight of stairs to the sixth floor, the nurse opens the door straight after the loud buzz. She welcomes me with a brighter smile on her face than last time and invites me to the lobby. What is happening? A smile is not a negative form of news. The nurse says nothing but disappears behind the doors that lead to the hall full rooms, with my mum sleeping in one of them. I step around impatiently, looking at the door, wishing for it to open. Finally, the nurse is back, but who is she holding hand in hand? It's Mum! Oh my goodness, she is walking. What? This is incredible. I give her fragile body a huge hug. We sit down and I listen to her speak weakly, but this time I can understand what she is saying. An incredible change of circumstances since last night. The nurse is sitting down next to us, telling me that Mum woke up a few times during the night asking for water and food. I am so pleased for her. If she has another day full of recovery, due to the medicine and minerals boosting her body, she could go home in couple of days. I have to extend my stay, as the state of her health petrified me, way too much, but she is getting better and she needs me, at least to see her home and see her how she does outside the hospital! Two more weekdays, and it will the weekend, so I return to work on Monday next week. The nursery can operate well with my assistant manager, and I will be on the phone for any support. I can also come back at lunch time, and bro will join too. Mum looks weak still, but much better than last night, and she has to start moving around, to start physical recovery.

Three vases filled with beautiful bunches of roses and tulips fill the naturally lit room, where my mum will be spending most of her time while she fully recovers, with cinnamon and cherry blossom candles waltzing aromas all around. A card that I personalised for my Mum's birthday, with family pictures, rests on the table next to the candle, saying *we love you all so much!* My mum sits there, seeming at peace reading a magazine and solving some crosswords at the same time, her favourite activity to pass the time. I am watching her from the kitchen, in gratitude for her life of support she has selflessly provided us. The hospital released her two days after my early morning visit when I saw my mum standing on her own feet, with strict instructions for medicine administration and physical activity. As I am about to put a batch of cream of mushroom soup into the blender – my mum's favourite – my phone delivers an email. I place the ladle back into the hot pot, lick my fingers off the leftover cream, and curiously reach for my phone, which is laying not far from the kitchen worktop, just on the side table in my mum's small kitchen. As I stretch my arm, I feel my exhausted body stretch along, and I suddenly realise that I am mentally exhausted just as much. Why am I feeling exhausted? I have allowed myself to become weak. I have to remind myself to stay focused on what I am fighting for, as my protective wall is down. I have walked with my mother, bathed her and cooked her mushy baby food. It is easy to take the wrong turn at the crossroads, but it is never too late to find the way back and continue in the correct direction. I will not lose my way, I have come so far, suffered so much agony, and yet my journey is still incomplete. Life moves on, and is severely unpredictable, and my mother needs my strength and energy, and I will give her every bit of it. The unexplainable energy that I managed to collect recently, will refuel me again. It just shows how much a human being can endure – there is simply no limit if there is will!

I unlock my phone and open the delivered email. I gasp, shriek from excitement and scream out loud *the report, it is here!* I run around excitedly! I suddenly feel so intoxicated, without any traces of exhaustion, my energy levels are reaching top levels. I have been waiting for this report for days, but my mum's illness distracted me, pushing my impatience to the background of my mind. Its arrival is such a glorious surprise. Strangely, something pops into my eyesight – as I am about to run and tell Mum about the report and read every single detail in peace – an onion skin peel that has been left on top of the pile of peeled vegetables, in the shape of a heart. The feelings surrounding the heart shape is not an illusion, it feels so surreal, and I embrace every part of it. I accept it as a sign to confirm that every bad thing will come to an end. Approaching my mum, now with a heart shaped onion peel in my hand, I can see her face all lit up and trying to smile to the fullest she has so far attempted to even try. My mum is smiling, however big it shows, the radiation of her inner smile is bigger than can ever be shown. She takes the onion peel and spits on it gently three times – something she does for good luck and protection from harm – not a religious ritual, more of a superstitious belief of its effect, it's just her thing! I shall accept the small ritual and open the email to access the report. I cannot wait! Oh blimey, it starts with my name in the box where it states *parent.* A parent! Feeling elated, I begin reading the report. I cannot believe the fact that I am being referred to as a parent, not only as an applicant, not only as a subject of a hearing. I am being seen as a parent, my visibility is slowly moving from the shadows, illuminating the person from the hiding, ready to shine once and for all. I have lived too long in the darkness of this title that I deserve the entitlement. The emotional torture I suffered, trying to gain my legal stand in the family union, will slowly disappear when replaced with the innocent presence of my baby. Often, I asked myself if the person I had decided to conceive Tia with, turned into a stranger who I no longer recognised. The threats, the twists, the conditions, the anger, all in one, that had almost wrecked my soul. People do change, in a relationship or not, but they do. It is inevitable, we are in constant change, a motion affected by various outside factors. Factors such as stress from a job loss, career change, financial imbalance, new hobbies or interests, the list is not exhaustive. These factors, necessarily don't mean negative effects on the relationship, but require a force, for the relationship to survive, and that force is the magic of compromise. The mutual understanding, that respect towards each other, that balances to support each partner's needs, is crucial, for a relationship to survive. How blind can we humans be, to bluntly ignore the obvious? Consciously choosing not to see, because it is better not to know, just to avoid the truth. If we could always know and see everything, that would mean perfection, right? Perfect is not ideal, nor is it real! Love is blind, it is a myth. It's our brains, that thinks it is love, and allows ourselves to temporarily let through what makes us feel great about ourselves and let everything else that can rock our ego and morals just float away. Letting us be at risk of complete blindness, subconsciously unaware of avoiding change and afraid of strife. When the eyes capture its first sight of a light, it wakes the blinded brain from the unconsciousness, then it allows one to begin the change for oneself. Once the transformation is fully achieved, the person may gain back that clear sight, make better choices, take back the lost respect and mostly, see things with a bright sight and face those fears with courage. This person, will not turn around again, will not be blinded anymore, this person will look straight ahead and thrive from healthy decisions made. This person becomes stronger and wiser as a central purpose of human life, respecting themselves to the fullest and owning that respect so that no one could ever take this away from them. Avoiding the ego to be in charge of decisions. This person today is me!

My mum pulls my hand to sit down right next to her, to tell her everything the officer has stated, every detail. Mum seems as if she had an energy boost treatment, her face muscles are making her smile. As if it were my moment of happiness that instantly energised her physique. The doctors did mention that her inner state of health will determine her recovery too.

As I read the report, it discusses the officer's assessment of Tia in the school setting and what catches my eyes, and immediately tightens my chest is this snippet of the report: *Tia is feeling sad, and talking about her Mummy, and that she misses her. Although she has settled into school well, and academically we have no concerns, there are times when she sits alone looking sad. Friends and activities seem to cheer her up and help her with the transition she has been going through.* My lips tremble, tears rapidly cause a waterfall in my eyes. All this time, my little baby is hurting inside, and it is now taking an emotional toll on her. I cannot bear to imagine her little precious face, sad, sitting in the corner, away from enjoyment and happiness where she should be at her age. The lioness just wants to rip out from inside of me and get her baby cub out of affliction! I cannot keep her inside for much longer, taming her has been a great mission. Tia is left feeling alone in a world where she may feel as if she doesn't belong. No one is telling her the one thing her heart desires to know, and that's *where I have gone and if I am ever coming back?* The school doesn't give her answers, and at home she gets no answers. The only place where she has answers is me. The report states that she asked about me and if she could see me, but the officer age appropriately explained to Tia that however wonderful that would be, it was not something she could do. Cafcass have a duty to protect children from further harm, and they should not ever build false hope and make promises, just in case things may not go in the child's favour, the pain from disappointment could cause greater damage. However, she professionally, but age appropriately, explored the opportunity to turn her answers the other way around and asked Tia, 'Would you like to see Mummy Vivien again?'

'Yes, I want to, I miss her. Mummy Vivien is nice and funny, I love her,' Tia answered from her little heart, to the point, and that is what the judge will be very interested in hearing. I think to myself, what a clever girl, she may have trusted the officer in hope to bring me back to her. So very proud of her, just honest, true to what she feels, that is my baby! Tia needs me back, the life she may have been adapted to, is not the life that has truly fulfilled her, as a big chunk is missing from it and it is beginning to affect her negatively.

Professionals working during custody battles have the responsibility to protect children's welfare and importantly, once able to speak, listen to their voice – what they want is important, but what they need is even more so. Tia wants to see me, and she needs me too! That is evident in my statement, and now in this report. On the other hand, I am so extremely relieved that there is no effect on her academic development, as that would mean, that the separation touched her fundamental core. Thankfully, she has remained on the surface and her resilience has kept that protected. Children can regress in their development when faced with severe emotional or physical stresses, including loss, abuse or illness. Tia may just be right on the edge of suffering, but shortly, I will come and save her.

I jump up from joy and hug my mum, feeling gratified. Tia has practised everything she has learnt from her little but meaningful experiences, which has formed a protective shield that disabled anything affecting her beyond the surface where she may have felt abandoned, lonely and vulnerable. The protective shield of her resilience has also allowed her to focus on her life as it is given, knowing that whatever is happening, however strange and scary it may be, I am coming for her and will be in her life and things will be good again. Tia has self-designed a support bubble that surrounds her everywhere she goes and lets her see the world a little more colourful. I am ecstatic, my heart is feeling an immediate sense of peace! I feel more powerful than prior to the report, due to my mother's illness! The findings analysed by the Cafcass officer may appropriately weigh the scales towards my side. The judge may pay close attention to these details coming honestly and directly from the child's perspective, regardless of her young age. Their responsibility is immense, the evidence and support material they need to assess is complex and the decision they have to make is arduous. That is because everything is child-centred, and they will decide what is in the child's best interest.

My case is not ordinary, my parental status is unusual, but am I important to remain in Tia's life? Undoubtedly yes!

The report mentions no signs of abuse and that is liberating! Tia is physically safe, and that worry can wear off for now, but emotionally there are signs of abuse based on the report findings, as Tia may in a way be emotionally threatened to be freely talking about me or asking questions related to my return. But soon I expect that I will be able to make amends and continue being the protective shield for Tia and further her life skills to help her tackle challenges that life may bring her way. Parents feel the biggest desire to safeguard their children from any form of pain, the truth is, parents can protect their children, but only protecting them will not teach them how to protect themselves when they are not around. Children need to be taught how to handle situations in life as the older they get, the more conflicts they will face, may those be socially, academically or physically. The aim is to teach positive life skills as a response to the diverse emotions that can flood children daily. Their mental health is the key to their future happiness. Mental health conditions can occur if children develop feelings of anxiety from learning or academic expectations, peer or parent pressure, forms of bullying they may experience. Friendship conflicts can lead to developing focusing, social, and behavioural, self-esteem and cognitive issues. Stresses that children may face in life are often unavoidable and parents can be utterly unaware of their presence until they may observe concerning behavioural changes in children or receive a concerning letter from the school. Children sometimes struggle speaking about their worries, it does not come to them naturally, so parents have the greatest responsibility to encourage them to share the worries they face, not to carry the weight around with them in everything they do. Teaching them what personality traits might not be healthy to be around, those that make us not feel very good inside or behaviours that cross respect, fairness and kindness lines. Implementing these life skills from an early age is a vital aspect of parenting; however, it is essential to know that children must learn to adapt theories to real-life situations, and they will only learn if they encounter some of the obstacles that will enable them to practice their knowledge and even support others. My dream for Tia, is to learn to love herself, accept her inner beauty, express her passion and interests, have quality friendships that match her liking and stand out from the crowd for her individuality rather than try to fit in and follow others. Have I set myself a tough goal to reach? Blimey! Frankly, yes, but I would rather watch her try and fail, then never try at all. Love and experience heartbreak, rather than never love at all. Take risks, rather than staying safe and never living life to the full. Compete by gaining success or failure. Tia, so young, is already experiencing the sense of loss, however temporary it may be, but what she is learning is how to cope with the feelings. Although not yet aware, her experience is making an imprint in her memory lane as the first building block in her block tower of life. May the tower be low, tall or crooked, the early foundations are the one that form the roots of a strong standing tower that can withstand life's storms. An ocean of feelings is stirring my heart as I reach the end of the Cafcass report stating the advice for the judge. The officer is convinced that Tia needs my presence in her life and advises the judge to proceed with a shared care order as soon as possible to prevent more risks to her wellbeing. I couldn't agree more, the triumphant ending to her findings. What a talented professional, she has written up all the evidence that supports the mothering relationship I have with Tia. I will be forever grateful for her allocation to my case. She has done a tremendous job with her analysis and concluded a phenomenal conclusion on her findings. If I could, I would joyfully hug her right now. This report means everything to me! She has seen me, I am becoming visible, given a title, and foremost my relationship with Tia has been rectified. Will the judge take on the Cafcass findings and agree with her conclusion? Why wouldn't they? Cafcass is there for that exact reason as judges hardly meet children or choose to directly speak with them at such a young age. It can be both upsetting and unsettling for young children, therefore as far as my research has shown, they in most cases trust and take on the advice from the Cafcass officers. Apparently, the rare cases when judges turn down the advice and follow their own judgments, is when their own findings and what children report directly to them during a hearing – if old enough to attend a hearing – differs from the Cafcass findings. Judges conducting custodial court hearings have to have excellent logical reasoning, analytical and decision-making skills to take on complex cases and make a fair legal decision in line with statutory law. Optimistically, after reading the report, I believe that the judge who will take on my case in the court, will be just as talented in their field of justice.

I have tried to reach Gloria, but her phone is switched off, she might be in court. I cannot wait to share my excitement with her. In my voicemail I encouraged her to read the Cafcass report first and then call me when she can speak. I turn my attention to my mum, who has patiently been listening to my translations of the report. She shed tears of joy and hopefulness with me. She suddenly takes my hand and squeezes it, the same way she felt my tight support when she could barely even sit up.

'Vivien, this report has given you the wings to fly and take that poor thing from the prison she has been captured in. She needs your love and affection, the life she ought to be used to right now, is not the life she knows. Bring her back to us all! I can't wait to hold her tight!'

My mum took a while to enable the words to come through, with many breaks and hesitations whether to try again or stop talking, but I could see the strength in wanting to speak and share her mind. I love hearing her words of wisdom, but it is surely difficult to see her struggling with something that is second nature to her – speaking her mind. Leaving her in a couple of days, seems just too early, but the support is being passed on to my brother, who has just arrived with some delicious Mexican takeaway – beef tacos, beans and salsa salad, something I actually fancy. His gesture is complemented with and ice cold Mexican beer, so I cannot wait to tuck in. Mum is still on a simple blended diet, but she suggests trying some different textures, as there is no harm – got to love the enthusiasm. A kind and an affectionate act from a man, who likes to seem like a strong shell to crack, but it is soft on the inside. My brother is a bit of an urban romantic soul, he does have his caring nature in place, given to the fact that he had grown up with two older sisters who cared for him, and had skills role modelled to him. Sis and I, we always tried our best to teach him to respect women, treat them well, be honest with them and not to worry about showing his sensitive side as he can be quite ego-driven but underneath that lies a compassionate man. He is indeed trustworthy and follows instructions well, so if he knows what our mum needs and wants, he will absolutely satisfy every aspect of the requirements. He might not be too big on hugs but he shows affection in his own special way, still making an impact. However, he finds his niece and nephew irresistible and treats them differently from how he would treat adults. He just goes utterly crazy, throwing them up in the air, asking for cuddles and chasing them around. He finds them hilarious and adores their unique individual traits. Seeing them happy and hearing their giggles pleases him. They both absolutely adore him! I wish for our family to be united, in one place, at one time, always, not a long flight apart. Dreams are allowed and never to be underestimated as they can become as realistic as we wish them to be! Sharing a nice evening with my brother, or any time in fact, is therefore special. Catching up with life, work and recent events mostly, are the topic. He feels angry over what Shona has done, as he is protective, just like Sis, and he had no idea of abuse occurring in my relationship. He is somewhat disappointed, not in me or in my mistakes, but in not being open to him about it. Confirming his blessing on my lifestyle choice, on my sexual preference, back when I came out of the closet, his only one condition was for me to be happy. Relationship discussions are not really his strength, but he understands that they can fall apart, their occurrence is not a secret. What he cannot comprehend is that Tia has been ripped from me, and directs his anger towards the law that allowed it to happen for so long despite my non-biological status. I pass him the report to read through but tell him about the best outcomes.

'Finally! Tia is a clever girl, she handled the interview amazingly, so did you, Viv. Now let's get the judge's ruling over and let Tia out of her sadness, to be free again, back where she belongs – with you, with us.'

My brother spoke seriously with a slightly quivering voice, very unlike him. Showing his emotions has been his personal barrier like a shell, but I could see his compassion and pain towards Tia and my pain from being apart. This is difficult for anyone to bear, so my family, closely connected to us both, are taking this to heart.

The past couple of days, Mum has improved so much, I am so proud of her strength. Healthy milkshakes, blended meals and short walks through the park have benefitted her mentally and physically. I prepared meals and put them in the freezer, as Mum can now warm up meals all by herself. Bro is going to get a few hours' sleep before he takes me to the airport in the morning, and I will spend my last few hours making sure Mum has everything prepared and instructions for her medication in the right place for her and Bro to see. I set a repeating daily alarm for my mother as a reminder to take the medication, as I think at the start in respect to her exhaustion, it can be quite overwhelming.

The faint light of dawn has begun to shine into the living room as I sip my morning coffee, all set to go, as my visit has come to an end. I wish to stay longer, but I will come back soon, with Tia. I hug my mother tight and pass on my energy to her for the last time, and whisper to her something more positive than on the day of my arrival. Something positive to drive her towards that courage to fight to get herself back on track: *'When you see me next time, Tia will be by my side waiting to give you the biggest hug ever."* That thought shall linger for as long as it needs to. My words have no expiration date. I find it difficult to part, but it is a must otherwise I will miss my flight and I have stayed for as long as I possibly could, my work requires me to come back now. London bound, here I come.

The arrival to London is very bumpy, as the weather is just miserable – strong winds mixed with heavy rain. The air is cold, in fact freezing for my liking. Trees look rather shabby now, with hardly any leaves left on them. Winter is almost upon us. The thought that the last time spent with Tia was early spring and now winter is approaching makes me feel fretful. It has been too long, months in fact. Tia must have changed in her appearance so much! Children change in a matter of weeks, months will surely be visible. I can barely endure the wait! My phone suddenly rings, and as I pull the phone from my bag, I see Gloria's name displayed on the screen. Well, that is something that I have waited for, as analysis of the report, from her lawyer point of view, is valuable. I pick up the phone and Gloria begins to talk straight away, firstly asking about my trip and my mum's health, but after a short brief update on both sides, she continues in a more of a high-pitch voice.

'Vivien, I read the report and it is fantastic. You have clearly made a great impression on the Cafcass officer. I must say, her advice for the hearing is exactly what we are after – the shared custody! Tell me, how was the interview? How do you feel about the report, tell me?'

Gloria is clearly very excited and honestly that is making me feel a lot more positive than I even had before. Knowing her excitement adds confidence to my case!

'Ah, it was a little nerve wracking at first, when I just stepped into the building, but once the officer assigned to my case – Nicole – collected me in the lobby, things changed. I was not nervous anymore and the interview was more of a pleasant chat. I literally answered some questions in advance, before she managed to ask as I answered each question with more than she expected. The reason for that is, because she asked about Tia's life, and I could tell her the number of times I woke up to help feed her when she was born to the latest moments of her not wanting to leave my side post separation. The officer recognised the sincerity in my answers and could see that I am not the person Shona described me to be, but how I described myself in the statement to the court – a mother to my daughter!'

I think to myself, as humans we cannot really tell a lie from the truth easily on the spot, unless we know the person whom we are dealing with or have sufficient evidence to prove the person is lying. It is a coin flip situation. If you hesitate and find yourself here, that is too bad, you probably may not feel like meeting that person again. However, if the person you face is a stranger who is claiming to be a mother but the actual biological mother is claiming otherwise, even to an experienced professional it could be super puzzling. Their position is extremely sensitive, and they are on a quest to ask questions and analyse the verbal and non-verbal cues to determine their perception of the circumstances. I had an urge after my Cafcass interview to find out about the scientific evidence on how one can judge whether the person sitting opposite them is telling the truth. Apparently, the stories they are telling are longer and detailed – in comparison to short stories that seem scattered and inconsistent, they are more fabricated. Next is the power of eye contact – liars tend to break eye contact and look around in crucial moments, whereas truth tellers will maintain it. Then it is the voice – a more steady voice may be the sign of the truth, if the voice pitch changes, it is linked to lying. Body language such as touching the nose – that is because when people lie their nose engorges, the same is for touching areas such as the chest and the throat. I was surprised, I mean some people are just good liars, as the little slips when talking more in depth during an interview, can give a liar away. When I read about these signs, I had nothing to worry about, as I am telling the truth and I am more than certain that I passed the truth test. My urge to search originated from the curiosity to find out about the way professionals need to form their questions, where they can judge whether the person is truthful or deceptive. There was nothing that made me come across as a liar, therefore the officer matched my story with my statement and ticked the match boxes.

'Excellent, I am thrilled for you, Vivien! We are moving in the right direction; your truth will get the results you want. Only two weeks to go and I strongly believe that the judge will only put a stamp on what the Cafcass officer suggests in her report. Vivien, you have come so far, it has been a difficult journey, but you have persevered. I understand, you have experienced a great weight of pain, disappointment and stress over these past months as you must miss your daughter very much!'

Gloria's joy and positive boost is bringing a range of colours to the grey skies on this blustery day. I feel jubilant!

# Chapter 16

## Pressure Is Rising

'The force within me is astounding.'

I place the guitar gently on my lap, I begin to strum some random chords to get the flow into my fingers. Teaching myself to play has been satisfying, somewhat it has served like an escapism from reality. When I strum the strings, the sound waves fill this void – the empty space between my own self and my busy mind. My guitar has a sense of creative attraction, it makes me want to pick it up into my arms and play along to my favourite songs – today's list has started with Birdy's song Wings. Songs that have made it to my playlist this evening are touching, powerful and encouraging. I play, I cry. Playing on the guitar does not stop my tears, it opens the dam that blocks my tears all day long. I hold back tears, as I cannot break down and lose my steadiness at work, as that is my protective wall. Crying doesn't make things go away, but it provides consolation and suppressing this need would cause a blockage of negative thoughts and tension that a dam could not hold. An amateur artist, with me and myself as the audience. I doubt that my guitar skills would deserve a grand round of applause, more of a wall banging from the next-door neighbour, but I feel satisfied, somewhat proud of what I have achieved. What

I experience is the melodies, their echo in the house as the strings vibrate my levels of stress away. A remedy for my disparity. Disparity that is soon to become the face on my armour, when I enter the war to fight for my visibility. One week, just one week! This pain will only be a memory and the bad days will be picked up like powdery dust in the wind. The final week of waiting, I am so exhilarated. I am going to save all of my energy for the big day, as beneath all that pain and uncertainty, the lioness is waiting to be released in search of her baby cub.

A sudden, gentle knock on the front door withdraws me from my stream of unconsciousness that has successfully detached me from the real world. I look at the clock, it is almost eight o o'clock, I move slowly towards the door, switch on the light and quietly ask who is at the door. A sense of safety fills my senses, and without an answer from a familiar person's voice, the door will remain closed.

'It's Emilia, let me in.'

'Blimey, Emilia, again! Have you picked up a new style of surprising your friend?'

I open the door and Emilia laughs directly into my face, clearly very pleased with her accomplished mission. Slightly relieved it is not my neighbour complaining about my loud and out of tune acoustic session. No one has ever dared to yet knock, maybe there is a slight joy instead of annoyance on the other side of the wall? She swings a beer bottle right in front of my face and tells me that she decided to get off the bus in my area, and surprise me for a drink. The idea is lovely, a gesture that comes easily from my lovely support bubble, and to talk to someone meaningful tonight will be just additional tension breaking that keeps rising more rapidly with each day as I draw nearer to the hearing day. I am nervous, confident, but the hearing day is just so ambiguous. Emilia needs nothing more than to have a bottle of beer with her friend, share a packet of our favourite crisps and chat on the sofa, about everything that comes to our mind. Emilia has obviously something very exciting to share, as she is way too unsettled on the sofa, pulling on her scarf left to right, talking fast and in a high pitched voice. After some rapid crisp munching and big sips of beer, she finally lets out that she has been promoted to a position she has always dreamed to achieve. I share the excitement with her. This woman deserves it, working so hard, to achieve something in life, to rise above herself, to survive in one of the most expensive cities with her fella and two children. We have become close friends, Emilia arrived at my friend zone without a prior reservation, just at the time when I needed her friendship the most. Friendship is not something that can be planned, it is something that develops with time, if all its elements are achieved with the need to be nourished and looked after to succeed. Like a planted seed, without all the elements such as sunshine, water or nutrients, the seed would only live a short life. Friendships, relationships in fact, including those between parents and children, require their own individual element – understanding, support, freedom, and love – in many different forms to meet everyone's individual needs, to grow, form a bond, to not only survive but to also thrive. That is what friendships mean to me. Emilia has a similar moral outlook on life, we have endless intellectual conversations where we delve deep into fascinating topics. The latter can only be broken by external sources – responsibilities.

'Vivien, how on Earth are you keeping sane? I love my

independence, but I would go mad not having my children to go home to everyday, kiss them good night and however annoying they are most of the time, god I would miss them.'

Emilia takes a sip from her beer bottle, sinks deeper into the sofa, and awaits my lengthy monologue with a rather compassionate but curious expression on her face.

Sanity? The ability to protect my health and the ability to respond to my circumstances in a rational manner, has extraordinarily challenged me in these past few months. Even just reciting *the past few months* out loud, shatters me inside! I often wake up, scared to open my eyes, as in trying to postpone the horrid reality and embrace that momentarily hope that what is going on in my life right now, is just a bad dream with Tia sound asleep. Braving to open my eyes, comes with the shock of the truthful reality. Keeping the sanity, to be able to get up and fight, I had to train myself to let go of what I cannot control and hold on to the things that I am in charge of – my truth, control over my own life, self-kindness and the ability to express myself freely without horrid consequences. I want all of it, but with my little darling by my side. I want to demonstrate to her, what happiness and self-love looks and feels like. I want Tia to know how much I fought for her and what a mothering strength truly is. I want her to learn what a healthy relationship is, how two people in love behave to one another, but most importantly that besides love, that can be very enchanting and emotionally uplifting, respecting one another is the core of a happy relationship journey. Unable to share my words of wisdom with my daughter, I have recently started to express myself through writing poetry. I allow *me* to flow free, to restore, to bloom, all to intensify my resilience to get to grips with this unprecedented time in my life. The mindset is incredible, it can form unimaginable miracles. I have resisted the term loss, I stayed away from reading forums and social media on this topic, as losing a child who will never return into mother's arms, is an indescribable despair, way beyond mine. That would break me into tiny shattered pieces, and I would never be able to default ever back to one piece. Broken, I would continue living a life, without meaning. Although, my despair, is the one from losing a child temporarily, and but the ability to have that hope for them to return one day. I have been doping myself with this aspiration daily, as my child is not gone, not from this life, and I have a chance to have her back. As I sit here today, I can assure myself that I have not only survived, without any health concerns, but I have become stronger and more courageous than ever before. It's almost like the lioness has thrived with me, multiplying into a herd of lionesses, in order to prepare for the approaching storm.

Emilia puts her empty bottle to the side and jumps up and gives me a big hug, one long-lasting one, that transcends verbal affection and as she pulls away, opens another beer bottle and throws in another question accompanied by a cheeky smile. Usually, the second bottle would last us a long time.

'So, who is this Lily? The curiosity is killing me Vivien.'

I suddenly feel that I am blushing, the name certainly has the stomach butterfly effect on me. Lily is this fascinating woman that has recently entered my life, been chatting to me for the past few months about herself, her travels, studies, shown a huge interest in my life, and offered a listening ear, understanding and advice. Our chats can last hours and hours, varying in lengths, but not ever brief or reaching a dead end.

We always end our chat with an opening to a next chat opportunity with a simple pause and later resume genuine attitude, and that is two sided. Sadly, she does refer to 'we' sometimes which indicates to me that she has someone in her life, I am pretty sure there is another woman taking her time so whatever sensations I can feel, outside of my painful turmoil, needs to stay in place. I can't quite tell, but what my intuition says, it is not a friend type, and she is here to stay, but what will happen exactly is unknown. For now, Lily provides me with a sense of comfort, support and personal light-hearted tranquillity. May that be a friendship fermenting, I appreciate what every stage offers.

'I do enjoy talking to her a lot and she makes me feel incredibly grounded, but at the same time, gets me that floating on a cloud feeling too. She is not single, so I'll stop you right there before you delve deeper! I am embracing her presence, in whatever way it ought to be. It is easy, cute and energising. I am in way too much pain and hurt to be able to focus on anything more, even if there is more.'

Emilia seems unconvinced and she only replies with a smirk as she sips from the beer bottle, but respects my explanation, as that is what our friendship is like – based on respect and complete understanding! However, that twinkle in her eyes tells it all. Love is in the air, kind of twinkle. What for now needs to be said, is an exchange of unspoken words, as we chin-chin and take a sip of beer from the cold bottle. Emilia changes the topic and attempts to explain the next tattoo idea she has recently had stewing in her mind. The images of her idea, shout discomfort and soreness to me. I shall not discourage this bubble of excitement and listen intuitively. Emilia, yet again, succeeded, I am distracted. Late or not, the sky is the limit. People that surround me, go out of their way, for me, to help me, and I take every crumb of their effort.

The week is whizzing by, the anticipation is growing rapidly, as most of my focus and thinking is on the court hearing. Feeling scared is slowly adding to the pile of emotions. The rollercoaster ride is moving on the lift hill and slowly approaching the highest point, to exploit my potential energy of gain or loss. I cannot help, but see Tia's excited face on the ride down from the top, feel her energy filling up the world around, screaming from the top of our lungs, as loud as we can possibly scream. Positive drive, is the route I take in life, no matter the circumstances. I believe that *what doesn't kill you makes you stronger*. Life does test our limits, it challenges our minds, builds obstacles and each and every individual gets a choice, and those choices we make, portrays us and our life. Acknowledging the problem is an important part of the process, as accepting the problem would mean nothing more than a new much larger problem. Accepting, is not an option, changing the mindset, to find a way out, is the way towards solving the problem. Often, the outcome is not in our control, but the positive attitude will lead the way, no matter how long it may take, how many failures we may face, it will find a way. The positive mindset will enable a clear vision, discover the untouchable, and see beyond the materialistic world that occupies our existence. The heart symbols that have showed up in my life, have truly made me feel so magical. No matter what type of belief I try to attach to the symbol, I only focus on the sensation I experience and embrace it every time. Their appearance has been a lot more frequent in the recent weeks, more often in a day, everywhere I have turned – heart shaped tree bark, stones, leaves, stains on pavements, food remains on the plate, clouds, shadows and so on, all shaped like a heart. Whatever we choose to focus on, are the instructions the brain picks up, and we follow them. I have felt as If I had some kind of signposting and confirmation of my acts and thoughts. Recently speaking to my mum about the heart symbol, her opinion is that it is my guardian angel that is watching over me. The reasons for more frequent appearances is because my hearing is close by, and the guardian angel is sending their affirmation through the heart symbols. To consciously attempt to believe in the meaning of the heart symbol, may seem somewhat odd, but provides me with good vibes. What have I got to lose anyway? Nothing.

I take a short break from the screen work, admin can be quite draining, very different from the joyful interaction with children. Although, it does count as a distraction, so I categorise it as a necessity and beneficial for both, my business and myself. I rub my eyes that are sore and tired from the prolonged exposure to the computer screen and lean back in the office chair and relax, watching the bubbles in the water dispenser bottle offers a rather relaxing experience. Eyelids slowly closing. Falling asleep is not optional, as I shortly have a meeting with a stakeholder. Not the time to nap. I slide out of the office chair, rub my face vigorously and drink the cooled water, in one go. Ah so refreshing. I go through my bag to look for my diary and find a postcard to fill in to send to Tia. When I search through the envelope, I realise that there are only two cards left. Wow! I feel elation from the possibility of gaining my legal visibility, in just few days. I grab my pen, and look out through the office window, to gather an inspirational note. The town is beginning to look like Christmas, lights have been lit and local shop windows have adapted a wintery decor design. I do love Christmas, and this year, as every year, I will decorate my tree with Tia. Knowing how much she loves Christmas, I write a message on the card: *Don't you love the light everywhere darling, how beautiful. I hope you are looking forward to your Christmas play at school. Hmm I wonder what it will be and the costume you will wear? I am at work looking at the sky through the window and wishing for snow! We do wish every year for some amount of snow, don't we darling? If you wake up to snow on any of the days, go outside and have a bucket full of fun. I will do the same and throw a snowball right back at you. Love you always!*

I gently kiss the postcard and I imagine my kisses sprinkle all over Tia like stardust. It has been my little weird ritual, as whatever helps the heart, I will follow. I seem to be surrounded by magical sensations lately, they feel wonderful and spread excitement through my body. I indulge myself while it lasts, it nourishes my aching heart. I recently read an interesting fact, planetary scientists confirmed that supernova stars contribute to creating elements of the periodic table, and very much including those that form the human body. I wonder, whether that light, live touch and sensations, is somewhat transferable from one person to another on a completely different level, beyond our understanding. There is so much to know, yet we just walk on this planet, survive and thrive, but each particle that makes us move, think, act, and is the universe within us. I imagine these elements, within me, each in a different colour. Fascinating! So, I choose to imagine the stardust sprinkling over Tia forming some kind of a colourful me, sending direct kisses to her cheeks. To some it might seem insane, but to me, in my desperate mind, it is very much making sense. I indulge myself while it lasts, it nourishes my aching heart, so in a way

I have hung on to that scientific explanation.

As I am about to drop the card through the letterbox slot, I notice a spider weaving a small web in the corner of the slot, and from the angle of my position I notice spider egg casings. At this point, the warmth I feel is different from the fear I feel when coming face-to-face with a spider. I only see a caring mother, who has spent time to wrap her eggs in many layers of silk to design a comfortable sack, to protect her babies from harmful species until the eggs have hatched. Nature is extraordinary! Parenting comes with responsibility to protect, love and care, no matter what. That's all I have ever done, and I miss this responsibility. Connecting with *me* has taught me resilience, patience and perseverance over the past few months that will always fulfil my existence. These past few months have not changed the person I was before, but manifested other layers of my personality that I had no idea were part of me. Realising that trust is deceivable, touched my core and it may take a while to recover from. When it comes to relationships, I think achieving that power of trust is important for its survival. When my trust was broken, I suffered a shock from no longer knowing the person I was with anymore and that realisation was portrayed to me in the worst possible way. Disrespect and abuse. The awareness that I have reached, due to my awakening in my relationship and beyond the separation, will pose as a healthy relationship guidance. The constant attempts from a person offering to change, are fake. As a genuine person is not defensive, nor endlessly talks about how much they didn't mean what they did or said following a hurtful emotional or physical action and especially if they would blame the victim for the reason of their actions. The patterns of the same behaviour and the useless promises, are a red flag in a relationship, may that be same sex or heterosexual, it applies to every relationship regardless. It is no longer a safe concept that women are more respectful and compassionate in a female relationship. I shall not view general female relationships under this concept, but accept the awareness, that anyone could present with mental health challenges, capable of any act against another. In fact, what has recently flagged up in my volunteering family support profession, is that there is a wide range of support delivered towards helping children and young people cope with distresses experienced or witnessed in their family homes. Support sessions which guide them with coping strategies, activities to turn their negative experiences into something positive and provide them with a listening ear, it is a prevention towards discontinuing these cycles of behaviours, and also making them aware of the impact specific behaviours can have on others. Stressing the importance of teaching the future generation, where to turn for support and the importance in talking and sharing about their mental struggles, is where it all begins. In order to recognise the wrong from right and attempt to build a healthy start that could feed into a happier future. In today's world, many adults that carry out various forms of abuse on their spouses and children but may have experienced the same distress in their childhood. Non-recipients of assistance may been more likely to conceal their emotions and have them surface later in life as a result of some kind of direct stimuli, reminding them of their childhood experiences. But, there is no excuse for their behaviour, only an explanation. Thinking about Shona's childhood, it makes more sense now. What needs to be taught is no longer a singular focus, but who should be taught is rather an important factor to bring to light. Bringing up children, needs to take another turn and that is boys and girls taught the same towards same or opposite sex. Meaning, to treat partners or friends respectfully, kindly and avoiding the enforcement of gender roles. Supportive of each other in pursuing a career passion and avoiding control over what an individual wishes to do for their own self-growth. When in a relationship, communication and compromise are essential factors. Children, from a young age need to be taught these skills, so to better navigate their life in adulthood. No one is perfect, and that shall not be expected from anyone, but treating each other kindly and respectfully, are two things that universally must apply in any relationship.

The postcard drops in a rather empty sounding letter box and leaves me wondering whether people still send handwritten letters. Personally, I still treasure the true emotions formed by pen to paper, it enables us to absorb what is being written or read, feelings that years later a letter can reconnect. I possess letters from friends I met in summer camp when I was only 9 years old, I have kept them in a little box, on the top shelf of the wardrobe in the family home where I grew up. If I am ever able to, I go through my box and the feelings take me back right to time when the pen was scribbling those words, right back to the times when we all got lost in the forest or when we first lit the camp fire or won the scavenger hunt. The memories are endless, but the paper form will always keep some record of what happened in a safe place. Priceless! That is the reason why I have put an effort into getting a postcard to Tia with an image that resonates with her character and things she likes, so she could maintain those memories until we can continue making new ones again.

Technology, in today's world seems to desensitise our emotions instead, however, it is also part of our evolution and it is in some way inevitable, but I will always cherish the hand written gesture of a letter. That moment, my phone rings, and as I scramble for it in my jacket pocket, I see that it is Gloria. I immediately feel gratified, as the technology also allows people to connect worldwide in an instant, enables research and have an immediate impact on people on a different level, it is incomparable.

'Hi Gloria, how are you? Is everything all right?'

Slightly worrying, as she mostly emails me, unless it is important or more so, urgent. Unsettled, I take a deep breath as I await her answer.

'Hi Vivien, I am aware that you are working but this won't take long. I will be sending an email from Shona's lawyer over to you shortly, but please do not worry. That is the reason why I am calling you now. It is a response to the Cafcass report advice that Shona disagrees with, and you may not be happy to read it. Anyway, rest assured, it will be viewed by the judge before they conduct the court hearing, but I can reassure you that disagreements from the other parties, who are against the claimant do in most cases disagree with anything that favours the applicant. To be honest, if Shona did not respond, she would have had automatically agreed with the Cafcass officer. So, as not to show agreement, she had to disagree, if that makes sense. I mean, the Cafcass report is fantastic, in your favour, and that must have threatened Shona, and may have pressed her to go against the advice. If it were the other way around, I would be one hundred percent be advising you to do the same. Read the email and let me know if you need any assistance. There is no required response from our side, but to wait for the court date, which is only few days s away now. Vivien, hang in there! The difficult journey is nearing an end.'

Gloria's confidence is unquestionably encouraging! The update from Shona on the other hand, unsettling. Opposing the Cafcass officer's views and advice, with yet again excessive lies, however, this does not challenge my emotions anymore. She has not changed anything in the past months, but it doesn't bother me as my resilience against those cruel intentions has intensified. Is Shona prepared to look into to the judge's eyes and lie? Tia speaks the truth, so do I and the Cafcass officer is going to back us both up.

'Okay, I trust that this negative response will not affect the judge's view on the case, they shall not be blinded to all the lies. Gloria, I did some reading, regarding custody hearings here in UK, although hardly any sources are available on same sex couples, but a biological mother seems to have a strong status in judiciary, and they seem to have an almost automatic right over the child. This worries me as I have always been more than what a status can give a mother.'

'I understand your worries, Vivien, and you have every right to question everything, but the courts in the UK do not favour one or the other parent, they do very strongly put the child's interests first. You have your statement that is your truth, testimonies that are your additional evidence and the Cafcass report based on your daughter's innocent words. These are confirmation of findings that form a concrete support for your claims. The judge will make sense between right and wrong; they are highly experienced and trained professionals. You may be finding it hard to trust the world right now, after what has happened to you, but there is justice out there and we are on the way to claim it for you. Okay?

Now, there is one more thing. At this stage, before the final hearing, it is necessary for our firm to assist you with a barrister, who has a greater degree of objectivity, to provide advice on something a lot trickier in your case, depending on the way the judge will be leaning. It is very common at this stage, especially if there are strong allegations against the applicant, even if we know and Cafcass believes, these not to be true. Rest assured, we work with one of the best barristers in the family law field, and as we promised to provide you with the best legal assistance to get your legal status visible once and for all. The barrister's name is Christina, and she is already going through your case and is happy to meet us both already tomorrow, to discuss the hearing with you and I will be present at this meeting as well. The law firm has more barristers, but in my opinion, Christina is one of a kind and the best suited for your case. She pre-organised in connection to your case and is ready to meet us tomorrow. Would you like to first meet her and see how you connect? However, if you do not feel that I have made the right choice, tell me and we will get you introduced to another barrister. I do think that you will love Christina though, she is a hard shell to crack in the court and has won so many complex cases, including cases of same sex couples.'

'I understand, I just wasn't aware that someone else would replace you for the final hearing, as I do enjoy working with you, I get a sense of legal comfort from you, something I will certainly seek on the day. Although, I trust you and your recommendations. So, if taking on a barrister is the right choice for me, then I unreservedly accept it. I need the best in every way possible and I only have one chance, one opportunity to rise up. Having to go through this ordeal again, if my claim is rejected, would break the shattered pieces into even tinier particles. I doubt my strength beyond this stage. So, yes, please I would like to meet Christina, and from the sound of it all, I am sure I will like her as I trust your legal and professional judgment in every way. What time shall I meet you and Christina tomorrow?'

'I will meet you at 17:30 at Leicester Square station and we can walk together to Christina's chambers where she will be waiting for us. Is that okay, Vivien?'

'Yes perfect, I will see you then.'

Wow, what an eventful break, my case has taken yet another turn. Rushing back to work, I quickly open the email to read Shona's response. I slow down my walking pace to regain some balance. Reading Shona's words doesn't come easy, the constant bitterness, the hurtful lies and the steady perseverance to cut me out of Tia's life. Word after word, slowly cutting the rope from under my feet, but I would rather risk falling into the deep of nothingness than ever give up. Making it to the other end, is my one and only focus, as that is where my little darling is cheering me on, however wobbly that thin rope gets, I will pull through. This response document that lists every part of the Cafcass report that mentions me in a positive light, Shona has of course disagreed with. To name a few: *I am not suitable to look after Tia, as I am irresponsible, aggressive and I am a risk to Tia's wellbeing* or *Tia has settled well and she does not mention me anymore* or *allowing me into Tia's life, will be disturbing and upsetting to Tia or Tia does not need me in her life and she never has before.* These are utter fabrications, targeted directly at me, to make my chances very fragile. I wonder what the judge will make out of all this. Will they recommend further observation on Tia and possibly delay the hearing based on these latest responses against the Cafcass report? Every time, that rope shakes, I recite to myself what Tia shared with the officer. *I miss Mummy Vivien.* At last, as I read towards the end of the response document, is that *Shona does not agree with the shared custody recommendations and urges the judge to strongly refuse this to protect Tia from further harm.* Harm is already done, Tia is deeply sunk in it, and it is time to get her out of there! She may be hurting inside, that may not be visible on the outside because she has had expectations that caused disappointment. I have confidence that Tia believes in me and that is keeping her hopes to see me again, alive. Time cannot separate two people who form a bond, it cannot just simply be cut by anyone, however adamant the attempts get, it is impossible. The love we share is an unending connection, felt deep in the heart, and the reason for knowing that Tia is not alone, she has not forgotten me. What she may have done is adapt to a routine that has been presented to her – routine provides a sense of security that helps children to adapt during hard times – and she has had no other option since I am not there as I promised. Is she allowed to ask about me, speak of me or is she silenced by stories about my absence? My chest tightens as I think of her waiting for me to one day, walking through that door, and the disappointment that fills her little heart, releasing in that instant. What a wait. Day after day, week after week, month after month! The time has been shockingly too long, and my heart panics when I think of it, with the desire to trust that Tia's age and her time perception may have not reached that development milestone just yet, so that months seem like days to her mind. Tia is just over four years old and her time perception may be slowly transforming, enabling her to sense the time frame slowly expanding, and that bothers me. No, I shall not put myself through this, not now when the time for our potential reunion is within reach. I picture that day, I imagine her little face when she first sees me, the joy in her delicate voice as she runs towards me saying Mummy Vivien. With one of her soft teddy's clutched tightly in her hand, as I catch her and embrace her in that moment that I hope to last a lifetime. Her soft little face buried into my neck and he warm little hands gripping around my shoulders. This little magnificent person makes my life worth living. Surprisingly, I react with a smile when I close Shona's response document. I straighten my posture and with powerful thoughts, I walk back to work.

Arriving at the barrister's chamber, and seeing Gloria standing there, makes me want to shout out of excitement. Apparently, the barrister that has worked with the law firm where I found Gloria, has succeeded in some high-profile cases and I can't wait for her to stand beside me at my hearing – that is only two days away – yikes! When the door opens, Christina, the barrister appears – this tall smartly groomed woman with her thick dark hair reaching down to her hips, loud but polite and direct in her speech. She stretches her hand out to greet me with a pleasant smile on her face and offers a brief greeting to Gloria and invites us both in. The chamber's walls are covered with neatly aligned shelves filled with books and files. Hanging on the wall behind her desk are qualification certificates and articles of her achievements, each frame perfectly aligned alongside the other. Her desk immaculate, with a walnut leather clipboard next to a matching pen stand and a thick file in the middle of the table that I assume is my case. All three of us take a seat and I predict that a monumental discussion is about to take place. Christina takes the lead, by highlighting how privileged she feels to be representing me in the court hearing, she also expressed her compassion towards the pain that I am experiencing due to the separation from my daughter. Christina feels extremely confident over my case, as she reassures me that what has happened to me is unfair, and she has witnessed cases a lot worse than mine. Worse than this? I think to myself, this is excruciating, I can't begin to imagine what worse things could have happened. On another note, she adds that she has studied my ex-partner and feels prepared to face all of the accusations that she has drawn against me. Then she moves towards the thick file on the table in front of her. The pages in her file resembling an evidence board, with red coloured notes of every single accusation made against me, accompanied by blue coloured notes representing evidence of Shona's contradictions hidden between the lines. The Cafcass report evidence in purple, connected to Shona's accusations or to my claims. This is incredible! I am astounded! A mind map, cleverly connected, analysing the lies, truth and contradictions where it is clear that Shona is going trip up at the hearing. How is her lawyer ever going to argue this piece of evidence against her client's fabricated story? Adding that she knew instantly the lying party in this case, but knowing is not enough, evidence to every claim, is the golden key. Awestruck, she is already proving to be incredible. I receive a *told you* kind of look from Gloria with her eyebrows smiling over her forehead, listening contentedly in agreement with Christina. Further, thanks to the experience and wide web of connections, she has managed to read up about the judge who has been assigned to my case. To my satisfaction, and advantage, the judge is not only highly experienced in custody cases, but has extensive knowledge of psychology and specifically has strengths in analysis and character judgment. What her advice is, is to be myself, as I have represented myself since the very start of my application, honest as he will be reading both mine and Shona's body language along with facial expressions. In her advice, she emphasises something that has not gone down well, in the eyes of this particular judge, is making grimaces when the opposition party says the lies that can naturally have this effect on the other party that is being targeted. Whether I will be taking the stand in the hearing, is something that for now remains unknown but Christina advises me to be clear in answers, truthful, stick to the script and if the opposition party crosses any lines, whatsoever, she will step in. Having such an experienced barrister, as advised at this stage by Gloria, is an invaluable asset. My complex case has very much challenged the judiciary system, thus as confirmed by Christina, in her many years of experience, she has seen much worse, including a battle between same sex couples. However, what she has never experienced, until my case, is a battle of a non-biological parent, fighting for a child, without any legal formal evidence. Christina, by the sound of her past cases, thrives on challenging cases and is certainly prepared to fight right by my side. She confirmed, that with all the evidence in her mind map file, Shona will be trapped in her own bait. There is only one question to provide an answer to. Shall I take on the barrister? An outright yes! The fireworks in my body are going off right now, I feel nervous about my hearing, but at the moment I am hopeful. We agree to meet an hour before the hearing on Monday, and Christina adds a humorous comment: *'I will be there bright and early with my baseball bat, just in case.'*

I laugh in response, as that is the inner power I need in someone who will represent me in the biggest case of my life.

Gloria, for the first time, pulls me in for a hug, to reassure my worries and the rising anxiety over the approaching hearing. She will not be there, and that makes me feel a little uneasy, but she will be on her phone, awaiting any news or support we may need on the day. Unfortunately, I cannot pay Gloria as well to be at the hearing as her assistance will not be required. I have already exhausted my savings, but for Tia, it's worth it. To send me off with good luck, Gloria invites me for a glass of wine before we both head our separate ways for the underground.

'Vivien, chin-chin and best of luck on Monday. Do not forget, you are a mother, and the judge will grant you that official title too.'

I smile back and raise my glass in response.

'Thank you, Gloria, for everything you have done for me and connecting me with Christina, no matter the outcome. You were right, I absolutely think that she is the best match for my case and her abilities along with her experience are truly promising. I look forward to bringing you the news on Monday. I am so very nervous over the result of my case, but simultaneously have all my confidence and trust in your team. Six months ago, I wouldn't have thought of this moment, as I had assumed my invisibility would just further defeat me. Your law firm has helped me to the surface, by believing in me and my story. Especially that my case must have initially sounded complex and almost impossible to solve, but you didn't let that judgment cloud your decision to present me in my case. From the very first moment, you witnessed a desperate mother who has had her child ripped from her arms, despite being the non-biological parent. To you, I am a mother and that is the reason I trusted you to be the lawyer who will get my daughter back. You are not only professional, committed and creative in the space of the law, but you listen to your client patiently, with a critical objective mind. While explaining the impossibilities, you opt to offer solutions or other ways, in line with what your client desires, keeping the case motivated and representative of the client's true nature. That is what makes you a great lawyer, thank you! Chin chin!'

# Chapter 17

## The Denouement, Part I

'My heartbeat awaits the beat of yours.'

Eyes wide open, mind wide awake, body restless and the time is only just nearing 5 a.m. on this particular Monday morning. Darkness defines the space outside, with streetlights forming patches of brightness on the road. There are no cars, no sounds, just me and my thoughts, which are louder than the typical bustling activity on the street. I wish to teleport to a realm where I live my life with Tia by my side, without accusations and cruel intentions. Wandering thoughts over a possible hypothetical existence is not a solution to the day I am soon about to conquer. Today is the day of my final court hearing, that will give me my legal parental title. The latter is what my heart desires, what my existence demands and my sanity thrives for. I am building some strenuous butterflies in my stomach, that is making me slightly nauseous. Unable to sleep, I mentally analyse the possible hearing outcomes over and over again. Concluding the facts, the judge's objective nature equals many possibilities. I successfully interlink some solutions to my case, and those seem as logical as possible in my state of mind. One outcome could be the judge believing in Shona's response to the Cafcass report and believing that my return to Tia's life may just be disturbing, this would mean going against Cafcass advice and my evidence making a decision solely from the perspective of the parent that has spent the past six months with the claimant child. This possibility is terrifying, but I have to prepare myself for the worst ever outcome of today's hearing. Better to stay safe and low, than fall from up high. The other possible outcome is more positive, the judge agreeing with the Cafcass advice, and following their own rational judgment in what is best for Tia, dividing the time between both parents. I calm my thoughts and remind myself that I am a confident mother ready for the hardest battle and I will have Christina by my side who has got her files and 'bat' prepared. Feeling the need to move the energy within my body and put my mind at ease, I roll out my Pilates mat, a short routine is going to be beneficial and prepare me for the day ahead. An emphasis on my breathing technique will sharpen my mental state and reduce stress. I am not an expert, but I am in tune with my mind and body, to be able to determine the affect it has on me. After a strong session, it is time to get ready, time to get my baby girl. I can sense the lioness' bravery and courage in her heart, as well as her agile mind, as she prepares to fight.

  I automatically go to Tia's room, sit on her bed and grab the soft rainbow teddy I got her for the day when I had my Cafcass interview, in the hope to give it to Tia fairly soon. I stroke her duvet cover, neatly adjust the soft toys in her bed and take in Tia's scent. Her bed is still the same, like she has never left. Oh my, she may be playing in her room and cuddling up to me in her bed reading stories soon. I cannot wait, the energy of this anticipation is excruciating. Suddenly, a single tear rolls down my cheek, it reminds me of the many tears I have shed over the past months. Tears also remind me of what I have been through, what I have survived. I was going crazy, insane, from being heartbroken and when I projected the months of wait, the pain that surrounded my existence was unrecognisable. I wipe my tears, squeeze the teddy really tight, and think to myself, how magical we humans really are. We can face the unimaginable, as life throws things in our way that we may not ever even think of. Whatever it may be, however scary it may seem, to give in to it is the worst that one could do in response. I have stuck with a determined mind, and fought my way to accomplish my plan for *visibility*, regardless of obstacles. I release the teddy, and get up from the bed, as I walk out I send kisses into the air, whispering *Baby girl, today is the day, I am coming for you! Stay strong for only a little longer. Mummy loves you!* I move towards my wardrobe to choose my outfit, I need a colour that shows my loving and nurturing nature. Hmm, I reach for the hanger on which my pastel pink blouse rests, ironed, ready to wear. Perfect, this is exactly what I need today. I continue searching my wardrobe, now going through my trousers and selecting a pair that match my determination for victory. Aha! My red trousers, the match has been completed. I must not forget my Amethyst crystal necklace, I will need its calming energy, to overcome the possible stresses of today. I reach for my jewellery box, and place the necklace around my neck, and clench the crystal stone in my hand, to transfer the heat that my nervy body has generated since the morning. I reach for my phone, to check for an email, that I have been waiting for the whole entire past six months, one from Shona saying that she has had a change of mind and is ready to mediate in terms of caring for Tia. I scroll through an incredible amount of good luck messages from my lovely friends, who have been the best support one could ever wish for. I will be ever so thankful to everyone who has stuck by me during this difficult period of my life. Madison and Helen have taken the next two days off, just in case they will be invited into the courtroom to take the stand to testify. Their loyalty and commitment towards my case, will be forever appreciated. I cannot thank them enough for coming forward with their honest supportive evidence on my mothering qualities, character and my relationship with Tia. I will forever express my gratitude to them, and their effort will never be forgotten.

 Madison, thank you for your round up on our long-term friendship, the way you described me, truly shows how much you know me, and how much our children have grown close in the past few years. You have specifically, focused on highlighting the points which reflect on my mothering qualities and on your observations during social gatherings, having Tia for play dates and explicitly stating worrying information coming directly from Tia, about her witnessing Shona's unkind behaviour towards me. Confirming your experience over the period of conception, pregnancy and birthing stages along with your recommendations based on what is best for Tia, is not only priceless but based on well gathered evidence that you supplied to the judge. We are similar in one way, we are women that are solid as a rock and have been through a lot in life, but we do not just give in easily, we are fighters. Our friendship is one of a kind that flows along as our children grow older, one that will always exist based on strong foundations. I will forever be in debt to you. Helen, thank you for your honesty on your positive views of me as a professional, mother and a friend. Tapping on what the separation is possibly causing Tia, based on your collected evidence of events. Your words are simply touching the points that support my statement in many ways. I will never forget your reaction when you discussed the accusations made against me, your eyes filled with tears that brought tears into my eyes. That moment truly reflects on the person you are, and that is clearly present in your testimony. You are a dear friend, with such a strong feminine power, dealing with your own life challenges, and still finding time to support me with my case will hold my forever gratitude. I look forward to reuniting Amber and Tia, they will be over the moon. Here's to more years of friendship ahead of us. Both of you are ready to take the stand, and in my eyes, you are both superstars.

As I scroll all the way to the bottom of my display, I realise no email or text from Shona, meaning that no change is taking place, today will go ahead as planned. Shona may just be very confident that being the biological parent will give her an automatic victory today. Whatever, she may trust or believe, will be challenged today. Today, her words and actions will face consequences as I am going in with full power and I am not leaving without a paper that states that I can see Tia again. At this stage, my expectations are quite realistic and anything that the judge will rule, with all the efforts of my barrister, that involves reconnection with Tia, will already be a satisfying outcome. Obviously, we are fighting for a shared custody here, and we will fight with every inch of legal strength that the judiciary system will allow. Given the complexity of the case, the judge has set two consequent dates, to allow time for the testimonies to take a stand if required. I begin to gather my papers, the teddy and extra evidence material just in case it is needed, when my doorbell rings. I rush downstairs and open the door to my sis holding two cups of coffee in each hand.

'Viv you cannot start without a delicious cup of coffee, here. I have fifteen minutes before I need to dash to work, but I think that is the same time that you need to leave for the hearing, great. How are you feeling?'

Sis places her cup down on the coffee table and hugs me tight and rubs my upper arm to provide some sense of comfort, as my nervousness is visible in my body language. The restless fidgets on the sofa, looking towards my phone display for the time or on any last-minute updates from Shona, Christina or Gloria as I cannot seem to shake off the desire for that change of a mind to avoid a court hearing. Why did things have to get to this stage? A question that has become my nemesis over the past months. Cohabiting, marriages, civil partnerships, whatever the union, can get disturbed for whatever reasons, but children are at the centre of these unions, and they do not deserve to be harmed during their parents' separation. They suffer a great ordeal of distress by witnessing the family falling apart. For instance, one parent walking out through the door, leaves them with a feeling of loss and sadness. Their little hearts want both their parents, in one place, always as they grow up, and that feeling from my experience is agonising. The decision to remain in the family home to co-exist for two to three weeks, was for settling Tia after the stressful abusive event of that terrible night that ended the relationship forever. As well, as to arrange a well-balanced childcare arrangement that will be the best for Tia. In our situation, the best would have been to pack my bags and walk through that door, never turning back, but having children needs discussions and thorough planning cannot go amiss. The latter depends on each individual. I left when the plan was formed, based on 50/50 shared care and Tia began to move between two homes. However, recently I have heard of the term *Nesting*, meaning when the children remain in the family home for as long as it possibly works after separation and the parents take turns with moving out when it is the other parent's shared care duty, to look after their children. It reduces the stress of the separation in the family home, provides some time for parents to practice single parenting and has that one space to process the separation. However, in my opinion, longer than a few months while arrangements bind, may cause confusion in children over not understanding the separation context and miss out on understanding what having two homes feels like. In my situation, even if we were aware of the nesting option back then, it wouldn't have worked. In such circumstances, minimum contact is necessary with a civil approach to discussions strictly focused on the child. Separation was a feeling of disappointment that we as parents caused to Tia. That had haunted me for a while. I still see the tears welling up in her innocent eyes, those sad little cheeks staring at me as she processed the awful news we brought to her. I have not regretted my separation from an abusive and controlling partner who greatly risked my daughter's and my own sense of safety.

Some couples opt for the cohabitating parenting option, in which they mutually agree on the relationship breaking, but remain together in the family union as a couple for the sake of their children. Can such mutual agreement actually work? Can two people, who either stopped loving each other or hurt one another causing the breakup, actually live together happily, respectfully and pretending to be something they are not just to put on a show in front of their children, families and friends? If the cohabitation arrangement continues to be filled with both parents feeling miserable, argumentative, presenting dislike to one another and spending time separately in the family, could potentially role model a wrongful understanding to the children that relationships are built on separateness not togetherness. I did not want to cause any more harm or confusion to Tia. Separately, building a happy life and providing love and support for Tia, however challenging at the start it was for her, was a healthy choice for everyone. It was ought to be a smooth transition to cause minimal disruptions in Tia's life. But that was ruined by Tia's abrupt detachment from the parent whom she formed a strong bond to, and the consequences of such an abrupt event, worry me, when I look into Tia's life ahead. Will I be able to fix the harm done to her? Will Shona let us live in peace? I cannot face more drama. I wish this ordeal to end, today!

Couples make their individual decision, based on what enables them to continue parenting their children, often financial commitments cause a great deal of separation dilemmas, as living separately can often be unaffordable. Children, on the other hand, whether parents do separate or remain cohabitating, should not be the ones who suffer, feeling like they are left alone in the thunderstorm with no shelter to protect them. Parents should pause, take the time to think of what is the best for their children, for their ongoing protection. Handling the separation peacefully is the healthiest choice for children. Offering them a clear understanding over the separation, age appropriately, to put their uncertainties at ease as children adapt to changes quite well if the separation is handled well and they feel loved from each parent beyond their separation. Feeling loved brings a sense of safety to their existence, and these foundations will reduce the risk in developing physical, emotional and social challenges (focus and attention problems at school; self-esteem and identity issues; maintaining and building friendships; depression; anxiety) in their immediate and wider social environment. If you are parents, who were or are able to separate under these above terms, you can take a golden medal and a round of applause.

In my opinion, from the perspective of a separated parent and a qualified professional working with young children, separation does not need to be a bad experience if you put children's happiness at the centre when discussing arrangements. Avoid staying together if you do not love each other anymore, if you do not have respect for one another and especially if you cannot stand each other's presence and however busy children may seem to be, they see, hear, and absorb everything that goes on around them, including non-verbal gestures and body language. Children are not temporary, they are the future, giving them the best start in life, is for a lifetime.

I take a sip from the coffee cup, the temperature is just right, it momentarily satisfies my overwhelmed mind that seems to travel thousands of miles in my world of wandering.

'How do I feel? Excited Sis, I could potentially see Tia today. I have to be emotionally well prepared, as my expectations cannot be too high, but given all the positives, it's promising. If things do not go well today, I will break Sis. I will need you to get me.'

Answering my sis, is making me realise that speaking about today's event is making my lips tremble, eyes tearful and my chest tight, and I guarantee that I will try to remain strong on the stand, it will be tremendously hard. Preparing for the fact that my story will be twisted in front of the judge, from my opponent, works well in theory but I shall not stow away my pain. If my resistance is triggered on the stand, my response will proudly present my maintained emotions. The judge requires witnessing honesty, to make sense of the case he is soon about to figure out, and my emotions are the honest portrayal of my statement. Should the situation cause any difficulties, my answers and story will not be changed, I will persevere confidently and bravely. A true story cannot be changed it can only be voiced and shared.

'Go and get our Tia back! Update me whenever you can, do not worry, I will share the updates with Mum. If you need me there, I will leave work and come to you. Good luck Viv, we love you!'

Sis is looking serious, emotional under that strong face she holds for me, although struggling to speak herself. Tia means the world to her. She gives me the biggest bear hug I have ever received and hands me a picture that Charlie drew for Tia a few days ago. I squeeze my sis tightly and admire the picture which shows Tia and Charlie as disproportionate stick people playing with colourful balloons. It makes me smile, and I trace the drawn happy face of Tia with my finger. I wonder if at a later stage Charlie will remember not seeing Tia for a long while. It has been tricky to keep away the whole truth about Tia's absence, not only from Charlie but Tia's friends too. They are too young to comprehend the full story. I cannot stand any other children being affected by this ordeal. Tia has a huge support team, who adore her dearly for that one little amazing being who she is, with a huge heart, creative mind and so much fun to be around. Today, everyone believes, in my victory and I will do everything to make that happen. If things turn out well for Tia and I, this experience will leave a footprint in the history of our family and social circle. I wave my sis off and embrace the moment. The moment I shut the door behind me, the journey of uncertainty begins.

  The city streets are filled with an endless row of colourful umbrellas moving in various directions, almost creating a choreography to the melody of the heavy rainfall. Taxis and buses in gridlocked traffic on the roads, filled with passengers eagerly awaiting the congestion to tail off. I attempt to hit the streets, with my funky red umbrella, fitting into the dance routine as I dodge the enormous amount of footfall hurtling in my direction. Rush hour in London is notorious for its chaos. To avoid the madness, I opt to go down a side street, a hidden gem of magical old style book stores, line the street in a neat row. Fascinating, a place to return to for a thorough visit, as I love to browse book shops, especially as these stores seem to offer a diverse selection of antique books. London is full of surprises! I doubt that I will ever be able to say that I have seen everything in this beautiful city, and the spontaneous encounters of the unknown, are remarkable. I can see the court building in the near distance. A lump catches in my throat and I find it hard to swallow, indicating that the reality of today's event is becoming as real as the concrete ground beneath my feet. With a heavy inhale and an uneasy exhale, I approach the court building entrance, shake off the excessive rain water and make an entrance into the lobby. Christina waves at me from the other side of the security metal detector, her long black hair is immaculately styled, her face painted with gentle makeup that goes well with the navy grey boucle blazer and skirt –

sophisticated with a smart edge. Successfully completing the security check, I gather my belongings and make my way to Christina, she instantly puts her arm around my shoulders, reassures me that everything is going to be all right and reminds me to keep my huge smile on, as the day will end with the same smile, she can feel it up her sleeves. I do admire the positive vibes. The lift takes us to the correct floor, and as the doors open, I find the crowded hallways shocking. The buzz of dialogue exchanges surrounds the air that we slowly attempt to pass though. Everyone seems way too busy to even acknowledge an addition to the crowd, heads turned either into papers or at what seems like client and lawyer conversation. The facial expressions of people vary, sad to anxious, some tearful, although, I can immediately tell the lawyers from their clients. The lawyers seem to be the one in charge of awaiting news or the next move from the floor ushers, presentably hovering around their clients, who seem to be focusing on managing their emotions, rather than the formalities. I immediately share these feelings and feel united with these strangers, my stomach since entering this floor, is a bulge of concealed anxiety. I made a promise to myself that today, I need *me* to be tenacious, buoyant and put together. To my surprise, Christina opens a door that leads into a small conference-like private room and shuts the door leaving the buzzing corridors behind us. The quiet room makes an immediate difference, I feel slightly more relaxed and extremely thankful for Christina's early arrival, who understands the busy court floors, and managed to allocate us a quiet room. Confirming that this room is registered with the floor ushers and will remain in our sole use for the whole day. An arrangement that seems well thought through, offering me a sense of comfort that I greatly appreciate. I sit down on the chair opposite Christina, who seems to be already well settled with some files partly opened in front of her seat, seemingly ready to be discussed upon my arrival. Suddenly the speaker on the wall, that I have not yet managed to notice, makes a noise announcing a court hearing. I pin myself to the back of the chair with my eyes popped wide open at Christina. She seems completely unaffected by the announcement and only looks up from her files to tell me to relax as that is a different hearing from ours. I take a note of the hearing number, although, I am certain, that every time that speaker announces again, I will be glued to the chair, attentively listening for that number and case name. I am handed a pen and a notepad, to use as a communication tool when other parties or the judge will be actively speaking, as to not unintentionally disturb the court hearing, unless time for discussion is required by Christina, in unforeseen circumstances when an interim will be essential. The note pad will be specifically for writing down disagreements, additional comments and questions, as these will be discreetly reviewed by Christina during the hearing, and she will automatically know what actions to take. I appreciate such attention to detail, as I am more than certain that I will have moments when I wish I could speak or shout up *No that is not true, that is a lie,* so it would be great to manage my inner thoughts and expressions by using a tool that is not so obvious, yet still professional. Christina tells me to avoid annoyed body language such as head shakes or frowning towards the other party in disbelief. However difficult that may be, the likeability of hurtful information will certainly fill the room in today's hearing. Can I ever be ready to face the forthcomings? Doubtful, but there is only one way to face today's dread, and that is to let my truth speak for itself. The hearing in August, crushed my heart, as the judge had no grounds of any evidence to permit any time spent with Tia. The judge had two opposing statements, both claiming abuse towards one another, therefore, he had no choice, but keep the claimant child in the care of her biological mother whom she resided with at that time. With all due respect to the judge, they had no understanding of who I am as a person and whether I had been a parent to Tia all the way until the day of the detachment. They acknowledged based on the evidence, that I had some kind of a relationship with Tia, and I was granted the parental recognition, which was superb, as without that partial victory, there would be no hearing today. The judge, saw the parent in me, but as explained to me by Gloria, they couldn't have granted visitation permission based on abusive allegations, that needed an in-depth investigation The latter was the reason for the court hearing rescheduling, to allow the Cafcass officer to carry out their assessments. In respect to Cafcass workload, the judge is obliged to allow the twelve-week period to collect data and prepare a concise report along with advise, to present to the judge. I am pleased, as often the twelve week period can extend, for any unforeseen reasons, but gladly not in my case. It was extremely unbearable, as I remember, to accept anything else than the reconnection with Tia, my heart was crushed and I have not yet recovered, as I have remained increasingly hopeful and motivated. Have I really had another choice? If I had gone against Gloria's advice, such as clandestinely approaching Tia in locations known to me, just to simply say hello and reassure her, I would have jeopardised the opportunity I have been offered today. Why? That's because Shona, just bumping into me once with my excuse of coincidence, would have led for further accusations of me harassing them and not leaving them alone. That would have added to her initial report to the Police, and her fabricated story would be much stronger today. So, the unbearable patience, has been the key to my potential success today. Fingers and toes crossed! On another note, I could have selfishly caused more pain to Tia, to whom my abrupt appearance would have not presented well. The joy on her little precious face and tender heart would have faded into sadness, and her refusal to let me go may have prompted Shona to finally call the Police and report me on the spot. Way too much of a risk, when I have a lifelong vision with Tia ahead of me. Poor little baby, what could I have told her anyway? Any promises would have been fake, unreal, as our future was greatly threatened then, and is still threatened today, whether I get to see her again is in the hands of the judge today. I reach for the soft colourful teddy that I have kept close to me since the Cafcass interview where my meeting with Tia was not permitted. I squeeze the teddy and squash it close to my upper body. An irresistible sensation to want and need to feel Tia close to me, instantly fills my heart. I respect the parents out there, who have this strong shield protecting their children from harmful partners, but I am not a perpetrator. In fact, it is me who is good for this child, the one who has provided this child with my everything, love and care, at all times, day and night. From everything I have gathered, throughout this ordeal, I learned that biological parents have an immediate right to the child, that immediate parental responsibility. That is granted, but I respectfully disagree from my point of view. A second parent who has complete input during the planning, conception and delivery, does not become an automatic parent to the child, unless married or in civil partnership. Outside of these relationship ties, it is solely in the hands of the biological mother who she allows to be entered onto the birth certificate, as that decision automatically provides the parent with parental responsibility. Parental responsibility is something divine, it allows the parent to make decisions for the child, may those be related to health, education, travel or any everyday decisions in the child's best interest. However, if the parent, for whatever reasons is not named on the birth certificate within six months of the child's birth, loses the rights for the child. To regain these rights, one needs consent from the biological birth mother, as without her permission, any name additions to the birth certificate or parental responsibility cannot be granted. Simply a matter of paperwork, that takes no more than a few weeks and a signature from Shona, that's all that was required. But, Shona's controlling nature encouraged her to keep that control over me and remain the one person in charge of Tia and I. This has kept me invisible the whole time since Tia's birth. No marriage or civil partnership equals no rights. Whereas, in the hospital I was registered as the second parent, we had the donor agreement to prove our joined conception as otherwise I would have not even been allowed into the delivery room. The papers I signed stated two parents – in fact two mothers – who conceived at home with the help of a known donor and these papers were filed in the hospital until the day Tia was allowed to leave the hospital to go home. However, from then on, none of the conception or Tia's delivery significance mattered, as only one parent had successfully made it into the birth certificate and that was not me. Only conceiving through a clinic gives same-sex couples the automatic parental right to enter the birth certificate. I wish,

I wish, I wish I wouldn't have cared so much about Shona's private matter, and pressed the birth certificate within the six months, until my name was visible on the papers, there in black and white. Don't we all wish for those wishes to be able to take us back into different times in our lives, to amend our mistakes, but then what would we become? We would not have an opportunity to continue evolving, learn from our mistakes and gain purpose in life.

Circumstances beyond the conception and the birth can change in many ways. Such as a relationship breaking up well before baby's due date or in the early years of the baby's life. Leaving that absent parent on the rightful papers, but not in the child's life. A child can be conceived in many different ways, it is for life, regardless of the relationship breaking down beyond the child's birth or not. The decision is up to the parent, and I was present at conception and my responsibilities for Tia were set for life. If we used the clinic and I had that automatic right to be entered in the birth certificate, Shona couldn't have played her emotional games on me, and her private matters which were dishonest anyway, wouldn't have been relevant. There are cases in which, the birth mothers become the least eligible parent to take care of the child, but the granted parental responsibility doesn't allow the other parent to take action to protect that child, in the relationship or if separated. In the eyes of the law, biology is superior. Today, I sit here, awaiting a decision to be made by the judge, whether I can ever see my daughter, how often that may be or for what length of time. Today, I have to fight for the legal title that I have always invisibly carried with me as I looked after and loved Tia with everything I had. I trusted Shona, it was the biggest mistake I made, and because of that mistake I have suffered great agony during the relationship and beyond. When I realised the six months of the birth certificate period allowed to add a second parent was over, my life had forever changed. I did, not for one minute, think that I will not be added to the birth certificate, or else, be permitted by Shona to acquire parental responsibility. None of these seemed uncertain to me back then, until the moment of the relationship when Shona, without any reasons, refused to grant me parental responsibility. From that very moment, I had begun to doubt her intentions, but that was too late. I stand here today, to plead with the judge to grant me the right to see my daughter, to have her back in my arms. There is nothing else I want more!

I place the teddy on my lap, squeeze it tighter to my body, and turn towards the clock on the wall that shows the time, just past 10 a.m. and patiently await the usher's announcement through the speaker.

# Chapter 18

## The Denouement, Part II

'Win or lose, is the question.'

It's almost 11 a.m. and the speaker has made no announcement in the past hour. Christina has left to gather knowledge over the delay, which she also confirmed, just like Gloria did, is very common in courts as each case is individual, and unexpected complications can arise that require judges to act outside of the allocated time frame. Suddenly, something hits the door from outside, that instantly makes my blood run cold and muffled shouting noises. I slowly creep towards the door and focus my hearing senses. The situation seems heated out there. Definitely an angry male having an outburst of profanity. What is happening out there, is Christina all right? Oh please, do not come back to this room and tell me, that the hearing has been cancelled because of this situation. The curiosity is unbearable. No, I must not get accidently involved. I am worried about Christina's whereabouts and whether we will need to be evacuated because of the situation out there. I wouldn't like to interrupt Christina, despite the drama out there, this is still a court, and she might be in the middle of something important. I drop her a text message and instruct her to kindly call me back, briefly telling her about the situation on the other side of the door. I keep my phone on ring, slide it back into my back pocket. Nothing will happen if I just open the door slightly, just to have enough space to peek through. There are people around the area of the door, so my visibility is obstructed, so I open the door a little more to gain some kind of vision in between the grouped-up shoulders. People congregated in the corners of the main corridor, resembling a crowd encircling a boxing ring in a match, but without the sound of cheering and booing. I am safe from where I am standing, and now I can tell, that several security guards are attempting to tame a gentleman who seems rather aggravated. Pieces of paper thorn all over the floor, chairs turned upside down. This gentleman, wearing a T-shirt, jeans and smart shoes. His face red, very angry looking and his body language translates dissatisfaction and fury. With a raised voice, trying to barge his way through the corridor that seems to be leading towards the hearing room, shouting, *'You can't do this to me, there is no justice, I am coming back, we are not done.'* The security guard is barely managing to resist his attempts, so they call for police on their radios. This is getting serious! Simultaneously I search for Christina, who is nowhere to be seen. The man is temporarily held back, and people are trying to stay as close to the walls as possible. The man is a regular size, but anger is his motivation, and he is not giving up. The police arrive within minutes, and although there was resistance, they manage to handcuff the aggravated gentleman, and successfully remove him from the corridor. Despite the authority of the police, he still braves himself to shout back, insulting the court staff, including the judge. The corridors fill up with people that have been forced to squash into the corners, to seek a safety. The buzz of people's dialogues take over the corridors again as things seem to have settled now and the security guards take their place to continue with their duties, looking shocked, outraged, but satisfied to have handled such a dramatic event where the safety of others was at stake. No sight of Christina, so I shut the door, as there is nothing more to peek at, and sit back in my chair. No message from Christina either. Maybe she got held back for safety reasons. I am sure she will be back soon. I will not allow myself to create worrying thoughts in my head or imagine scenarios that can negatively affect my, so far relaxed mind. I decide to send a group message to my waiting friends who ought to provide testimonies, to inform them that the court hearing has not yet commenced and their required presence to take the stand is currently unclear. Also, a good moment to update family and friends who have been closely following my journey, and inform them about the current delay. Just as I press *send* to all the group members to deliver the message, Christina walks through the door, looking breathless, like she has run a marathon. Sweeping her hair to the side of her face, she settles back on the chair opposite mine and leans over the table with some freshly printed papers in her hands. Christina begins explaining the reasons of her disappearance, which seems to be the situation that I witnessed not long ago in the corridors. She left to look for Shona's lawyer, gather their positions and to begin liaising. Nothing that I need to worry about. Apparently, the dramatic incident already occurred in the courtroom, and he was asked to leave the court and was escorted by the security guards The hearing was carried out by the same judge that has been allocated to my hearing, but Christina reassured me that everything seems to be fine and the delay shall not be for much longer. The judge has only got my case for the rest of the day, and the case before me, was only allocated for half an hour as it was a decision ruling hearing only. Based on the recent event, the ruling didn't go in the gentleman's favour, who seems to have lost his case, and because this is a family court, he has probably lost contact with his children. Related to his anger management issues, the judge may have ruled against his wishes that hopefully will keep the children safe as a person with such behaviour problems could not be a positive influence on a child, nor could possibly provide a safe place for a child to reside. The father was probably refused contact with his children but based on what I witnessed, he made the correct choice. This is a great example of excluding someone from children's lives, who poses a threat and a possible future filled with abuse, has no place in a family home or in fact anywhere near a child. I truly hope that the judge will have his gut in place when judging me as a person and a parent, and make sense between the truth and a lies. He has some great evidence to rule on, that is not solely my own statement, but those of others close to Tia and I and the Cafcass officer themselves. Christina reaches over to me and rubs my shoulders.

'Do not worry, this will be a piece of cake, everything is on your side and this judge is one of the greatest. They will not overlook the evidence nor misjudge the lovely person you truly are and the importance of your presence in your daughter's life. I am sorry that you had to witness the scene earlier. These things can happen in court and are not uncommon. People often hear verdicts that are against their wishes, although, aggressive behaviour is never the way to handle it. I am glad you are all right.'

Voice of a motivator, so encouraging, she sweeps her hair

to the side again and shares a comforting smile with me. I feel her genuine words fitting well into my vision, but I cannot let that over excite me. I would rather use that energy to feed into my confidence in the hearing room, as I will need every inch of my existence to be visible in that room. That is the person and the mother I am. What more do I need than raw, pure honesty! My thoughts are interrupted but the speaker that finally makes an announcement, Christina perks up closer to the speaker and listens to the hearing list.

'Yes, that is our hearing, room twenty-one, let's go Vivien, it is time to shine and be brave, just be who you truly are, and the judge will see you.'

Wow, the time I have been waiting for has finally arrived. I cannot believe it! I feel so nervous, I can barely get my legs into motion as the great unknown of how I will walk out of room twenty-one, is surely petrifying. Will I win or lose everything? The thoughts in my head are running wild! I immediately send out the group message to my witnesses, so they can be prepared to be called in if necessary. I feel humbled as my two lovely witnesses have devoted all their time today to my case. They have both been in the area since ten am and are prepared to be called in by the judge at some point today. I would do the same, if that was ever asked of me as a friend. The saying, that's what friends are for, is true to life. The court usher collects us from our private room and directs us to follow him towards to courtroom twenty-one. We arrive at the door and stop for a moment. Oh goodness, I can just about hold the nerves in my stomach in one place. This is it. The final moment. It's go time. The towering doors open wide, by another usher from inside the court room. The doors lead us into a somewhat of a less formal court environment than I imagined. A room that is well lit, with large windows and light oak furniture all around, including the tables and chairs lined up in five identically arranged rows, each row facing the oak wood decorated bench awaiting the judge to take a seat behind. Christina and I are ready for the hearing, and just as I begin to look around impatiently fidgeting with my pen, at that moment the doors open again, and Shona walks in with her lawyer escorted by the court usher to the opposite side of the front row. I immediately look away facing the judge's bench instead, automatically rejecting any eye contact with the person who has caused Tia and me so much torment that we will never forget nor fully recover from emotionally. Anger is now adding to my nervousness, as that is the only emotion this person can trigger out of me. So upsetting, that she has let this situation get this far. I need to put a full stop to the end of this long wait. I will not let it go any further. I take an inner deep breath, to cut out all the negative forces present in this court room today. I cannot understand how Shona's lawyer can just sit there, supporting a person, a mother who has been nothing more than selfish and emotionally harmful to her own child. Christina captures my expression that I am having difficulty controlling the inner worries, so she takes my hand and squeezes it gently, reassuring me with a whisper into my ear. '*Try not to worry about her presence, block all your anger towards her, focus on your sweet little Tia instead and place her at the centre of this room. Imagine she is here with you. Stay strong and brave to face your ex-partner's accusations because that is only if you are called to the stand, otherwise leave everything to me and just follow through. I have my baseball bat ready, remember?*'

    Christina's energy is fiery, so encouraging and I shall

follow her advice to bring the best out of today's hearing. The doors open again, this time a very pleasant surprise fills my soul, it is Nicole the Cafcass officer, and she has made it, meaning she is ready to take the stand. The presence of the Cafcass officer is making me feel elevated, as her report findings and advice to the judge, are greatly in my favour as she agrees with the shared care order which is in Tia's best interest and agrees that I am important to Tia, and she needs me in her life. Nicole shares a gentle glimpse and smiles politely at us both, neutrally offers the same to the other side of the row at the other party. She sits down right in the middle of the back row, prepares her case file and patiently awaits the hearing to start. Naturally, I wish to run over to her, give her a massive hug and thank her for finding time to attend the hearing, as it is not mandatory for her. In my opinion, I think this hearing is significant to her, as she probably has not represented two mothers before and the case seems unusual and sensitive. The Cafcass officer believes in what is right for the child and that is the reason why she is here today, to witness that she does her best to express her opinions based on evidence findings. Just as I settle myself, both mentally and physically, the bailiff announces '*All rise. This court is now in session*' and asks everyone to stand up in respect to the judge, the court and the law. Since King Henry IV established the Royal Arms, it has been used in every court in England and Wales as a symbol of tradition. It indicates that the monarch is the source of justice, and that the law is a component of the Royal court, hence judges are the official representatives of the Crown. The presence of Royal Arms urges attorneys and other court officials to bow to the coat of arms rather than the judge to demonstrate respect for the Queen's justice. As to my witnesses, and myself, it is customary when taking a stand to raise the right hand and take an oath to tell the truth, nothing but the truth. Witnesses can choose to either swear to tell the truth in the holy book of their religion or to affirm, as to promise to tell the truth. The very same applies to Shona, but will she continue with her lies under oath? This is going to get interesting! Is she not scared about the consequences, has her lawyer not clarified that getting on the stand may be mandatory for us both today? I can stand strong with dignity anywhere, as I am the one that holds the truth, and truth shall prevail today!

The judge places his reading glasses on and begins reading from the paper file in his hand, by introducing the case. In that instant, goosebumps appear all over my arms, so I take a deep breath, but can hardly swallow the large lump in my throat. Intensely looking towards the bench, in agreement with the judge's announcement. As he finishes the hearing case introduction, he takes off his glasses and looks in my direction, rather relaxed in his chair with a compassionate look on his face.

'Hello, are you Mummy Vivien, the claimant?'

I politely answer with a *yes* and he nods his head in response, accompanied by a warm smile. He seems like a nice man, down to earth, and that immediately decreases that formal pressure and positively exceeds my expectations. I feel more at ease, the lump in my throat is slowly getting smaller and I can breathe a bit easier now. He places his glasses back on again and takes a deep look whilst looking through details on the papers. The courtroom is momentarily filled with silence. But the judge gathers his thoughts and begins speaking again.

'Miss Vivien, so you have not seen your daughter Tia for six months. It must be difficult, I understand, I have three children myself. I must say that I have read every single page of your evidence that you seemingly took a long time to gather. I appreciate it. I am going to be very honest; your statement and witness testimonies are a great match. I can see that you experienced abuse, but there is no evidence of any records, therefore I will need to bring your witnesses to stand shortly today. I will also be bringing the Cafcass officer to the stand, who has kindly managed to find time to attend this hearing today, to discuss her report findings. Thank you for coming, I appreciate it.'

Something else is happening deep within me, is this some sort of an inner cheer? Super thrilled, I feel a flutter in my chest, my heart leaps out of joy. Christina shares a delicate side look over her shoulders too, as she can sense my tiny joy of excitement and she reads my note in front of her; *the judge said Mummy, Daughter, OMG!* Christina responds with a gratified face expression, that means more than the world to me right now. I feel as if I could go out and conquer the world! My hard work to gather the most unusual evidence the court probably has ever received, paid off, it worked. The judge believes in me, and he is compassionate towards the time I have spent away from Tia. I cross my hands and place them on the edge of the table, straighten my posture and proudly continue listening to the judge, who is looking into his file again and he may be about to address the respondent on the opposite end.

'Hello, so it makes you Mummy Shona.'

I still refuse to look in the direction, but I do turn slightly towards the side, capturing the lawyer sitting in his dapper suit, right beside Shona. I can only see Shona's light hair poking out from behind his masculine build. Perfect blockage, as this way I can seem easy looking in that direction, purely out of respect but still avoiding direct eye contact with Shona. She is a reminder of all the past months of emotional turmoil, and the cause of my separation from Tia. The anger is traveling to the surface at high speed, as I look in her direction. How could she sit there, smiling, when all she has done is lie? Lie after lie, to make me look like an abuser and a stranger to Tia. Suddenly, I realise myself and straighten up in my chair, take an inner deep breath and refocus on the judge's speech again.

'I have also read through your response and every evidence you provided, in support of your claims against Vivien. So, to understand, you claim that you decided to have a child on your own, and met Vivien just recently, who spent some time with Tia which provided them an opportunity to get fond of each other. I am a little puzzled here, as the donor Gregory, who both parties agreed not to get involved with this case, confirmed that you and Vivien both agreed to have a child together. Looking at the witness statements from Vivien, and the Cafcass report, there is no evidence of abuse towards Tia and that is important in this case today. Whether abuse occurred on either side, or both, I will need to examine carefully and determine my conclusions. I will not require to meet with little Tia at any point in this case, although it would be an absolute pleasure as she sounds like such a lovely and smart child. I have sufficient evidence from the Cafcass team who interviewed all the parties separately. I can see Shona that you also disagree with the Cafcass report outcomes and suggest that I should not grant the shared care order to Vivien. As well as this, you believe that any changes at this stage would disturb Tia's wellbeing, as she seems well settled at school and has got used to a new daily routine without Vivien in her life. Again, if Vivien, as you claim, had not had such a deep input into Tia's life, why would that disturb her daily routine? Vivien has witness testimonies which do claim some aspects of controlling behaviour and reported Tia witnessing your abusive behaviour towards Vivien. Things here do not add up, and may need clarifying, but we will be going through that shortly and that is why we are here today. I can see no testimonies filed to support your claims that you are making here today. Thank you for coming.'

The judge smiled at Shona politely the whole time when he addressed her in his speech, the approach to us both is equally polite. However, I cannot stand the situation Shona has got me into and what I need to prove in the eyes of the law today to get my visibility to shine, but I wouldn't appreciate any bias from the judge to affect the hearing. Justice is what I am here for, and I seek it from someone who is objective and bases their ruling on pure evidence, without prejudice. I want to win fair and square, and this judge seems to be the perfect match, as he seems like a people person, experienced and knowledgeable in the field of family disputes. Yet, too early to say the least, the day ahead is long and will probably be dragged out to the next day, as there are many details for the judge to investigate before he can make a decision. He will need to rule an order that will be the best for little Tia and for her life ahead until the age of eighteen and beyond. As what Tia will experience in her early life will feed into her adult life. Tia, and children in general, need security – the feeling of safety with their needs met, love – the emotional support and the sense of stability, education and positive role models in life, and who is able to provide these for a child, is no doubt a parent that child needs to bring out the best in them and enable them to develop to best version of them as possible. May that parent be male or female, single or in partnership, biological or non-biological, regardless, children need their needs met beyond feeding and providing shelter. Their voices need to be heard and applied in their everyday life and their worries put at ease by a person whom they can trust and rely on for unconditional aid. The judge has a tremendous responsibility to not oversee these qualities in a parent, and that requires detailed analysis of every single piece of evidence as their decision equals a child's future life.

'Miss Counsellor, can your client's witnesses be ready to take the stand after a short ten-minute break?'

The judge speaks in a serious tone when addressing the lawyers, but again their exchanges are purely formal and related to sections of the law.

'Yes Sir, both witnesses are in the courthouse, ready to take the stand.'

Christina's voice also changes to more baritone when speaking to the judge, it is that invisible mutual ground of respect towards the person who represents the crown and the person who represents the client asking for justice from the law of the crown. The law has a power to define a person, to remove all they have ever had from them, and give individuals a sense of who they are. Without law, in my case, what would I do? Demand Tia from Shona and enter a lifelong battle, probably making Tia's life a misery? Honestly, however painfully long it has been, I am thankful to the law. Wishing for the law to act faster? Yes. Do I admire the thorough attention to safeguarding concerns and the well-being of a child? Yes. Christina leans towards me with a smile, and just confirms that the judge is about to leave and will be back in ten minutes and our witnesses will take the stand. I gently nod in response and ask her opinion on how the hearing has been going from her point of view.

'I think the judge is great, and you are in an immense position so far, and I cannot see that turning around. Fingers crossed! Are you all right? You seem beaming over your title of *mother* being acknowledged in the courtroom, and you have every right to be *Mummy Vivien'*

'Yes, oh my, I could not be happier, it has automatically lifted my anticipation Christina, I am speechless. Fingers crossed indeed!'

As I am turned towards Christina, from this angle I spot a disagreeing discussion between Shona and her lawyer, although, the distance muffles the words so I cannot understand the matter clearly. Something is about to go down. Shona's lawyer is unsteady, working hard to keep their discussion private. Shona is unhappy, shaking her head. Oh, she is looking in my direction. Jeez, there is a wave of fury travelling fast to my shores. I quickly turn back to face the judge. Shona's lawyer suddenly departs from their seated position and makes his way towards the judge's bench. It startles me for a second, and so does the hesitant look on my lawyer's face who is in that instance called to the judge's bench. Christina slowly walks over, and the two lawyers and the judge begin a discreet discussion that no one hears, as intended I guess. How much do I wish to be a fly on the wall right now, to hear what is being said, unnoticed. I am rather impatient now, but I remain steady in my seat, fidgeting with my pen that is my good luck pen from my sis. I was given this pen with the purpose to use it to sign something significant in my life, and today could not be a better day for that purpose as I am leaving this courthouse today with a signature. That's my tuned in attitude and I am not willing to change it. My knees, shaking, oh no, please stop. I need to practise some mindful breathing. Inhale and exhale, gentle motion, invisible on the surface to other. Phew, it is working. I grab my pen and gently begin to fiddle with it. Finally, Christina returns to our table and synchronously the bailiff announces *all rise,* and we all stand up as the judge leaves the courtroom. I am beyond baffled.

'What is happening, please do not tell me the hearing is postponed?'

My voice sounds in distress, my body filled with cortisol.

'Something incredible has just happened, come on, let's go to our private room and I will explain everything. Do not worry! Could you please say a huge thank you to Madison and Helen, but they will not be required to take the stand and can go home. Please tell them that you will soon follow up as you will get that opportunity in the meantime.'

What? My witnesses will not be called to the stand? It is not the same tone of a voice, when Gloria announced the postponing of the hearing back in August. Christina sounds at ease, uplifted, reassuring, but ambiguous. The latter is the way I currently feel. I reach for my phone, which has a display full of message and send a quick message to my lovely witnesses, that they will not be required to take the stand, so they can go home. I also added a massive thank you to my message, and that I cannot explain the reason of the cancellation just yet. My dearest friends, they must be so confused. I ought to add a sentence of reassurance, that the reasons are all positive, in my favour and the news couldn't be any better. I wish for them to feel appreciated and worry-free. I bet they had a nervous wait. None of them has even been to the court before, nor stood on a stand and interrogated. It's a relief not having to see my friends being treated in this way. However, both of my witnesses were confident with answers based on the truth. Regardless of this, both got tearful over the thought of having to look into Shona's eyes after the hurt she caused Tia and me. I am just glad that their role of a being a witness is ending here, in this very moment. The written testimonies fulfilled their purpose. As of now, I have no idea what is happening but apparently it is something incredible, so bring it on. My head feels like an overinflated balloon that is about to pop at any second. I quickly follow Christina to the private room, and she shuts the door behind us. We both take a seat, an action that keeps reoccurring today. Christina tosses her files to the side of the table and begins with a huge smug smile.

'So, your ex-partner withdrew all her accusations against you and that is the reason why the judge no longer needs the witnesses to take stand for further questioning as it was more about the abusive allegations as that questioned your suitability to take care of Tia. The judge has sufficient evidence from the written testimonies and because the abuse is no longer in the picture, he is putting it down as a malicious act which he did give credit for to Shona, for coming forward and telling the truth. Whether she has come to her senses in Tia's best interest or because of her lawyer's advice is unknown to us. What we shall celebrate is that you are already winning this case. Vivien today, could possibly be the only day we need to attend a hearing. If everything goes well, the judge shall announce his decision by the end of the day. Too early to confirm, but you can cheer a little in your heart for now. This is a remarkable moment. You ex-partner had a change of mind and that deletes all of her fabricated statements. You stand now, as a mother, who awaits a confirmation and decision from the judge about a shared care order.'

I sit back in my chair, cover my face with my hands, and let out the tears that were awaiting to flow from the exhilaration. Unable to control my emotions any longer, this is too good to be true! What a turn of events! My heart is certainly cheering, my mind is in a sudden shock. I lift my hand towards my upper arm and pinch myself. Yes, this is reality, not a dream, not an illusion. Omg, what a moment to already celebrate. Christina walks up gives me a big hug, reassuring me to take time to let it all out first. The overinflated balloon did indeed pop at the end and as a result confetti burst out all over the place in celebration.

'I am completely taken aback, that is all I can say. What made her change her mind after so many months of utter torture? If she didn't make up all the allegations against me, this hearing didn't even have to take place and I would have probably had Tia back after the first hearing. Shona could have saved Tia the emotional harm. Our detachment. The wait. The turmoil. The unknown. The heartache. It was unnecessary, just as I said at the very start. Lies cause pain to others but come to an end eventually.'

'I understand and I very much agree. When I read your statements, I immediately distinguished the truth form lies. Honestly, I felt your pain in between the lines. I am also a mother under this hard core lawyer and losing my children for such a long period of time, would destroy me. You are a strong woman, Vivien. You did it. Not me. You did, with your truth.

But we cannot change what already happened, let's embrace the change that is taking place now and focus on what needs to be done next. The judge will resume in an hour, he may need to retune his case approach after this abrupt change of circumstances. Let's take a coffee break and prepare for what is to come. It is highly possible that you may not be asked to take the stand, but if you do, just respond to all the questions in a clear and honest manner, as we initially planned.'

Christina seems relaxed, placing her metaphorical bat down to the ground and rolling up the sleeves of her blazer. Although our game is far from over, this turn of events has changed everything. Just one hour ago, I entered the courtroom, to defend myself from all the fabricated allegations and prove my innocence to the judge, with the help of my witnesses and my proficient barrister who was ready with her 'baseball' bat for the worst. Now, I am walking to get a cup of coffee and it feels like I am walking on floating clouds, passing the space effortlessly. Unbelievable, as what I had waited for the entire six months' time, is now here. It is now only a matter of what the judge will see as being suitable regarding the care for Tia and plans for the future. I must not get too buoyant, as what the judge is brewing in his chambers right now, remains unknown until we are asked to rise again. So, psst, conductor, calm that exciting orchestra awaiting a phenomenal performance. In the meantime, I allow myself to share my quiet excitement with my family and friends, including Helen and Madison, who are stars in my eyes, and always will be. I can imagine their faces upon reading my message, knowing my close peeps, tears will be shed. We are an affectionate bunch.

Sitting in the first row, clenching the soft teddy in my lap, refreshed after the hour break, ready to embrace what is to come. The judge has rounded up the recent events and asked the Cafcass officer to take the stand. This is an extraordinary moment, as apparently the officer can change direction from her report, if she finds that appropriate. So, I pluck up my nerves and draw all my attention to the stand where the officer is ready to respond to the questions coming from three different directions. The judge takes the first step and begins discussing the interview findings with the officer.

'What a smart four-and-a-half-year-old, she is clearly missing her Mummy Vivien as she made that very clear in her interview. The evidence shows no signs of child abuse and no concerns from Tia's teachers, from academic and social perspectives. That's great. What is the opinion regarding the abuse reported by Miss Vivien, is that of any worry into the future as a possible risk to Tia's wellbeing?'

I gasp a small amount of air like a fish left abruptly on dry land longing to return to the oxygenated water space, and look straight at the officer, who has been facing the judge the whole entire time. Interesting, that respect, towards that one person, whatever the professional's position. Every answer matters, as it seems to have a pronounced meaning to the judge, his agreement with the Cafcass officer is crucial as her advice goes hand in hand with my initial application to the court for the shared care order.

'No Sir, based on my findings, there was no sign of abuse when I thoroughly assessed Tia during the interview process a few weeks ago. I believe that physical abuse is not a threat to this child's wellbeing, but I would like to highlight that possible emotional abuse is evident in the way Tia was worried to speak out loud about Mummy Vivien. I shall advise the respondent Miss Shona, to refer to Miss Vivien in a more positive manner and create a positive environment in which Tia is able to share her feelings and emotions towards Miss Vivien. The same applies to Miss Vivien, although there is no evidence of her speaking of Miss Shona negatively in front of Tia.'

My little darling, she is certainly smart for her age, and no way would abuse have passed unseen, and I am relieved that she is safe. Terrified over the thought of how Tia will respond to me after such a long time of possibly having her whole life routine changed that hasn't involved me for six months and the possible further negative portrayal of me and my departure. What Tia has been told, she may have just believed as she had no other option but to adapt to those changes. I still believe that she has been waiting for me, right there in her little heart. Six months of lies can only temporarily overshadow a child's mind, at such a young age, but they cannot wipe out over fifty months of a bonded life spent together. The truth I carry will clear the dark shadows and Tia will hopefully settle back to the life she had before our detachment. I do wish to have been able to do more and do something sooner but the legal path was the only way to find my way back to my baby. Will she be able to understand my disappearance from her life and find peace in her innocent soul? I will continue keeping my promise and will not allow anyone to distance us from each other. Not again, not ever! One question remains, will I have her back in my life today? I bow to the coat of arms, pleading for the justice that stems from the monarch, to be granted to me so I can go and save my baby from her wrongful life.

'Thank you, Ms Nicole. Does your advice still stand, and you believe that this child will thrive from a shared care arrangement?'

'Yes, certainly, the claimant child is missing her other parent, in this case her other mother, and she needs her back in her life as soon as possible. The longer this separation is taking place, the longer this child will suffer. Ms Vivien can only positively impact this child and my observation confirms Ms Vivien's significance in this child's life.'

The judge nods his head, folding his delicate looking brown glasses in his hands simultaneously glancing in my direction, which seems in agreement to the officer's response, but it may just be an acceptance of her opinions and a polite acknowledgment. Such a neutral response is hard to analyse, but that just may be his motive. Misleading his crowd could potentially develop false hopes or cause misinterpreted excitement leading to unclear dissatisfaction. The judge looks up from his files and welcomes the opportunity for the respondent to raise any of their concerns regarding the Cafcass report outcome. The Cafcass report is in my favour, so we have not much to add at this stage but wait for Shona's lawyer's next action. If necessary, Christina will object to any unfair diversions targeted at the Cafcass officer that could change my position or threaten my shared care for Tia.

'My client, despite withdrawing all her accusations against Miss Vivien, still disagrees with the Cafcass advice for granting the shared care order. My client finds Miss Vivien unstable to have Tia in her care for any consequent time and suggests a couple of weekend days each month to be spent in Miss Vivien's care, and that shall be without overnight stays. My client is asking the Cafcass officer to reconsider their final decision.'

Oh, what a joy kill! What? Two days a month, and no

overnight stay? Absolutely no way, that is unacceptable. We cannot settle with such a suggestion, which is far from ideal for Tia and miles away from Cafcass' advice. I quickly scribble down for Christina *are we not going to object to their statement?* I get a quick response back, *do not worry, let the Cafcass officer respond first.* I return my gaze to the Cafcass officer and wait for her response.

'I stand by my advice to grant shared care order, as my assessment with little Tia and Miss Vivien, shows evidence of a strong bond and a relationship that Tia will only benefit from. I find Miss Vivien a suitable person to look after a child, she is loving and caring, and has been in Tia's life since her birth, which is evident in the depth of knowledge she holds about Tia into the smallest details, such as her favourite food, play times, toys, activities and what has convinced me the most is the knowledge of Tia as a character, including her behaviour traits. Miss Vivien was able to predict how Tia possibly entered her interview room, and her reaction to a stranger and her choice of items Tia would choose first to interact with, it matched Tia's actions on that day when I interviewed her. Tia, said herself, that Mummy Vivien is caring, fun, loving and she misses her, and I strongly believe that this relationship needs to resume as soon as possible in Tia's best interest. Sir, I have no concern over a matter of suitability. Thank you!'

Blimey, the officer nailed her response, she is not budging, and these strong grounds should be impressing the judge as well. The judge looks in our direction, the opposing team, to allow that space for additional comments. Christina did not have the need to object but waited for Cafcass to respond first. She knew, that the Cafcass officer will not change her mind based on her report and already confirmed facts to the judge. Christina acted respectfully, presenting confidence in our claim and the Cafcass findings. I like this smooth tactic, instead of immediately objecting to Shona's lawyer in response. Christina begins in a calm, assertive manner.

'My client initially applied for a shared care order, based on her life that she has shared with Tia as her parent, as a mother, since the day she was born. In fact, since the day of this child's conception. My client does not accept Miss Shona's suggestion of a two days per month visitation. My client has suggested the great pain of being separated from her daughter, as a possible revenge for breaking away from the relationship, but she believes that their child is being harmed in this ordeal and deserves to have her other mother back in her life. My client believes in a civil relationship with Miss Shona, as going forward and providing a steady positive co-parenting routine to support Tia's needs in her best interest. Thank you, Sir.'

The adamant tone in Christina's voice, showed the use of that baseball bat, her response echoed across the courtroom, and it certainly delivered my voice in a splendid fashion. She was me, not only spoke for me! I receive a confident squeeze to the side of my arm, and that has partly settled the flapping of the hundreds of butterflies in my stomach. I take a deep breath and exhale, quietly, just in my own space and turn towards the judge again, who is looking right at me and then taking a turn and looking to the opposite side at Shona. He removes his glasses and places them on the desk in front of him, takes a deep breath and rubs his eyes, before he puts his glasses back on. The judge excuses the Cafcass officer from the stand, who addresses the judge with a thank you sir and walks towards the back row, sharing a compassionate but brief smile at both, Shona and myself. To me that smile means everything. Whatever Shona feels from the same smile, I could not care less about. I return a grateful smile and eagerly await the judge's conclusion, as it does not seem like he will break again. I feel as if I could just shout out really loud *oh come on, please just tell us!*

After a short while of silence that seems like an eternity the judge finally clears his voice and begins to talk. Omg this is it. Decision time.

'Miss Vivien and Miss Shona, I have carefully considered both of your concerns and claims, and after examining the evidence from the Cafcass assessment and the witness statements, including Miss Vivien's detailed evidence in support of her relationship with the claimant child, Tia. I have made my decision.'

My heart is grabbing every beat intensely, my eyes wide open in expectation. This decision is going to determine my life beyond today. How could a mother possibly see her child only for a couple of days per month, without the opportunity to be able to tuck in her child for a good night's sleep and rise to the child's morning innocent self? Children are barely removed from their biological mother, unless the court finds evidence of risk of harm, to the child, neglect, substance use, but otherwise they will keep the child in their mother's care. Why should I as a mother be treated differently, just because I am not connected to my child with my flesh and blood? It is our hearts that bond us for life! Regardless of gender or sexual orientation, maternal instinct is either innate or the keen nurture for a child can be developed and maintained during the parenting experience. Even then, the attachment when a baby is born, does not always happen instantly, it can take days, weeks or months, but the continuous effort shall not be aborted. Babies are sensitive human beings from the very beginning of their existence in their mother's womb, and when they are born their social, emotional and cognitive development depends on that bond with their primary caregiver, whether the parent is the biological or non-biological mother, father or other form of a guardian. When Tia was born, her huge eyes looked at me and I instantly felt that bond with her. It was the most magical moment in my life, and my mothering instinct immediately kicked in, whether it was innate or triggered, makes no difference to me. Biology or non-biology did not matter. I became a mother who provided their child with every aspect of their needs, and that continues today and will never stop as the bond between a child and mother is for life. As children grow older, detaching socially from their primary caregivers, is a sign of healthy development, but that primary person will always be part of their life wherever they will go, whatever they will do, and this person will always be here to come home to, in good and in bad, that protection is for life. To focus on the authenticity of parenting, rather than on labelling, is how a person can become the greatest parent.

Impatiently, I shake my legs in a rhythm to soothe my nerves, as I feel absolutely flustered. The judge has a rather long way around announcing the decision he has made, and he seems relaxed while explaining and expanding on various sections that seem only clear to lawyers present in the courtroom. Christina's facial expression is deeply devoted to the judge's bench, occasionally nodding her head in agreement and making notes in her open file book. The names of the sections in law make no sense to me, or am I supposed to be reading these riddles to understand the judge's decision? Clearly not expected of a parent who is awaiting the decision of her life! Christina suddenly seems very excited when she registers a section read out by the judge and she quickly scribbles a note for me while this interesting law-jargon filled monologue seems to have no end, the note says *he is about to announce his decision.* I change my crossed over legs, straighten my posture and gaze right at the bench, where the judge is now removing his glasses ready to make a speech, looking in turn taking in both sides of the front row. Here we go!

'I believe that Miss Vivien is proven to be a wonderful parent is evidently a significant person in the claimant child's life. With respect, Miss Shona, I considered your objections, and I understand that you may not wish to have Miss Vivien in your child's life, but this child was born into this world to two parents. Your child can only benefit from all the love Miss Vivien has dearly gifted her since her birth.

'Therefore, I grant Miss Vivien with Shared Care Custody and Parental responsibility, which is an unusual combination in one very same order, but I could not have granted one or the other, without granting it as a joint order. I will be resuming this hearing at three o'clock, to allow plenty of time to orchestrate a parenting plan with the support of the Cafcass officer who has kindly offered to help. Thank you everyone and see you back in the courtroom shortly.'

All rise, the bailiff announces, and we all watch the judge leave the courtroom, politely smiling at everyone equally in response.

What has just happened? I cannot believe what has just happened! Am I just imagining this moment or is this real? I pinch myself, and hard this time. The pain sinks right away into my arm. No, this is very real. I won! I won! I won! I am in absolute shock, in response I excitedly grab Christina's arm with the biggest grin on my face and I whisper as quietly as I can with an eek in my voice.

'What, I was told that I will need to apply for Parental responsibility if today's hearing is successful. Omg! This means I have it all, all that I needed. We did it, I won the case and have Parental responsibility! That means I have an equal right as a mother and time spent with Tia. This is a ground breaking moment. I cannot believe this Christina. Thank you, thank you so much!'

Fireworks enter my bloodstream, and I feel my body elevating in celebration. All I wish to do is hug everyone who made this happen for me and run as fast as I can through the streets of London, all the way to Tia. I want to stroke her little face, cover her in kisses and hug her tight with all my mighty heart and assure her that no one will ever be able to take her away from me, ever again. I want to lift her up high in the air and swing her around in joy, to hear her excited screams. I cannot wait to share this ground-breaking news with her. I cannot wait to see my baby girl! Oh, my heart that is nothing like a shrunk prune anymore, is beating out or rhythm from happiness and my chest is about to explode from the inner satisfaction. It is all over, no more court, no more wait, and no more agony! I survived the worst time in my life, but what I have done has made me stronger as a person and stronger as a mother for my baby girl, who needs me now, more than ever before. We have plenty of catching up to do, but we have all the time in the world, without any threats and troubles. I feel a euphoric sense of freedom! There is justice in today's world, and I was given a chance, the true mother has spoken, and her voice has been heard out loud by The Royal Court of Arms. Today will become history not only in our family, but in the history of the family court.

# Chapter 19

## Super Trouper

'Determination can conquer all the obstacles.'

This triumphant achievement will remain with me forever. Finding it impossible to contain my excitement, I have this incredible urge to dance to this victorious beat from within me. Why would I want to tame my excitement, when I want to pop a celebratory champagne bottle, shake it madly and spray it all over everyone around me whilst dancing all the way to my baby girl. Swooping her into my arms, and together embracing this cheerful melody that will forever play into our ears. Nothing can compare to this very experience. I love my life, and I love the person I have become, but I have insanely missed my mothering responsibilities and being a mother is part of the person who I am. I love being a mother, and without my sweetheart, a huge part of me has been deserted and only the love and hope kept that empty space alive. I always proudly carried my mother badge, but I never had to justify myself to anyone, nor was I ever questioned. When you introduce yourself to someone as the mother of the child you are with, unless for official reasons, no one has the right to investigate whether you are biologically connected to that child. To speak of the nature of motherhood has never been a problem, to tell my non-biological tale has always been an absolute pleasure. I am proud to be a mother to my child and have devoted my life to this responsibility. Whoever thinks otherwise can honestly speak their mind, but I will respectfully stand my ground. Not everyone will ever understand your life choices, but it is your unique life and so your choices will simultaneously be unique too. Carrying a child and to be biologically connected to your child, does not make an amazing parent, 'other' mothers, fathers and guardians out there, are not less worthy of the title. I have come across comments, such as *Oh so you didn't carry* or *I see so you are the second parent then* or *Do you feel like the third wheel or Are you a family?* These were comments from absolute strangers, and however surprising these may have been, I found a crack of an open opportunity to educate and raise awareness in the minds of those who may not comprehend such arrangements in the world. The fight for equality is a constant mission. The fight for LGBTQIA+ equality is not history just yet, as the society we live in still struggles, in some places, to accept the community and additionally, families or relationship arrangements that stand out from the stereotype. Who we are, how we look, who we choose to love or how we decide to settle down and start a family should never lead to discrimination. LGBTQIA+ communities are collectively establishing alliances and promoting pride worldwide. Pride occurs in the form of a carnival or march, whatever the event, it promotes a moment for LGBTQIA+ communities to celebrate and show that they are out and proud to be who they are. In some countries pride is banned, but where it is permitted to take place, the celebration on the streets is spectacular. Personally, the vibe during pride is phenomenal, all communities, celebrating as one, people hugging and dancing, regardless of race, gender, sexual orientation. Sadly, in many countries, LGBTQIA+ communities do not receive legal protection and experience a great level of hostility, but on the other hand almost fifty countries, worldwide recognise homophobia as a type of hate crime, with almost thirty countries having same-sex marriage legalised. Yet still many countries need convincing, the change is slowly adapting into the modern society. To live by the established norms, is no longer the norm. There is no *normal* out there, people are waking up to the new wave of freedom, choosing to live however they wish. I am respectful towards everyone's own choice, as long as it makes them happy and does not bring harm to others, and I accept nothing else from anyone else in return. Respect, not necessarily agreement, but respect. Don't point, don't stare, don't criticise, and if you don't like what you see, turn away and mind your own world. So, to answer those unexpected questions, it has every time taken a great effort of resilience, to handle them without feeling offended or coming across as defensive. It is best to manage these situations respectfully, allowing space for knowledge building and indirectly diverting the conversation to another topic. This approach has proven to work well for me, as I retained the conversation and could proudly face the person again if I had to. I stand up for my rights and proudly present myself in the world.

Christina enters the room, and finally we can share a professional, but triumphant hug. Her excitement is just as visible as mine, and her ecstatic joy for me is out of this world.

'Vivien, you have everything you came to the court to ask for today, and more. I have not experienced two orders to be announced by a judge in a single hearing. I was prepared to suggest for the Parental responsibility as a follow up hearing after the judge's decision, but there was no need. Oh Vivien, I am so happy for you. What an incredible mother you are! What a moment for a celebratory drink, but we have some work to do so best to grab some coffee and lunch, then we shall begin planning with a Cafcass officer, who will be meeting us in half an hour.'

Perfect, coffee sounds amazing, a large one is what we need after the morning we had. I ping a concise message to everyone *I won*! Everyone in my court support bubble must have been sitting on pins and needles and impatiently awaiting every inch of the news. Gloria will be ecstatic, once she finds out about the verdict! Coming across this incredibly experienced lawyer was a true blessing, she had a vision from the very start, and I have trusted her every step of the way. I was promised to have my daughter back, but warned about the possible wait, that right now does no longer matter. The months of waiting have vanished, when I look back, I see light instead of darkness and it seems as if I have only just seen Tia the other day, what a miraculous mind twist. I lift my jacket off the chair, but pause for a thought, and follow an inner instinct that wishes to find out whether the judge could change his mind about his order.

Apparently, the judge handed down his judgments and announced his final order, even if that is not yet sealed by the court, the judge will not change his decision. Unless, in the worst circumstances, the decision is appealed by those unhappy about his final order, in this case it would be Shona. However, the order is effective from the moment the judge announces his judgement and will not change unless the appeal is accepted on some strong grounds and assessed by more senior judges. Yet, the appeal process can take months and the outcome may just not justify the applicant. Christina is reassuring me that today's events, in which the respondent – Shona – withdrew her allegations that she strongly stuck to for months, her appealing against the judge's decision is not out of the question, but improbable. The latter is the one that will remain with me, and continue in the back of my mind during my celebration. As for now, nothing can take away my victory, and apparently my daughter will be reunited with me in a matter of days. As I lift my water bottle from its place on a newspaper, I notice a smudged ink mark in front of me, shaped as a heart, but ever so beautifully as if it was a piece of art. My guardians, who have not left my side, filled my journey with enlightening warmth and positive vibes. Their frequency has risen in the past few weeks nearing the court date. I wonder whether they will decrease or disappear as a result of my completed harrowing journey. I wish deeply for their appearance to never end. Satisfied with Christina's summary, I throw a brave smile across my face, and allow confidence to fill my steps as I cross the corridors, no longer filled with the buzz of people. The whole building seems to have quietened down, but our judge that holds the torch lit up, determined to complete his order and reunite two aching hearts before the sun sets on this glorious day.

It is time to get into the swing of things! Planning a 50/50 arrangement that has equal day and nights for both parents, requires considerable analysis. Concurrently, both lawyers and Nicole will need to liaise between the two rooms where each parent resides, as given the circumstances, we cannot possibly be in one place together. I cannot yet describe how I feel towards Shona, as upset and enraged are descriptions that barely reach the hilt of how I feel. To choose rage as an exit towards a personal failure, is not brave, but sad. To cause pain to an innocent heart is despicable. To make someone meaningful invisible to gain power, is revolting. Such people have no place in my world. My mind is now preoccupied about what matters to me after this dreadful torment, and that is to get my daughter in my care, and close my eyes to the negative past and approach the person who I would rather avoid, with a simple acknowledgement, nothing more. As a parent, I have an obligation to role model positive behaviour and kindness, and demonstrate that two people can be civil to one another, despite the past. Continuous bickering beyond separation in front of children can cause further harm, and they have emotions to deal with that may not even be visible at the early stages of parental separation. Children sense the way parents feel already, and the best is to avoid disagreement in their company. Providing loving support and encouragement is what they may need the most, however hard it can be, separated parents must step up beyond selfishness and view their interactions as a friendly encounter however pretend it may have to be. What will matter to the child thereafter, is the quality time spent with each parent, an important factor that will determine the wellbeing of the children involved. Reconnecting with children after the separation is an important phase, as their whole life they have known, turns upside down and they require time to adapt to these changes and find a way to positively carry on. Therefore, I explained to Christina that I only want a plan that is best for Tia and her happiness going forward, with a formal and minimal contact with Shona involved. I am taking slow sips from my very large cup of coffee, as I retain my attention at the spreadsheet opened up on Christina's laptop, and share a *ready, let's do this* look with the Cafcass officer, who looks eager to begin. To figure out an equal plan that is 50/50 is going to be a puzzling experience, as the weekly rotation needs to be considered equal weekdays and weekends. Academically supporting Tia regarding homework, and having that input in her learning, is just as important as the fun family weekends together. Tia has developed from a tiny baby into an incredible, almost five-year-old. I have been part of every single milestone and I am not ever leaving out any aspect of her development because of the separation. Full-time business employment that permitted me to have Tia close by daily, following her development closely and having an input into guidance as well as teaching her the vital foundation skills for the best life ahead of her, will forever be treasured in my mothering process.

There is no right or wrong in parenting, each child is a beautiful unique gift and how to parent them, a book may offer guidance, and that will be the start, but the child will show you the magical path that satisfies their needs. It can be a stressful experience, but what may take the pressure away from the positive focus is parents listening to the society, rather than their child. That is when the difficulties kick in, as doubtfulness questions the competence, and the child is the one to suffer. Tune in to your child, look into their eyes when they talk to you, don't just hear them but listen to them and find the time to take part in their world through the way they see it. To see the world with the children's eyes, is not ever going to be entirely possible, as to understand what their views and opinions can be closest translated only through the child's voice. To misinterpret or misunderstand their intentions, to satisfy these expectations, may lead to a confused journey in which the child could smile on the outside, but cry on the inside. Living up to a parent's expectations can be a mentally exhausting journey for a child, and a great distraction from focusing on self-growth. Not to worry over the word *no*, that has become so sceptical in the parenting world in the past years, it does not need to be portrayed negatively, but applied clearly, without guilt or to rather avoid anger outbursts, otherwise the child may struggle understanding and accepting boundaries. Simply to explain the why nots, avoiding negotiations and giving in, shall lead to an enjoyable parenting experience. Make a mistake? To become a parent takes no training for what is to come in real life, but role modelling the apologising approach and learning from the mistakes with the ability to reflect on them, may just teach that magical trial and error practice to the child. The special ingredient in parenting is sharing memories and building new ones! Telling tales of a parent's childhood is the best story to tell, as the child will listen with enthusiasm, appreciation and a sense of pride. A child is a social construction, vacuuming everything they see and hear and applying it to their world, even if unaware of the process. Every experience builds towards developing identity and character. Be part of that growth, witness the transformation and watch those wings take off in directions the child desires! I have been part of that growth, and wish to observe every fraction of Tia's transformation until the very moment when she is ready to spread her wings and fly high above all the expectations, above the crowd and shine brighter than the sunlight. If her wings ever break and need a place to repair, my heart will always be a place where she can rest at peace.

I have been fiddling with my pen once again, and trying to draw up some of my ideas on a piece of paper. I am a bit old school when it comes to brainstorming as the sensation of the pen touching the paper resembles the drawing actions and enables the relaxing mode in my system and delivers creative ideas to mind. Unsatisfyingly I stare at the timeline I drew, showing the seven days of the week, with various arrows pointing in different directions. Nothing makes sense! We feel completely befuddled! Nicole has so far managed to offer days in the week and days in the weekends spent with each parent based on weekly rotations. However, after a short realisation, we notice a glitch, as to how would the weekend parent then pass on the turn and begin the weekday's rotation that would only mean that the weekend parent would continue to the week. No, this is not going to work. Equal amount of fun and responsibilities. Neither one nor the other parent should settle for anything because Tia needs a well-balanced routine with both parents. I wish the bottom of my coffee cup said *want some more?* Rather enthusiastic flashes pass through me, but stop at a dead end, and that makes me feel a little blue as we have such little time left and no sturdy plan to put in front of the judge, in just over an hour's time. Then out of nowhere, Christina shoots up from her seated space like a thunderbolt. Flicks her hair swiftly to the side of her face and exclaims:

'I got it, why not look at the amount of sleeps and rotate these on a weekly basis?' Looking at Christina's spreadsheet rolling rota, that is impressively colour coordinated, it makes sense. Bingo, we hit the jackpot! Nicole gives me a huge smile and rubs my arm gently, indicating that we are finally moving in the correct direction, looking at the time, all three of us group up towards the screen. Nicole adds her professional input into the planning process.

'Tia's young age relies on a consequent fixed routine that will help her to settle into the shared home lifestyle. Additionally, a continuous uninterrupted routine provides security and a firm sense of belonging in each of her homes. Because of her age, I can only suggest to the judge a maximum of four sleeps to be away from each parent, as anything less or more may cause potential separation issues for little Tia. Although she is such a smart child, we must assure she has the best plan that supports her long-term wellbeing. Mummy, are you happy with the four nights sleep routine?'

I do not want to seem difficult, but I cannot seem to be able to hide my slight disappointment over the fact, and there is literally no other choice for an equal routine rotation, that there will always be two weekends in each month that I will not see Tia. On a more positive outlook, annually the shared care order will become even. This plan will work and I just need to accept that.

'It sounds incredible, and I am happy with this arrangement to go ahead, but I will miss Tia when the weekends don't fall in my hands! Currently any time without Tia, is horrifyingly unimaginable, but I believe in the routine eventually settling my detachment anxieties.'

Nicole looks compassionate, as she must see many emotions that parents present in her custodial cases.

'I understand Vivien, I do but look at Tia's whole life ahead as a routine, instead of a single month. When you picture a whole year ahead for instance, you will have an absolute equal share of Tia. There is no other way to do this, unless one or the other parent agrees taking on only weekdays and other only weekends. In my experience, some fathers or in fact some mothers, have opted for the weekends only, starting with the Friday afternoon. Would you like to have this option open and see what Shona thinks of both arrangement suggestions and also see what their party has orchestrated as I will be going over to their room in a few minutes, we don't have much time left. There is no pressure, but if we do not impress the judge with an agreed shared care plan, he will postpone the hearing to the next day. That will be costly for you, just to hire your lawyers for the planning hearing and sealing the court order.'

The whole custodial process has already cost me tens of thousands of pounds, which has affected my bank balance but has not bothered me, as I would have given everything I possess to get Tia back in my life and obtain my legal visibility in the eyes of the law. However, it doesn't need to get any more costly, if there is only one thing to do now and that's the shared care plan. I am pleased to have this amazing team around who keep me motivated and focused on the tiniest detail. I feel in good hands, of caring professionals who view me as a mother, parent and a person who has worked hard towards affording such a costly court hearing process. I can only be grateful! It is disheartening that my savings could have been donated towards other memories spent with Tia rather than a court battle. An act that was not only unnecessarily hurtful to Tia, but also futile in a way as eventually Shona withdrew all the fabricated allegations against me. Why do I get a feeling of maliciousness behind this all? By all means, Shona may have concluded after the Cafcass report and the witness testimonies that the truth would have come for her. Why wait for the actual hearing date and prolong the separation, causing pain and suffering? What really disturbs my mind over and over again, is how Shona could deny my significance in Tia's life, just out of spite! I had spent every day and night with our child since the day of her birth and dedicated my time, effort, character, skills and knowledge to support her. What shocks me the most is how one can turn the story around, smudging mud all over someone's face to make them seem dirty, while being empowered by their biological label. It is an utter shame that it had to come to this, as everything could have been avoided and Tia didn't have to be affected by this ordeal. It is too late, what's done is done. I have kept myself away from these disconcerting thoughts, and it has served me well indeed. I am here today, with proven visibility and with pride that reaches out to the highest of heights as I have conquered the greatest battle of my life. I had perpetual dreams, night after night, where Tia disappeared from my sight, and I would be running around looking for her, that panicking, that emotional torture in the dream resembled the living truth. However, I would find Tia in places such as play areas or her bedroom, looking happy and content, and I would awake with a feeling of relief. Although, often, I would wake up panicking, calling her name and checking whether she was in her bed, only to discover that she was not there and the harshness of the dreams resembled the cruel reality. When I searched about the dreams, in fact answers confirmed that it is not something that will happen in reality but more likely offers a confirmation of how much love I feel for my child. Also, the meaning of these dreams indicates whether something is lost in real life, it is missed and the lack of control in life. The meaning did match the reality, but not for too long, as I hope for those dreams to settle too. When I think about dreams not meaning that I would lose my child in real life, is a little untrue. I have lost Tia indeed, but when she was in my care, I had never ever taken my eyes off her. Although the dream does not stand as a prediction to the future, it certainly can cause short term anxiety in any parent experiencing such a dream.

Nicole has spent the past half an hour in the other private room where Shona resides with her lawyer, but is now back to share the outcomes. She seems flustered, so the news may not be the best. She sits down, on the edge of the chair, with her hands between her thighs, a body language that demonstrates a departure shortly again.

'So, Vivien, please do not be alarmed, as this is very common in custodial cases, especially in a case where one parent is against the other. Shona disagrees with the 50/50 custody of Tia, and she is still fighting for the right that she shall have majority of the care and offer some arranged weekdays or weekends to you. What we can do is to stick with the two ideal plans you have created and the ideal plan that she sees right for the plan, and let the judge decide the most suitable option. I, as the Cafcass officer allocated to this case, will continue in supporting the equal 50/50 shared care for Tia. Not to be mistaken for taking any sides, I am simply a mediator who agrees in what is the best for the child involved. Additionally, one more detail needs to be added to your plan, and that is the time of something called as the handover, on each day when Tia will be due to change homes – my suggestion is somewhere after lunch time. In respect to the handover, it is also important to state that the parent should always take the child back to the other, rather than having the child collected. This affects the handover process because the child views it, as the parent is removing them from the other parent, so it can get distressing for Tia.'

'Okay, disagreeable, yet still. Thank you! Christina and I both agree with either of the two plans, but I strongly prefer the four sleep rotation and therefore we shall stick to one plan as a suggestion to put forward to the judge. In my opinion, the 1 p.m. handover sounds reasonable, so each parent gets to have lunch with Tia and carry out the handover thereafter. Sharing food is a comforting experience and it may provide a sense of calmness to little Tia. What do you think of that Nicole?'

'That sounds doable! Fantastic, we are ready for the judge, just in time. See you in the courtroom and best of luck.'

Shona is standing her ground, despite removing allegations, she may not want to let Tia be in my care for the same time length as in her care. Is it some kind of a biological entitlement issue? Clearly she may have not viewed me as the equal parent in this family arrangement. If we view the family arrangement and the reality of its functioning, then I would get one hundred percent care of Tia, as responsibilities did not share out to each parent equally before when the family was united. I had the biggest part in working, taking care of Tia and the household, so the custody arrangement, based on the past, should put me in the majority of days group not otherwise. I am in no position to fight for the majority of the days, as there is no evidence of threat on Tia from her biological mother so she is in lead. The biological title has advantaged Shona, even if that was in a negative projection, but I hope the judge will not agree with Tia living with her for the majority of the time.

The judge is sitting behind his bench ready to seal the deal, without his glasses on, indicating that he is ready to listen. I wish for this last part to be over swiftly, so I can see Tia as soon as possible. Bring on the finale! Christina is offered to speak first, so she repeats the shared care arrangement to the judge, along with an explanation of how it will benefit Tia and the importance of the arrangement is in Tia's best interest. The judge looks pleasantly taken and adds,

'Four nights sleep routine rotation is not yet heard of in my family custodial trials, but I must admit, it does sound appealing. Over to Miss Shona, do you agree with this plan?'

Shona's lawyer seems exhausted and frustrated to be pushing a very much unrealistic version of a shared care arrangement, but hesitantly with a deep exhale begins

'My client does not agree with the 50/50 share of her daughter Tia, and wishes to propose a plan that allows Tia to spend two consecutive days a week such as Tuesday and Wednesday and every Saturday of the weekend with Miss Vivien.'

The judge yet again shares a similar facial expression, thanks everyone for working hard to get a plan together in such a short time and shows appreciation to the Cafcass officer, who has dedicated over-time to help with the planning. He then asks the Cafcass officer for her final advice on the shared care suggestions from the two parties.

'Thank you, Sir, I have carefully considered and examined both shared care plans and I only primarily stand by what I found the most appropriate for Tia and what best supports her settling back into Miss Vivien's care. Given the importance of both parents in Tia's life, and avoiding unequal weighting of their responsibility to meet Tia's needs, I favour the 50/50 shared care arrangement with 1pm handover from one parent to the other.'

I am the one now sitting on pins and needles. The judge shares a look in both directions and places his glasses on and dips his hand into the files in front of him. Licking his fingertips and turning pages, seeming to seek something relatable that could help his decision making. What is he looking for? Then as fast as my thought is over, he removes his glasses, leans on his forearms onto the table and pulls himself up on his seat behind the bench.

'Thank you for your patience! I have already recognised Miss Vivien's significance in Tia's life, and I acknowledged the importance of the biological mother's part in Tia's life also. Therefore I believe that a 50/50 shared care of their child Tia will be the best for Tia's wellbeing and her happiness, as she needs both parents in her life, and both parents will individually have the opportunity to spend an equal time with Tia with the shared care order to commence from one p.m. Wednesday 6 December and will be in place until Tia's 18th birthday. Place and settling to be discussed within a parenting plan, which should be filed to the court no later than eight weeks from today's hearing date. I do wish my sincere best of luck to both parents, and a happy new start to little Tia with both of her mothers. The court is now out of session.'

We all stand up in respect to the judge's exit and sit back in our seats. I couldn't be happier than I am right now! There is nothing quite like this gracious feeling of victory, the dopamine is increasingly fuelling my body making me feel as if I have conquered the world. I am rewarded with the ultimate outcome that is far greater than what I expected it to be. I have my baby girl back, now and until the end of time! I am going home with a 50/50 shared care order in my hand and with the parental responsibility that means by law that I have all the same rights, responsibilities, duties and authority for Tia as her biological parent. Relating to the future ahead, simply Shona will not be able to make any decisions without me, and will never be able to not return Tia back into my arms. The true mother has gained her legal visibility and defeated the non-biological mother prejudice. I believed I could, so I did!

# Chapter 20

## The Alignment

*'Sunshine is not a source of happiness, learn to smile in the rain.'*

I shake Christina's hand, with respect, glory and pride! What a successful and talented woman, whom I feel extremely privileged to have connected with. She may have not needed her baseball bat, but she absolutely smashed it in that courtroom and secured me not only the reunion with my daughter, but got the best shared care arrangement. This arrangement will not only allow me to share the same amount of time with Tia as Shona, but make me an equally same parent, no matter the biology. Legally I will be added to the birth certificate, something that has been long overdue and my name will appear in relation to Tia, as a parent without Shona being able to make any changes. Parental responsibility is the golden cherry on the cake that surprised not only me but Christina as well. That was initially the plan to apply for in due course, following today's hearing, but the judge found my suitability to carry such a title already during the hearing, and granted it to me as part of the shared care order. He even stated that it is something unusual that has never happened in his courtroom, but he was confident that I deserve it, and as

Christina confirmed due to the unordinary ruling, that the judge trusted my story, and could see the malicious intentions of the biological mother post separation that caused suffering to a young child and granting me the parental responsibility in a way sealed the protection to Tia, as she will not be removed from me against my will, as that will be against the law and breaching the court order. Any individual that deliberately breaches a court order in the UK, which makes contempt of the court an exercise of crime and sanctions could include fines or even temporary imprisonment. The court order will always be our saviour, our shield from harmful acts. We will be free to live our lives at peace, uninterrupted.

 I suddenly move from the handshake into an exciting hug, and thank Christina for everything she has done for Tia and I. I will be eternally grateful! Exhilaration fills every single cell in my body as I exit the courthouse. Unaware of the world around me, I throw my arms in the air and let the beat of my voice out loud. I *won, I won*! Careless of who hears or not, the busy streets of London are used to the dynamics of its diverse population. Who to call first? I am way too elevated to even think straight, to be able to focus on my phone. Besides, the rain is heavily washing my phone display so I put my phone away for now and spin around in the rain, letting it wash through my hair, lifting my face directly into the downpour. Currently, I define myself as a pluviophile – a person in love with the rain, as the joy and happiness surrounding me would make a storm feel like a sunny resort. My suppressed energies from various diverted emotions of my harrowing journey are being released into the great grey skies and washed away by the rain. I feel reborn, cleansed and ready to take on my new role as the visible *true mother*, whose aching heart will soon be repaired by the warm presence of her truly loved child. Life can get us sometimes, and we can never be prepared for what can truly come but to not give in is the only way to find out what awaits in our story. Got to keep on the fight with courage until there is a light showing you the way towards new chances and opportunities. Otherwise life can fly past and may just seem meaningless, unhappy and full of sorrow. Live, give the chance of everything there is in ones' life! I am dancing to the sound of every rain drop as every drop has a rhythm and I can feel them. Today is my triumphant day, everyone, hear my screams, follow my dancing steps, this is the happiest you will ever see this person be!

Completely drenched, but the adrenaline still bubbles through my bloodstream and I have successfully made it to the underground station. The same underground station has the famous doughnut shop right opposite, the reminder of the day when I lost the battle and was not reunited with Tia. The heart aching news that crushed me to pieces as my hopes were dissatisfied and the next months of waiting were ahead of me. Indeed, I converted the disheartened event into the fact that I was recognised as a parent, legally in the eyes of the law, and I had to prove my mothering relationship to Tia by being interviewed with Cafcass to determine my relationship with Tia. The wait beyond the first hearing was excruciating but I had new hopes to fight towards and I did not give up, however hard it was. Now it does not matter, not one bit, my baby girl will be in my arms as early as tomorrow, and we will continue where we left off. The green man indicates the safe crossing, and I walk over to get two doughnuts, for tomorrow as it will be a special victorious treat, symbolising perseverance, determination and courage. Tia will get the doughnut with the colourful sprinkles topping, Tia's ultimate favourite and the other donut with caramel glazing, mine. Tia may not exactly know just yet what this significant day means, but with time and age she will learn to understand everything. As of now, she will celebrate with me, as she will certainly gather the fact that she has not seen me for a long while. How long has that meant in her comprehension is difficult to predict, the reunion day will begin a new chapter in our lives and close the door on our agonising experience. The new chapter will forever be the evidence of our story, which will lock in the story of the love and truth that had defeated the wicked. I run across the road in between the heavy traffic, back to the underground station and head over to the tube line, that is not homebound, but to my sister's who is waiting enthusiastically for the news. Hardly much of a wait, I jump on to the train, take a seat and hold on to Tia's soft teddy, really tight, and close my eyes. I feel way too restless to be enclosed in the underground, wishing to be out there, flapping my wings like a wild bird soaring into the high skies. Feeling way too customary, sat in between people looking tired and bored, reading newspapers, listening to music through their headphones or sleeping with heads dropped into their chest, their day may be just an ordinary one. Today is not an ordinary day, today deserves everything but the customary.

 Sis opens the door and jumps at me, with her bear hug, nearly plummeting me to the ground. Charlie, hearing my voice, runs straight at me, landing right in my arms grinning from happiness. He has no idea, but my excitement is contagious and everyone coming my way, will just join the beat. On another note, my little nephew doesn't need much of a trigger to get absolutely bonkers but what more would I ask for, that is perfect and even more so than on a usual day. Today, he is celebrating Tia coming back in our lives and today is the day when I can start answering all the curious little voices of those who have missed Tia, but had no comprehension of the reasons for her sudden disappearance.

'Is Tia here with you Vivien?'

'Charlie, not today, but she is coming tomorrow, just one more day.'

My heart is beaming with pleasure, he looks at me with an investigative expression trying to count two on his fingers and says, 'Tomorrow is too far away, I was waiting since yesterday for Tia to come and play?'

Bless him, that just gives me the giggles, he is clearly not aware of the days that have passed since her disappearance. That fills me with such a relief, as Charlie is like a brother to Tia. What if Tia was just Charlie's age – three and a half years old – would she view our separation so bluntly, thinking I had just gone away for work or to see our family for a few days? Tia will be the only one able to comment on my mind wandering thoughts, and she may tell me more than I am expecting to find out.

Sis has a chilled champagne in the cooler bucket, right in the middle of her living room coffee table, surrounded by delicious meze style dishes and snacks that will last hours. Fabulous, just what I need as I am ravenous. Scanning the amount of food, is a sign that Sis indeed wants me to share every single detail, and she knows with food I will be seated for a while without any distractions. Charlie comes off my arms, after a humongous cuddle, and grabs a handful of pretzels and runs after his daddy, to play outside in the rainy puddles. Great, I can share every detail without being too aware of Charlie listening. Sis passes the champagne bottle to me, to give me the honour to open it to mark my successful hearing today. The champagne pops, and the liquid bubbles pour out from the neck of the bottle. I quickly reach for the first glass and begin pouring, then repeat for the other two glasses. David runs in and with a massive grin reaches for his glass and we raise our glasses and toast to my reunion with Tia. I fill my plate with vine leaves, pork meatballs, flatbread and spoon some dips next to the mountain of food, and begin to talk. I try to capture the event as realistically as possible, and with my dramatic input, it is portrayed as meaningfully as it happened. My sis is just amazed by the true nature of the judge as we all were, and is grateful for his knowledge and skills to recognise honesty from the lies. If it would have been a different judge, we may have had to fight much harder. I'm deep in the middle of my discussion with Sis, when my phone rings. It's Gloria! She was in court all day, representing a different client, and told me yesterday that once she is out of the court, she will call me. I did at least text her that I won, so she must be over the moon right now, and cannot wait to hear more, although probably she has an email of the hearing summary already pinged over to her from Christina. I press the incoming call icon and I am prepared to launch a tsunami of excitement over the phone to Gloria.

'Hello Vivien, sorry for the late response, but I got stuck at the court, but I have managed to catch up with your case as Christina has already sent over the hearing summary and the temporary shared care order. We will receive the sealed document directly from the court, in the next few days. How are you feeling?'

Gloria sounds astounded, as what she promised, she has

delivered. At the very start, she did clearly say that she can make it happen, and I will have Tia back, and she asked me whether I trust her. Trust was the least of my abilities, but I had a good gut feeling about this lawyer. I listened to every single piece of advice, and I pushed myself away from actions that could have jeopardised my case. As from my heart I wanted to go and knock on Shona's door every day, appearing at the school gates if I could until she answered and explained herself. Barely able to handle the circumstances, I wanted answers, as what I recalled was that we had baby Tia together. I wanted to demand to see my daughter, and tell her that she had no right to take her away from me. I wanted to see Tia, and I would have done whatever it took! If I had done what my heart desired, I would have sacrificed today's victory. All thanks to Gloria, she had a clear vision of how to get my Tia back, and did indeed warn me about the possible time length, given my, at that time legal invisibility as a mother, including no birth certificate, parental responsibility or the original signed donor agreement. I had nothing, but my story. Gloria believed my story, and however strenuous it has been for the whole entire six months, I followed every single direction. There was mutual trust, and I had no doubts, not once! Grateful, for my intuition, as I am here today, and I won the almost impossible! Undeniably, the best day in thirty-seven years of my life!

'Hi Gloria, I appreciate your call anytime in the day, no problem. I am ecstatic! I was literally dancing in the rain after the hearing! The judge was amazing and so was Christina. You were right about her, she had such a unique approach towards everything, that Shona's lawyer had no chance for objections. The shared care plan, based on sleeps rather than particular days in the week, was also her idea. The Cafcass officer was just phenomenal, she really did agree with most of our suggestions, and not because she took sides, but she found them to be the best for Tia's happiness and safety going forward. Gloria, thank you very much, I am sending you a huge virtual hug, and I hope to see you in the next few days for our last meeting!'

'Of course, we can meet on Friday and make it a lunch meeting, to celebrate. There is also an email from Shona's lawyer, suggesting a time and place where Shona will bring Tia tomorrow. I will send the email to you after our chat. You will be meeting Tia, on your own without Shona's supervision, and you can spend a couple of hours together as directed by the judge. Given the six months she has spent apart from you, a settling period needs to apply. Okay? The rest of the settling-in routine is explained in the email and the settling plan is drawn up by the Cafcass officer. Let me know if there is anything you may disagree with, otherwise I will confirm your agreement back to Shona's lawyer. This needs to be confirmed before 1 p.m. tomorrow, so I suggest you do this as soon as possible. I wouldn't like to take up much of your time, as I bet you have got lots of celebrating to do with your family. I am extremely happy for you and your daughter, and best of luck tomorrow, have an amazing time together. You both deserve each other! See you on Friday, Vivien, and if there is anything, please email me or call me if it is urgent.'

I take a big sip from my champagne glass and apologise to Sis as I need to read the email Gloria has sent over. Sis has been patiently listening on the side. Somewhat of a *déjà vu*, as the scenario was similar, when Gloria called me late in the evening to discuss my enquiry in the very beginning, my sis sat next to me the same way. We have come so far since then, but my sis is in the same place, here with me! I love how much we both can laugh until we cry, yet bear hug each other when genuine tears fill our eyes. I often tell her how richly blessed I am to have a sister like her. A sister who has always accepted my quirky habits, and has understood me in a way others couldn't. She let me in her bed when we were little, and thunder struck above the roof of our family home, and scared me dearly. I found shelter in her nearby presence, and I still do the same today and always will do, as sisters are forever.

The email is brief, not requiring a long eyeful to read, it also seems structured and straightforward. I whizz through quickly, to gather the summary of the email, and the end of the email says *See you tomorrow at 3.45 p.m. in Finsbury Park Cafe. I have told Tia that she will be meeting you tomorrow, and she is very excited.* My baby girl, finally her day to see me is nearing, of course she is excited. What a positive ending to Shona's email, is she finally thinking about Tia and not about her vengeance? Well, we are going to continue to co-parent Tia, and we both ought to be positive role models to provide her with the best life she deserves as a child. Honestly though, I may not be so convinced just yet, and will examine the shared care situation closely. I am not reassured that Shona will not go and appeal against the judge's decision today, even if she hardly stands a chance of a change of mind on the judge's ruling, as Christina explained earlier at the court. I scroll back to the start of the email, and carefully read the outline of the settling arrangement designed by the Cafcass officer for us both to follow until the full four sleep routine commences. So, as I read, Tia will be dropped off to my place on Wednesday at four p.m. again in respect of the school ending at three-thirty p.m. to spend her first night and will be required to be dropped off to her school the day after, and Shona will be collecting her from school to spend the same amount of time with Tia, so one night. This means only one thing, oh my goodness, I am going to go to her school and finally be introduced at school as her mother. I cannot wait. The email describes the instructions for the school classroom location drop off, and the time. Given the fact that Tia went to the same school nursery, I have knowledge about the school, office and the entrance. Tia is in a reception class called *Mint* and the teacher is Miss Rodriguez. Adorable name for a class! Tia needs to be in the classroom by 8.55 a.m. Shona has already sent an email to the school, to notify them about the changes and permit my collections from school. As six months ago, the nursery teacher announced that I was banned from school to safeguard Tia, on whatever grounds Shona claimed then, so the nursery teacher could no longer continue communication with me. However, the school will require a copy of the shared care order, once it is received from the court. I ponder the question of what other parents may have heard, and the rumours surrounding the background of our separation. Hopefully, no one knows anything and I get to start afresh, with parents that may have transferred from the nursery and potentially new ones that got placement at the school. It is only a small two entry school, so I will get adapted in no time. Thereafter, I will be collecting Tia from school, and Tia will be with me for three nights this time, meaning that Sunday she will be dropped off at one p.m., as stated in the shared care agreements for weekends and holidays. Following the pattern, by next Wednesday, I will collect Tia from school and the full four sleeps will commence. There is nothing that I disagree with, the settling is reasonable and assuredly reflects Tia at the centre of this arrangement. Not that she needs any settling with me, but I have to respect that she has been apart from me for six months, and got used to a different life without me. However eager I am for more days; the settling routine is gentle and understanding of Tia's needs. I reach the end of the email, so I respond to Gloria to accept the settling routine agreement and to confirm the meeting point tomorrow. My fingers shake a little, as the is causing a feeling of suspense. The reason is not Tia, it is the fact that I will have to face Shona for the first time since she harshly stopped my contact. I can slowly feel the anger filtering through to the surface, from the depth where I had buried myself to be able to remain optimistic in order to deal with my emotional turmoil. Better to hold back that negative feeling, as I want to be the same happy Mummy Vivien that Tia has always known. I would not in a thousand worlds wish for her to feel uncomfortable in a potentially hostile environment by picking up on some peculiar vibes. The moment needs to be as natural and positive as I can possibly keep it, then when Shona leaves us alone, it will not require any hard work. It will be us two, just as before. We will chat for a while; I cannot wait to hear her little stories and see how much she has changed. Warmth covers my soul from picturing her little smiley face, she must have grown so much, and six months is a long time in children's development. Baby, Mummy is coming, sleep tight tonight and I will be giving you a *good day* kiss tomorrow!

  Sis suddenly jumps over to me and squeezes me tightly, and exclaims, 'I am so proud of you, you nailed it today! You are one of the best mothers I have ever known, and the best sister in the whole entire universe. I always believed that you would bring Tia back, and you have! Brave and a fighter, my sister!'

'Thank you, Sis, for always supporting me, I love you so much.'

We both cherish the sappy moment we have just shared. We continue discussing the court hearing via a group video call, as our mum has called to hear the good news. Mum is wiping happy tears from her eyes; she is utterly delighted by my success today. She confirms that her candle lighting has enlightened the energy in that court, and allowed the judge to see the truth and order justice to the person who deserves it. My mother can get superstitious and quite poetic, when it comes to dramatic events. We always smile about it, and accept her views and explanations, as her perspective will often be one of a kind. As I retell the story of today's hearing, a sense of fulfilment and pride fills my mind. I will retell my story over and over again, word by word, with honour and pride! Mum is constantly cheering at everything I share; she cannot comprehend how everything has fallen into its place. The biggest moment for my mum is that Tia will always be safe in my care, and she cannot ever be taken from me again. She knew how long I was pleading for the birth certificate addition, and the parental responsibility, but always had an argument in response. Having had a civil separation, Tia would be settled in a well-balanced shared care, as arranged at the time of the breakup. Anyhow, I tell Mum that we cannot mourn the past but heal towards the future! She is feeling well now, and happy to share a glass with us through the screen. My mother is a great example of a lioness, she is a fighter and does not give in to any confrontation in life, and she has faced the worst! The chat is interrupted by little Charlie, who is now after a bath ready to say goodnight, but notices grandma on the tablet screen and becomes joyful. Not the best to get him hyper before bed, but hey it is not a customary day today, let him fill in the happiness that is surrounding us all today. I share a huge smile, as I observe the silliness that Charlie is getting into from the excitement of seeing his grandmother. So, I grab my champagne glass, deeply inhale my inner peace and relax back onto the sofa. I suddenly feel as if my struggles are washed away and my soul is whole once again. The places we'll go, the laughs we will share, the memories we will build, I can't wait, darling Tia, I can't wait! Tomorrow is a momentous day, and it is time to put the broken pieces of so many yesterdays back together.

# Chapter 21

## The Reunion

'Hand in hand, heart to heart.'

I open my eyes to a new day; the thought of the wonderful upcoming event makes me feel immediately energised. In just a few hours, I will make my way to Finsbury Park, and be reunited with Tia. A few hours seems like the length of a second, in comparison to the 4380 hours of my wait. Today is the most beautiful day in my life, only the second after the magical moment of Tia's birth. Finally, I get to hold my baby in my arms and reassure her that my absence was not by choice! I was advised to not speak of the court process just yet, and to keep the settling period just about the reconnection. Knowing Tia's curious nature, and however long our separation seems to her, she will ask where I have been in the first instance. Meaning, that I will be required to keep my answers general, avoiding any confusion. I cannot and will not make up lies to cover up for the past six months, but I will adjust my answers carefully, as to create an open window into the future, when Tia will be ready to hear about the truth. Unquestionably frustrating, as I have to limit myself, where I have always been open and honest with Tia. It is in her best interest and upsetting her is the least I wish for her. I yearn for her happiness, for celebration to commemorate our reunion, and that shall control my desires. Elation surrounds my mind again, letting no worries influence this extraordinary day that I waited six months for. I spring out of the bed, no time to waste, it is time to get the day started.

Last night was a late one, as the instant I placed my fingerprint on my phone, it entered me in the world of unread group messages from my dearest people. I felt at ease, as before I got on the tube after my hearing, I sent a brief winning message to the group. Of course, everyone wanted to hear more, so I got myself into a messaging marathon, unaware of the late hours, driven by the victorious adrenaline that pulsated through my bloodstream. I did manage to sum up the event to everyone in the group and reassure them of a get together to welcome Tia back to our lives. I signed myself up for a party, that is, better get those words into action soon, first things first, let's settle little Tia into her four-sleep routine, as that is my priority, nothing else matters more. However, after the successful accomplishment of satisfying my lovely people who had waited for the news to come so patiently, I moved onto a single standing message from Lily. When I responded to her message, I was pleasantly surprised by her almost immediate response, mentioning her impatience all day and her fingers crossed for me and my hearing. When I shared the news with her, I could sense her celebration vibes on the other end, somewhere in Brighton, where she is from. We kept on messaging until the late hours, and it felt perfect. Lily can keep me fascinated, somewhat different to a friendship, but not yet sure of what that is, in fact I let the syrup effect take over this delightful new encounter. We arranged a date in a few weeks' time, close to Christmas, to finally meet in person, I imagine we will be talking for hours sitting side by side, as opposed to texting online, and to celebrate my victorious court outcome. Finally, I get to meet this fascinating woman! Speaking of Christmas, it seems early, but it is just a few weeks away, and will be the first Christmas since my separation, and Tia's first time to have two Christmases. The court order states a shared day celebration with appointed days to spend with each parent this year by the judge, and the rest of the upcoming Christmas holidays left for the parents to agree upon. To agree with Shona, is an already frightening thought, but hopefully the parenting plan will guide us smoothly, without any issues.

    I feel my body is in need of a great stretch, so I pull my arms into an eagle shape, one of the best arms stretches that eases pinched shoulders. My aching shoulders is the sign that I went into a deep sleep, something that my body must have been craving the past months, as that is the only time I unconsciously sleep with my lower arms under the pillow. I decide to start my morning with a Pilates session, to enhance the strength of my body and mind. Pilates, that combines control, concentration, precision and breath flow combines the elements that bring spiritual harmony essential for healthy mental wellbeing and physical strength. I jump out of the bed, stretch out my mat, load the online teaching video, and begin. Thanks to my aching muscles, I am giving my body and mind the greatest start to the day! Things do happen for a reason in life, precisely the right time, when it might not yet be clear. It is that moment, when everything just makes perfect sense. I do not simply wait for things to roll my way, but I do believe in that old superstitious myth, that what is meant to be, will find its way. Meaning that I try my utmost to accept what life throws my way, open my eyes to it, appreciate it and view it because of past positive or negative actions. In my opinion, it aids that ongoing personal growth process by learning from mistakes and learning what is wrong and right for our individual wellbeing. Everyone's needs are different, I simply have grown to a stage in my life, where honesty, respect and trust are at the core. To love, or not love, is a question that cannot be simply answered. Love and attraction are a beautiful combination, but the evocation of my core values will be at the centre of any future affairs in my life. As of now, all the focus is centred on my daughter and assuring her happiness and safety, everything else will fall into place when the time is right.

I am now in the car, driving towards Finsbury Park, with plenty of time on my hands, in respect to the possible traffic that is inevitable on London roads. I'm reminded of the beginning of my ordeal, when Tia did not come back into my care, my calls and messages were unanswered, and I drove to Shona's place to see Tia and try and encourage Shona to reflect on her unreasonable and hurtful actions. The visit was unsuccessful, and sadly, it was the day that began the six months long wait! Nevertheless, today's drive is anything but sad. Instead of the puddles on the road side, that I drove through six months ago, today it feels as if driving through The Aurora Borealis, lights of shimmering colours arch over the road ahead, mirroring the lights of my inner optimism and excitement building rapidly as I am approaching the time of our reunion. The excitement creating huge waves of sound into the open sky, as deep inside I am screaming from the top of my voice *my fight has prevailed!* Visibly in an ecstatic mood, I shall not tame my naturally vibrating *me*. I spot a suitable parking space poking out from between cars parked up in the car park, so I pull up and take the empty space near the cafe. Looking at the time, I have fifteen minutes to spare, but I wouldn't like to rush or be stuck in traffic, this is way too important to me. I walk into the cafe, which has a cosy feel to it from the Christmas decorations placed all over the counter and the windows, creating a festive atmosphere. I take a seat at the table near the Christmas tree, which Tia will appreciate, and wait patiently for three-forty-five p.m. to arrive. A cheery waitress skips over and asks for my order, but I explain that I am waiting for someone. The moment the waitress turns around, to serve the table next to mine, I capture a little bobble hat that appears in the door, looking slightly confused and staring in various directions.

'Tia baby, here!'

When she spots me, her beautiful bright blue eyes light up and she runs towards me like a fireball, shouting, '*Mummy!*'

I jump from my seat, my heart skipping a beat, and I bound towards her, avoiding every chair in my way. The time seems to be frozen for us both to cherish this moment and everything around us seems to have vanished, leaving only us two in the room. Auroras of lights in colours of blue, pink, and white arch over the space and a subtle sound of fireworks fills the surrounding space above us. We land in each other's arms, and I immediately lift her into the air and spin her around in circles. Giggles of joy fill the air, and in this moment I feel completed. Oh, how much I missed her laughter, her smell – that forever reminds me of that tiny, fragile baby I held in my arms just a minute old and her little face – cute little chubby rosy cheeks carrying two ocean blue eyes. Just as I had imagined. As I put her down, she wraps her little arms around my waist, clearly in a long-needed cuddle. As she presses on my leg, I can feel her little mighty heart beating so fast, my heart matching her beat. When she lets go of my waist, I crouch down to her level and pull her little cold cheeks into my hands, and give her thousands of kisses, she chuckles as she is very ticklish, and I know exactly what she enjoys the most. Kissing those little chubby cheeks!

'I missed you, Mummy.'

'Oh, I missed you too, my little angel.'

We share another humongous hug, we cannot seem to let go of each other, and frankly why would we want to? The harrowing six months apart, doesn't have enough hugs in this world to even make up for it! This remarkable moment provides a real snapshot of what our relationship has always been like and confirms that no forces can cut the invisible thread that connects mother and daughter. I exhale what feels like gallons of air that has been trapped inside of me for six months, holding onto this moment, waiting to be freed. I lead Tia to the table, and assist her with taking off her coat, hat and scarf. She seems to snuggle in her warm outfit, to brace the temperatures that have lowered quite intensely, just in the past week. Instead of the free chair, she charges straight into my lap, where I welcome her with a massive squeeze and gently squeeze her little cold hands to warm them with the heat that is erupting from my heart. She pulls out a grey teddy, and introduces it to me as *Furry*, and describes it as her favourite teddy that she got from the fun fair she went to the other day. Tia begins telling me about the rides she went on, and excitedly describes how fast some were, but she wasn't scared and the arrow on the measurement board said, she can soon go on much faster rides and how she can't wait. I recognise Shona standing to the side, waiting for some kind of acknowledgement so I politely greet her, and she just hands me Tia's bag with items she wanted to pack to show me.

Tia pulls it out of her hand, and says, '*Yay, I want to show you something.*'

Shona may feel slightly awkward, and as this meeting is primarily about Tia and me, she leans in to say bye to Tia. Who seems so excited and preoccupied that she only manages to offer a quick look and say goodbye. Thereafter, Shona confirms the time she will come back to collect Tia, we both say our goodbyes, and she walks right off, out of the cafe. I'm relieved. I still cannot seem to face her, to look into her eyes, as I am afraid of the words that would come out, regardless of the surrounding audience, *how could you have the heart to do this to Tia, cut me out of her life and completely disregard my existence! I will never forgive you for what you did to us! Though, now, I am the mother who is legally visible and have the same rights to Tia, just as you do, and just as I always had but you kept that away from me. My truth, honesty and love for Tia won over the fabricated lies, and this now past harrowing event will never repeat!* There is a time and place when I can speak my thoughts and the experienced pain out loud, but that is not today. Today belongs to my baby girl only, and to our shared happiness. I turn my attention immediately back to Tia, who is lining up things from her bag, on the table. The soft blue backpack we got on holiday in Italy, she still has it and has chosen to bring it with her today, each and every detail means the world to me.

'Mummy Vivien, remember this bag? I take it with me to school as well, you know I go to school now. I put my water bottle inside, but we are not allowed to take any toys to school anymore, so I have to leave them at home. I don't go to gymnastics anymore; I didn't like it. I was upset because you didn't pick me up from the lessons, I was waiting for you. Where were you, Mummy?'

I barely manage to hold my tears back; they gather in my eyes in response to her sweet words. Bless her little heart, she must be full of questions and wants to share so much with me. In support, I take a deep breath, and try to smile, although I cannot and don't want to fully show my true emotions, but somewhat balance it with happy vibes. Trying to block the tears, I attempt to explain.

'I had to take care of a few things, that took longer than I thought but I am here now, and I am never ever going to leave your side again. Trust me, it was very difficult for Mummy to not be able to see you, but you never left my heart, and I know you believed that I was coming back soon, didn't you?'

'Yes, I knew you were coming, it just took a long time, and I missed you!'

'I know, sweetheart, and I am sorry for taking so long. Clumsy Mummy! You are in school now, yes, how is it, are you happy there?'

'Yes, Miss Rodriguez is nice, and I have some friends there from my nursery. Not from your nursery. I miss your nursery, I miss Rachel and my friends. I miss Grandma, and Charlie. Can we go and see everybody?'

'Oh darling, I wish we could today, but we are only meeting for a short while but next time, only in a day – you need to only sleep one night – and with time you will get to see everyone you have missed, don't worry. Guess what? I am going to pick you up from your class, which I have heard is called *Mint*. Does it smell like mint?'

'Ha ha! No Mummy it doesn't, but it does have green

walls like mint. I still like mint ice cream, but it's too cold for ice cream now. Can I have hot chocolate with marshmallows?'

'Oh yummy, yes let's have some hot chocolate.'

Pleasantly surprised and pleased with how I managed to steer the conversation away from my absence, the explanation may have satisfied her only for now. I lift my hand to notify the waitress who is walking around, cleaning up some tables, to order two mugs of hot chocolate. Tia seems so happy, relaxed and apart from being slightly taller than six months ago, she hasn't changed a bit. The same little monkey that she has always been. I was so afraid to find her being withdrawn or even reluctant to stay with me. Obviously, I trusted our special relationship, but I was slightly wary that Shona may have tried to turn her against me. Super happy, that if she may have tried, it didn't work. My baby girl is the same as I left her, and I am the same as she last saw me. Just like nothing has changed, no time has passed!

'Mummy, do you remember this dolly and this little wolf, so cute and this snake, maybe not, and do you remember this colouring book, I finished all the pages – do you want to see? Aww and look at this snowflake I made at school, I know how to make a snowflake now, I will show you next time.'

I cannot get enough of her little chatter! Tia has clearly prepared for this meeting, and that warms my heart, that is still beating all over the place, as my excitement is blasting out of me with every movement or words I let out. I keep randomly kissing the side of Tia's head, who seems to lovingly welcome them as she each time responds with a smile or a kiss in return, on my cheek. We go through every page of her colouring book, dearly impressed with her colouring skills and some drawing as well on the side, so I can tell that her skills have certainly matured. The waitress places the two cups of hot chocolate on the table and brings attention to the one that is for Tia with extra marshmallows. Tia's little face lights up with appreciation and she digs in with the spoon, slurping the hot chocolate and eating the small marshmallow pieces with every spoonful. I take in every moment, as I missed everything about Tia, including even the way she drinks and eats. She isa tidy type, who doesn't spill anything, something Sis has always admired as when we would go out, Charlie would be absolutely smothered in food and drinks, including the table space around him. Tia moves the tissue paper from under her cup and takes out one of the pens from the bag, pointing out that blue is her favourite colour now and that she doesn't like yellow anymore. I respond in a gentle laugh and patiently watch her little hand move, printing letters on to the tissue that says *TIA* and she gives me the tissue to keep in my pocket. She has a habit of giving me random things – a stone, leaf, flower, stick – that I funnily always keep, as I appreciate the gesture. She is very chuffed about being able to write her own name, without any help and reminds me, 'Mummy remember, in your nursery I couldn't write my name, now I can, because I go to school now. When can I go back to your nursery again, like before?'

'Well darling, you go to school now, and many of your friends that used to come to the nursery, also go to school now but you can of course still come to visit after school, okay? Rachel is still there, and she has a new team of little troublemakers now and she is looking forward to seeing you, as she is asking for your arts and craft ideas. Has Mummy Shona explained the routine ahead?'

'Yes, I want to help Rachel, and you Mummy, as I am a

big girl now! I don't know what is routine?'

'Okay, do you remember when Mummies separated and you started to live in our two homes, with a few sleeps with Mummy Shona and a few sleeps with me? We will continue the same way, but first you will sleep in my house for one night, then two, then three and then four, and in between the same with Mummy Shona. Then you will stay the four sleeps and only go back to Mummy Shona, when the four sleeps are finished. Okay baby?'

Tia's little face drops, and she puts the spoon back into the hot chocolate cup. Her little eyes gather with tears, and her lips turn downwards, ready to cry.

'I don't want to go back to Mummy Shona, I want to stay with you. I wanted to see you and Mummy Shona said that you are not coming because you left us.'

I feel a stab to the heart, Tia's words penetrating deeply. Just what I thought, Shona may have planned that I would not win the court and never return to Tia's life but she was wrong. Tia's delicate shaky voice makes me want to cry with her, but instead I give her a motherly hug and offer reassurance in a positive light.

'Baby, listen, you have nothing to worry about now, Mummy is here, and I am not going anywhere. Yes, that is true I did leave the family home, and left Mummy Shona, but I never left you. Now what is very important, we will work together, as you will need to go back to Mummy Shona when it is her turn to look after you okay? You can take and bring any toys with you whenever you want, okay?'

'Okay, but I don't want to. Can I go back to your house now?'

'Not today darling, but tomorrow as I will pick you from

school and we will come straight back to Mummy's, okay? We can even drop by the nursery if you would like, but Mummy is not at work tomorrow so we can spend lots of time together at home.'

Tia seems momentarily settled in her mind, certainly not easy to take on so much information at her age, so I tried to be as simple as possible. It probably doesn't make sense in Tia's mind right now, but the information she has managed to grasp today will arise when her mind is prepared to understand it fully. For Tia to settle into her new routine, and reunite with everyone she has missed, will be at the forefront of her comprehension in the next few weeks, even months ahead. What will stimulate her mind and trigger memories in the meantime, will show with time. The important fact is that whatever will trouble her mind, will always get an honest answer and from today, I will always be there for her, just as I whispered into her tiny ears on the day she was born. I squeeze her tight in my arms, and cover her with my mothering kisses, wanting for her to feel my inner words, and not ever feel abandoned by me. To lighten the mood, I offer to go over to the small pop up Christmas market to see if we can get something special to remember our special day. We both truly love Christmas, so it straight away puts a smile on her little face. The cafe is like a sauna, it will surely be a shock to our system when we go outside, so we zip up our coats and put on our hats, and for the first time after six months, walk hand-in-hand. The feeling of holding her small soft little hand, all warmed up, is like a thousand Christmas Day joys in one. I stroke her hand with my thumb, something my mum used to do to me, and that habit just stayed with me. She still takes my hand, strokes my face and puts my hair behind my ear as we talk, reminding me that I will always be her baby, no matter my age. That is so very true, as that is how I feel now as a mother. Only a few stalls are set up on the street, with one very attractive spot where all the children seem to be gathering, and that is the light up toys and the candy floss stall just opposite. Of course Tia points straight in that direction, so we walk over, pass some people who are viewing items by other stalls with Christmas decorations, mulled wine and handmade baked goods by the looks of it. I can hardly lay my eyes on anything as Tia is pulling me so fast, in fear that the stalls will shut before she gets to buy anything. She picks a light up spinning windmill toy, and asks me if we can get it, and what can I really tell this super excited almost five-year-old, other than a yes! We get the candy floss too, but not until after her dinner, and Tia happily agrees. We are skipping side by side, spinning the light up toy. She surely seems cheered up, but she suddenly stops at the next stall.

'Mummy, can we get these letter decorations for our Christmas tree, when we get one? Letter T for Tia and letter M for Mummy. Please?'

We get the decorations, the letters are hand knitted in colours of orange, green and blue, I think it's a beautiful idea. We also pick a little hanging glass angel decoration for Grandma and a small hand-crafted wooden car decoration for Charlie. Watching Tia's smile spread up towards her rosy cheeks, holding her little hand and hearing her soft voice makes my heart feel alive again. I look at my watch, we only have half an hour left so I offer to go back to the cafe so we can have a bite to eat before she needs to leave as it most definitely close to her dinner time. I know for sure, as I could always tell when she is hungry, since she was a little bean. Her eyes somewhat sink in and her face literally says *food*. So, we take a seat and look through the menu on the cafe wall, which has some selection of toasted paninis, pasta, pizza and soup. Tia hesitates for a second, but quickly snaps tomato pasta with cheese.

'Cheese still on the side, darling?'

'Yes, Mummy.'

Tia's expression speaks for her mind, my *Mummy knows me*! We take a seat at the table, again next to the Christmas tree, Tia's choice this time. She sits in my lap, as she unwraps her coat and takes off her hat, playing with the light up spinning windmill. I take the opportunity and ask Tia for a selfie, she holds on to her spinning toys, grabs me around my neck and grins for the picture. Beautiful!

'Mummy, when will we get a Christmas tree, and will you be with me at Christmas? Will Santa know where I am going to be, as I wrote him a letter with my present list, what if he does not know where to come?'

Oh, one of those questions, when a parent needs to answer fast but carefully! I must think quickly as Tia is waiting for my response. Luckily the waitress brings our food order to the table, phew what a moment saver. Tia doesn't seem to want to detach from me for a second, as she wants to sit on my lap and eat. That's not usually the case, but today is not a usual day. The pasta dish seems only warm, not piping hot, which is perfect for us, and Tia enthusiastically adds a handful of grated parmesan cheese on top of her rich tomato sauce pasta and hungrily digs in. I can tell she has not forgotten her question, and I would not allow any distractions to interfere with my ability to answer her questions.

'The pasta looks delicious, darling, enjoy! So, we will get

the Christmas tree not next week, but the week after and we will put all our decorations on, including the special ones you got today. Regarding your letter to Santa, Santa is very smart, and he knows all the children in the world and he knows that you have now two homes. Don't you worry, Santa will know exactly where you will be asleep the night he comes. Children who have two homes, not only one, he makes sure to visit both homes. Why don't we write a list to Santa after you eat your pasta, and we will post it. Does that sound like a good idea?'

'Yay, I will get double presents.'

Children and the excitement about presents. That settles the worries, so great! Tia loves finding presents under the Christmas tree, but on another note, she loves the Christmas spirit and the festive build up. Taking all the decorations out of the boxes, and making the whole house look like a fairy tale. This year will be our first Christmas together, after the separation, and the first time that we will be decorating my house, Tia's other home. The dish is empty, all the pasta has gone down well. So, I pull out a piece of paper from my bag, and ask Tia to write the letter for Santa. She begins to draw a sledge because it will snow. Then she draws a dog with a string attached to it, saying that she has seen it in an advert and that the dog can walk and bark. Then she draws a scooter, saying that she really would like one as the one she has is too small. Satisfied with the list, she asks me to write down a message to Santa, that this list is for the Christmas tree at Mummy Vivien's, and she folds the paper ready to be posted. I can see Shona's car pulling into the cafe car park, and the time shows exactly 6:45 p.m. and that is our time coming to an end, but no reason to be sad, as tomorrow Tia will be coming home with me and sleeping in between all her soft toys. The excitement fills my heart, when I think of her all cosy in pyjamas, snuggly in her bed, ready for her good night story. I couldn't wait for today, and I can't wait for tomorrow, and for all the days to come! Tia spots Shona, walking into the cafe, so she clings on to me right away, refusing to get her coat on and leave without me. I was prepared for this, and Shona should have as well, as she will need to have huge input from her side as well to make the handovers easier with time. Given the history, the handovers were not ever smooth, as Tia was still settling into the separated childcare routine, and they may just continue where they left off. Reluctance is imminent and I can read Shona's expression clearly, she is not pleased with Tia's behaviour. To be blunt, I do not care about how Shona may feel, and to make the hostile moment, a little warmer, I offer Tia that I will come to the car with her to say goodbye, and we can post Santa's letter on the way. Walking in the company of an ex-partner, who hurt the two people walking beside her, is not ideal. Tia is chatting away about the Christmas market and the things we bought, holding my hand and that makes everything just all right. My focus is entirely on Tia, and I lift her up to reach the letter box, to post Santa's letter. I cannot help but reminisce over all the postcards I posted through this very same letter box, but as confirmed at the court, have never reached Tia. I have to at least try to believe that each individual post card held my energy and my kisses and thoughts reached her through a different plane. I barely speak to Shona, besides filling the awkwardness between us with talks about school, and how Tia has been settling into her reception class. Hearing positive feedback is pleasing, and I am so delighted that she has not been affected in her development. She is a tough cookie and had prepared for school since she was three years old, with activities that boosted her resilience, social confidence and some preschool academic skills such as counting and writing. Apparently, Tia is one of the children that is succeeding at already writing her name, recognising numbers, counting, and can write some numbers. These small snippets of her progress are heart-warming, and Tia seems certainly proud of sharing her positive feedback from school. Frankly, from now on, because of what Shona did to Tia and me, only conversations related to Tia will take place between us. To me, Shona, with all due respect for her being the other parent to Tia, is a ghost to me. Someone, who made me invisible through an unforgettable act of harm, has become invisible to me. Meaning, that nothing she says or will do in spite, will affect me, it will not ever touch me! Unless her acts may hurt Tia in any way, then the lioness will come to the surface to protect us. From a legal point of view, there is absolutely nothing she can do to us, so I am no longer threatened by her. The fearful times are over! Obeying her rules, for the safety of us all, is over! Feeling panicky for not having Tia returned into my care, is over! I fought for my rights, with every inch of strength I found within me, and beyond! I am done with being mistreated and I will not accept any more harm to my daughter, as I will be closely monitoring her recovery from the past six months of this ordeal and assure her happiness and safety at all times. Tia squeezes my hand as we near Shona's car, and it only occurs to me that she has held only my hand the whole time. Not to repeat history, I kneel to Tia's level and explain to her that after one sleep at Mummy Shona's, I will be picking her up from school. Reassuring her that I will be here tomorrow, the day after and every day from now on, to reduce her worries. It is only expected that she will find detaching from me difficult for the time being, especially on the first day. She begins to cry, and exclaims, 'I want to only be with Mummy Vivien, why is no one listening?'

'Baby, we are listening, and we understand, but you always had two mummies and it may just be a matter of time to get used to it. I will be there tomorrow, waiting for you, outside the *Mint* classroom with a yummy snack for you. We will go to the nursery, see Charlie, video call Grandma and you will go to sleep in your bed in Mummy Vivien's house. Okay?'

It has seemed to work, as Tia has accepted the letting go, but still holding on to me tight, sobbing gently. I gently explain to Shona, that there is no rush, let her take her time. I pull at the teddy I had for her, but was not sure whether to give it to her, as I am afraid it may not return. However, I got it for Tia, it has a purpose to provide her with a sense of closeness and comfort in my absence.

'You can call this teddy Mummy Bear, and cuddle up to it tonight, and any night you will need to. It is filled with my hugs and kisses, topped up with as many as you need.'

I kiss the teddy, and give it to Tia, who immediately takes it and hugs it tight, wiping away her tears. Finally, she lets go of me, and I put her into the car seat. She is clenching tight to her Mummy Bear. I watch as they drive off, Tia waving sadly from the car window. I send kisses, until she can't see me. Once they are out of sight, I drop on the nearby bench, and allow my tears to flow freely. Difficult to deal with seeing Tia sad or upset, as her little face shows so much emotion, that I can barely hold myself strong. However, we will both cherish the beautiful time spent together this afternoon, the time of our continuous time together has begun.

The settling period has gone partially well, many tearful

handovers still occur but that is something that will be part of Tia adapting in her new life routine. She was detached suddenly, and didn't see me for six whole months, and now all of a sudden, I have popped back into her life. None of this was by my choice, and Tia is working hard on understanding that and learning to trust that I will always be there after her fourth sleep, and not disappear again. It may need, weeks, months, even years of getting used to a steady routine, where she sees me there, welcoming her with my hugs and kisses. What I can do, is be the living proof of my promise to her, as actions speak louder than words, that applies to children too. I am collecting her from school today, it's the third week into her settling routine, and its Friday so I have arranged for everyone who loves and cares for Tia to be in our house, as a surprise to celebrate our reunion. All of Tia's friends will be there, everyone except Grandma but she will be soon flying over on a separate occasion as the doctor confirmed her steady health to handle the flights. I have planned to take Tia, supposedly, to get a few bits and bobs, which is only to allow time for everyone to arrive at our house after school. With plenty of notice, everyone will be at the party with food, drinks and party decorations already set up. Thanks to Sis who arranged an afternoon off work and has my key to let people into the house. As we agreed on a text message signal, I receive a *ready* message, so I pack the shopping into bags, and we walk back to the car. Feeling rather excited, Tia will be super happy to see everyone! I can hardly manage my emotions, but I need to be careful because Tia is looking suspicious. We drive up to our street, I leave the shopping in the car, and walk towards the door. As I open the door and let Tia in, a massive group scream fills the living room: 'Welcome back, Tia!'

As Tia and I enter the living room, the sounds of party poppers and exuberant cheers from friends fill the air, making her leap from surprise. Moments later, her friends, who've been notified of the idea, enthusiastically bring over a stick and present Tia with a rainbow-coloured unicorn piñata that is stiffly hanging from the ceiling above. I can only imagine how many sweets it holds, and the children's faces light up with delight as they surrounded Tia. As Tia takes the first strikes, others dash to the corner of the room and return with sticks, ready to completely destroy the piñata, which appears to be sturdy enough to withstand the exertions of ten or so children! The instant, when the strikes open the piñata, it tosses confetti at everyone followed by a massive waterfall of sweets. Children automatically leap to the floor like bees to nectar and begin grabbing onto as many sweets as possible. Let the amusement begin! I lean against the wall, taking in the atmosphere and watching every tiny detail, Tia is joyful and all I can feel is the air of love in the room. Tia's eyes meet mine, and she smiles brightly before sprinting over to me and leaping into my arms. We are both speechless, as no words are necessary to experience this connection, which will forever unite us.

# Epilogue

Tia's gentle arms wrap tightly around my waist from behind, a moment of peace in a world spinning around. Tia is still breathless from jumping on the trampoline in the garden, I can feel her beating heart, pounding fast on my back, as she pulls in tight for a hug. A comforting embrace, as if all the troubles in the world have been erased. Tia fulfils my existence; she is my sweetest essence. Past pain is nothing more than a vision of blossoms fallen on the ground. The pain in my heart is no longer the reminder to fight and to fight is no longer the goal of my life. Tia is right here, tightly wrapped around me, not going anywhere. I turn around and kiss her warm rosy cheeks, Tia smiles in return, with her right arm slowly leaving my waist and wrapping around Lily, who is standing near me in the kitchen, pulling us all together, exhaling "Group cuddle." I kiss Lily gently on the lips and we bask in this pure moment. The smell of pancakes fills my nostrils urging me to swiftly grab the spatula and flip the pancake over in the pan. Phew just in time!

'Mum! Are the pancakes ready yet? I'm *so* hungry.'

Tia begins rubbing her stomach animatedly.

'They're coming! They're coming!'

I chuckle at Lily, as she hurriedly prepares the condiments for the mountain of pancakes that will undoubtedly be devoured.

Over six years have passed since our reunion, and often Tia asks questions as her curiosity to understand her story is part of her identity. Answers to her questions need to be honest, as I have always been honest with Tia, but each stage of her age unravels a more complex understanding.

'Why did you and Mummy Shona break up?'

Tia's eyes widen with a glint of anticipation. The story of my life, so the answer to her question has not ever been easy and required an effort to navigate the answers. With a creative twist, I would go down the route of different relationships, character traits and how certain behaviours impact on others negatively. My story is an invaluable lesson taught to Tia, as my goal after our reunion will always be to educate her. My protective instinct is stronger than ever before. Tia is soon to become a tweenager who will explore the world around her independently, making her own decisions and I can only protect her by preparing her for the life challenges she may be faced with. Tia needs to know how to recognise controlling behaviour and to connect with her inner intuition to recognise people or situations that would make her feel unsafe or unhappy inside her little heart.

So, my answers to her question have been more extensive as Tia is now getting older. Besides her utter curiosity, I have remained a positive parent as her happiness and well-being has always been in the forefront of my mind.

After the reunion, Tia had caught up with her previous life, and the people that she missed dearly. Friends who had been by her side when she was a little baby, were waiting for her when she returned. Tia is a social butterfly; she thrives from time spent in her social group. She has strong views, creative ideas, a caring heart and is solution driven with a flexible approach to situations. To me, Tia's perfectly imperfect, she learns from her mistakes and has learnt to talk about her diverse experiences, and with guidance she is becoming more mature and able to navigate her social interactions positively. What more can a parent offer, than a shoulder to cry on and a place where she will always feel safe and talk about happy moments or troubles in life. A place that is her home. Home where the love that surrounds her is not only nurturing but makes her stronger.

Over the years, Tia has grown very close with Lily, and their relationship is beautiful to witness. It is what makes me feel warm in my heart, as this person, who makes me feel happy, loved and free, is favoured by my child. Not only does Lily love me, but she also loves Tia as well and Tia feels the same way. The only way to know how the child feels, is the way they behave and hearing the words "I love you Lily", whilst throwing herself into her arms, is very clear to me. When the judge mentioned during the court hearing that *the more loving people around the child, the better*, it is so glaringly true. Tia would be happy and feel loved by me no matter what her world would be like, but having so many people close to her that adore and love her, is truly special.

Tia would often remember, 'When Mummy Shona looked after me, I missed you, Mummy, and I wanted to see you every day, but you didn't come.'

All I can do is hug her tight and reassure her that Mummy Shona will not be able to repeat those actions again. Following my explanation to Tia regarding the court hearing period, with the evidence support from my friends that delivered a victorious win for the truth, Tia would often say to me "Mummy I am so thankful and happy that the court people believed in our mummy and daughter love."

Those six months of my life seemed like years to Tia, as that has remained as a memory in her mind, and that breaks my heart, still. Tia would often need answers repeated, as her mind is hungry for the truth, given the confusion that had been embedded in her mind over the six-month period. All in all, I feel that Tia may be in the clear, regarding those six months, but I don't feel so sure about what she may be hearing from Shona. Tia has had moments, where she would say that she is checking if we say the same thing, and we would explore the slightest details to minimise her confusion. I have taught my baby about the importance of honesty, and we trust each other. Tia knows that I would not lie to her, and she understands that I would like the same from her. When we *pinkie promise* to each other, it is valid, and that *pinkie* is kept intact. What matters now, is to focus on the present and future. Whatever may trouble Tia's mind about her past, will always get an honest age-appropriate answer from my heart.

Generally, over the past few years, Tia settled with the shared care routine, and has established a strong sense of belonging. She is much happier with her two homes and is happier going back to Shona's house. That was the aim, my goal, as one thing that was always addressed through the court process, is that Tia has two mums and she has the right to continue that bond with both of her parents, regardless of their broken relationship and hurt past. Tia needed an enormous amount of encouragement during handovers for at least two and a half years following our reunion. Tia continued with upset moments caused by the feeling of detaching from me, and I understood how hurt and scared she must have felt every time she left me as she would always say "Will you be here, what if I will not see you for a long time again?" This fear needed time to heal, and the fear of it happening again may still be buried deep inside her and occasionally resurface. Despite her apprehension, she is maturing cognitively and has grasped to her best abilities that the arrangement is stable and that I am not going anywhere.

Tia is a sensitive soul with the tenacity of a lioness, and she already lives for equality and opposes unfairness. She stands out in a crowd, her barrier of uniqueness firmly in place, and she is beginning to believe in her own abilities. She is learning about herself as she grows older, learning to embrace and love oneself is something she should treasure for the rest of her life because it is the only way to live a happy life. Every day, I am proud of her, regardless of her achievements. I am proud of the person she has become and will continue to grow into.

As we gather around the breakfast table and I take in the moment, it is as if time has slowed down to allow me to feel every precious second. Tia's face is frozen in a perfect picture of pure joy and laughter and the same is reflected on Lily's too. They both turn to look at me with so much love and adoration that I am filled with complete happiness. Finally, after so much time, I feel that my shattered heart has begun to be pieced back together again.